This book is part of the Goodyear Series in Education, Theodore W. Hipple, University of Florida, Editor.

OTHER GOODYEAR BOOKS IN GENERAL METHODS & CENTERS

AH HAH! The Inquiry Process of Generating and Testing Knowledge
John McCollum

A CALENDAR OF HOME/SCHOOL ACTIVITIES
Jo Anne Patricia Brosnahan and *Barbara Walters Milne*

CHANGE FOR CHILDREN Ideas and Activities for Individualizing Learning
Sandra N. Kaplan, Jo Ann B. Kaplan, Sheila K. Madsen, Bette K. Taylor

CREATING A LEARNING ENVIRONMENT A Learning Center Handbook
Ethel Breyfogle, Susan Nelson, Carol Pitts, Pamela Santich

THE LEARNING CENTER BOOK An Integrated Approach
Tom Davidson, Phyllis Fountain, Rachel Grogan, Verl Short, Judy Steely, Katherine Freeman

ONE AT A TIME ALL AT ONCE The Creative Teacher's Guide to Individualized Instruction Without Anarchy

OPEN SESAME A Primer in Open Education
Evelyn M. Carswell and *Darrell L. Roubinek*

THE OTHER SIDE OF THE REPORT CARD A How-to-Do-It Program for Affective Education
Larry Chase

THE TEACHER'S CHOICE Ideas and Activities for Teaching Basic Skills
Sandra N. Kaplan, Sheila K. Madsen, Bette T. Gould

TEACHER FOR LEARNING Applying Educational Psychology in the Classroom
Myron H. Dembo

OTHER WAYS, OTHER MEANS Altered Awareness Activities for Receptive Learning
Alton Harrison and *Diann Musial*

WILL THE REAL TEACHER PLEASE STAND UP? A Primer in Humanistic Education, 2nd edition
Mary Greer and *Bonnie Rubinstein*

A YOUNG CHILD EXPERIENCES Activities for Teaching and Learning
Sandra N. Kaplan, Jo Ann B. Kaplan, Sheila K. Madsen, Bette T. Gould

For information about these, or Goodyear books in Language Arts, Reading, Science, Math, and Social Studies, write to

Janet Jackson
Goodyear Publishing Company
1640 Fifth Street
Santa Monica, CA 90401
(213) 393-6731

BEATRICE GROSS

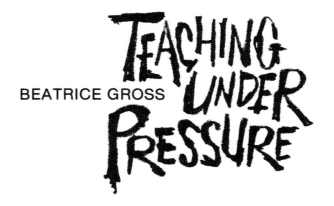

TEACHING UNDER PRESSURE

Goodyear Publishing Company, Inc.
Santa Monica, California

Library of Congress Cataloging in Publication Data

Main entry under title:

Teaching under pressure.

  (Goodyear series in education)
  1. Teaching—Addresses, essays, lectures.
I. Gross, Beatrice.
LB1025.2.T427   371.1'02   78-13238
ISBN 0-87620-888-X

Current printing (last digit):

10 9 8 7 6 5 4 3 2 1

ISBN: 0-87620-888-X
Y-888X-5

Printed in the United States of America

This book is dedicated to Peter Gross who has always sympathized with the pressures on parents and teachers, and taken responsibility for so much of his own learning and growth.

Both my children have contributed material to this book and contributed materially to my own understanding of the complexity of taking one's own learning and destiny in hand.

INTRODUCTION

"This book invites us to join the conversation," said John Calam in *Saturday Review* about this book's precursor, *Will It Grow in a Classroom?* "And I hope we do," the reviewer added.

You did.

Among the many letters from teachers who took up the invitation, most spoke of *pressure*—pressure from parents and administrators; pressure to go "back to basics"; pressure that made it difficult to maintain a human, warm classroom atmosphere that respected the subtlety and complexity of how children really learn and grow into decent human beings.

Times have changed since 1974, when *Will It Grow* first appeared. "A book for teacher's hearts rather than their heads," said the *Christian Science Monitor.* But today, teachers must use their heads as well as their hearts if they are to survive. This book has been written and edited to help teachers, survive—to make difficult choices and find new ways to teach under pressure.

I have found material, or written it when it was not available, that should help you not only in better understanding current educational research, but using it to reassure parents and administrators that what you are doing is educationally sound.

I have made clear the choices you must make, based on conflicts in the findings, and pointed out attractive goals that are mutually exclusive. I have provided concrete examples of how research translates into practical advice.

Even the most gifted teachers often differ in their approaches to children, yet at times I find we must all justify our practices to a critical audience. So I have culled material from current research on learning which will enable you to reexamine your work in the light of authoritative studies and explain your practice to professional and lay critics.

I believe that the material collected here is highly readable and for the most part, charming. But I will feel I have succeeded if you can use it to calm a concerned critic, to keep your job in such a way that you still want it, to increase the will, the enthusiasm and the "paper" results of the children in your classroom.

CONTENTS

VI   IT MAY BE ENGLISH BUT IT'S GREEK TO ME!

VII   MODIFYING CLASSROOM BEHAVIOR

VIII OTHER PEOPLE ARE ALIVE AND DIFFERENT

IX   RELATIONS WITH RELATIONS

X   EPILOGUE

I
SOMETIMES IT'S JUST TOO MUCH

I Thought You Said You Wanted To Be A Teacher?

In New York City the public and the Board of Education were shocked and unbelieving when two of every three teachers who were "excessed" the year before expressed no interest in returning to the classroom.

Most were resettled into jobs that were considerably less exhausting. They did not want to get back onto the "firing line" (pun intended). Some were still twitching from stress. Some perhaps were victims of beatings, (sixty-three thousand teachers were estimated by the NEA to have been attacked each year in the schools). And many were eaten up by the unending meetings, mountains of tests, forms, and extra duties and details they attended to.

I know from experience that you probably get time to do good grousing in the teachers' lunchroom, but when teaching under pressure you need plenty of time and space to say how difficult things are. You deserve some tender loving care and someone to put up with an occasional whine before you roll up your sleeves and get back to work.

Terry Lynn Nagle

Once there was a young man named Nathan. He wanted very much to be a teacher. So he went to seek the advice of the wisest, most highly respected counselor in the land.

"Wise counselor," Nathan began, "it has always been my dream to be a teacher. I want to stimulate the minds of the young people of our land. I want to lead them down the road of knowledge. Please tell me the secret of becoming a teacher."

"Your goal is a commendable one, Nathan. However, it is also a very difficult one to achieve. First you must overcome three major obstacles."

"I am ready to meet the challenge," answered Nathan bravely.

"First you must swim the Sea of Children," directed the knowing counselor.

Nathan started off to swim the Sea of Children. First he had to learn their thirty-eight names. He had to send the line cutters to the end of the line. He

This article was originally published as **"An American Educator's Fable,"** in *American Educator,* Winter 1977. Reprinted by permission of the American Federation of Teachers, AFL–CIO.

made the paper throwers stay after school to clean the room. He commanded the name callers, pushers and punchers to apologize to their victims. He gave M&M's to those who finished assignments and stars to those who were sitting in their seats quietly. Nathan checked passes to see how many children were in the bathroom. And he tracked down students who were gone longer than was necessary. He arranged the desks in alphabetical order, then boy-girl, and finally into small groups of four. He lined his children up for physical education and music and library and lunch. Then he stifled a cry when the secretary came into the room with number thirty-nine.

Tired and shaken but still undefeated, Nathan returned to the counselor for his second task.

"You are a very determined lad," said the advisor. "However, now you must climb the Mountain of Paperwork."

Nathan set out at once. He wrote objectives and drew up lesson plans. He made out report cards and graded papers. He filled out accident reports, attendance reports and withdrawal reports. He completed inventories, evaluations, surveys and request forms. Finally he made dittos and more dittos. He ran them off until he was purple in the face.

But the courageous boy's resolve never dwindled. He went to the wise counselor for his third task.

"You are indeed very strong, Nathan. But this third task will take all the courage you can muster. You must now cross the country of Duties and Commitments."

At first Nathan was hesitant. But his convictions remained steadfast. He began his long journey across the country of Duties and Commitments.

Nathan took lunch duty, bus duty, and recess duty. He was on the social committee, patrol committee, and the faculty advisory committee. He was the adult supervisor of the student government and ran the United Fund and Easter Seal drives. He went to P.T.A. meetings, N.R.A. meetings and inservice workshops. He organized bicentennial programs, talent shows, and book drives. Finally he was elected the building representative of the union.

At last Nathan reached the outskirts of Duties and Commitments. Exhausted but happy, he returned to the knowledgeable counselor.

"I swam the Sea of Children. I climbed the Mountain of Paperwork. I crossed the country of Duties and Commitments," Nathan proclaimed. "Am I not worthy of the title of Teacher?

"Why, Nathan," began the counselor, "you have been a teacher all along."

Nathan protested, "But I have not stimulated any minds. I have not guided anyone down the road to knowledge. I have not had any time to teach."

"Oh, you say you want to TEACH! I thought you said you wanted to be a TEACHER. Well, that is an entirely different story."

Mrs. Cole's Bad Day

If Mrs. Cole can have a bad day, you can too. Her books, *The Arts in the Classroom* and *Children's Arts from Deep Down Inside* have had great impact not only on children's arts but on teaching in general.

The following material is taken from her current manuscript which tells of her twenty-five years working with a therapy approach to children's writing.

As the children learn to accept and forgive themselves they can accept and forgive others including the teacher.

Natalie Cole

There is so much energy spent in making teachers aware of the emotional needs of children and so little spent in giving him an antidote to combat feelings of frustration and guilt when he is unable to give all that is needed. The teacher works with thirty or forty children at a time—the psychiatrist with one—and with no other teacher's kids shrieking right outside his window, "It's an out!" "You're a liar!"

I'm saying all this because the day before I was feeling rather good about myself. I was loving my own speech for our young pregnant teacher at lunch time. I had remembered a party given by Elsa Maxwell, everyone to come dressed to represent some novel. She had come with a huge blown-up photograph of the Dionne quintuplets on her back—the novel title being *It Can't Happen Here.*

A neighborhood doctor had come by to tell me what a child had said when he asked his stock question, "Do you like your teacher?" Little Stanley who spent one hour each week with his psychiatrist and thirty with us had gone up to dance for the first time. A mother had said, "What have you done to Sylvia? She dreams about you nights."

I knew it wasn't my youth or beauty, my grooming or my bulletin board. It wasn't me at all. It was this approach. But, as I say, I was feeling good.

This next day is awful! It begins with an art supervisor's meeting in the office before school. I run my eye over the latest adult-conceived art ideas put on display for children and listen to, "We must give the children experiences with many, many different materials and techniques."

This article, originally called **"Now I'm All Cleaned Up Inside—A Classroom Therapy,"** has not been published previously. Copyright 1977 by Natalie Robinson Cole. Reprinted by permission.

I sit asking myself a childlike, "Why?" Experiences can be hollow. Material things haven't made the adult world happy. If a teacher can't reach the inner child with a simple painting or clay lesson, how can she hope to do so with such difficult materials and techniques? With the meeting still undigested within me, I go back to our room for the art lesson to follow.

Aaron waves his hand violently to ask, "Can I paint the nurse giving me shots yesterday?"

"You had shots?"

"Yes. Sixty-four." (The children laugh.) "Allergy."

Thickly-built Herbert calls out, "Can I paint the operating room?"

"You were in an operating room?"

"When I was born." (More laughter.)

"Oh," I continue, "He remembers his own delivery table. Before he was off it he was stretching and peering to make note so he could paint it ten years later."

Peals of nervous laughter, the same exaggerated laughter as at the beginning of our dancing when embarrassment is high. We siphon it off in the dancing.

Little things begin to annoy me. Tony spills paint on the floor and his shoes and makes a big fuss about it.

"Forget about your shoes and think of all the paint you've wasted."

A boy stomps into the room to see our ball monitor. Without looking his way I say, "Will Big Feet go out and come in quietly?"

He goes out and comes in the same way.

"Will Big Feet go out and stay out?"

At recess time girls come in to report that Jess is flicking his fingers at their clothes saying, "This can be wool, this can be cotton, and this can be felt"— as he arrived at their beginning bosoms.

Recess over, a safety comes to report two boys jujitsuing in the basement lavatory. I say, "I would think it would block traffic and be dangerous. Every other school I've been in has had a rule against it." Embarrassed looks, then from several, "It's against the rule here."

The projector is misbehaving so we can't show our science films.

Lunch time comes. A teacher remarks *she* would like to do nice things with *her* children but they have so much WORK to do. Wasn't it WORK when I had David up on a chair for a pulpit expounding the principles of religious freedom and social justice and feeling that he really *was* Roger Williams?

Back in the room I learn Tobey is ill and waiting in the office for her father to come. I remark about a father having to leave his work to come for his little daughter. Children shout, "Her father's retired." "He owns a whole string of hotels."

Little Stanley is up snapping a wall map up and down, the children remonstrating with him loudly.

The day goes on getting worse instead of better. A notice comes reminding teachers that no children are to be in the building before school—meaning *me*, I'm sure. Even while I call off the rule the children sense I don't really mean it. Before school is the time I can welcome back those who've been absent, admire the new shirt or new dress. It's the time I can give a child that little extra bit of attention. He wouldn't come if he didn't need it.

The music teacher suggests the song they are to work on. Some children groan. She plunks herself down feeling the lesson hopeless. I am embarrassed and call for someone to speak for us and ask that we be given another chance. The music teacher says she'll be happy to work with us if we enjoy it but not if we are groaning and belly aching.

The lesson over, I jump on the biggest belly-acher. He says, "I don't like music. I don't get any fun out of it."

"You're not *you* any more. You're part of a group with a job to do."

Yap, yap, yap.

Judy has brought her cat to school and I haven't the energy to overlook the distraction.

"When can I bring my kitty again?"

"Never!"

"She loves you. She loves white hair."

"I am touched."

The wellsprings of warmth and spontaneity are dried within me. I am just an old empty sack. I tell myself, forty children day after day, I have a right to a bad day once in a while—I shouldn't flagellate myself. But it does no good.

Finally, Zara, a very intelligent child, sensing the general futility of the day, speaks up, "Couldn't we just read our library books?"

That does it. I go to the board and write,

MRS. COLE'S BAD DAY

I say, "Children, I'm pokey-headed and disagreeable-feeling today. I want you to write it out of your systems."

It seems there is enough carryover from better days for some children to pretend, at least, never to have noticed. Some spring to my defense. One child writes, "If anything happens the teacher thinks it is her fault. It also shows you are a *cheap opportunist.*"

At the beginning of the term, I had had occasion to remark that to fool around when the teacher was there was tiresome and time-wasting, but to do so when the teacher was out of the room was something else again. There was a term for such a person, and I had written it on the board.

Burnout

It happens to most teachers in late February. Some experience it only for one day. Some never come out of it, and some of those go into administration...

I used to care,
But I don't care much any more.
I used to care
That children had to sit still and be quiet
And read pages 9 to 17
And answer the odd-numbered questions at the end of the chapter;
But I don't care much any more.

I used to care
That finishing the assignment is more important than learning the skill,
And getting the right answer is more important than understanding, and
    apologizing is more important than being penitent;
But I don't care much any more.

I used to wake up in the night
And think about ways to teach children
To set goals and work toward them,
To make decisions and live with the results,
To work together.
But there were those who felt threatened
And those who felt frightened
Because my classroom was different.
Parents did not understand.
They listened to the evil insinuations and the confidential criticisms.
Their protests overwhelmed my sand-based supports.
I used to care,
But I don't care much any more.

Now I say
Sit down
Be quiet
Read pages 9 to 17
No exciting ideas disturb my sleep.
I haven't had a complaint in over a year.
Nobody seems to care
That I don't care much any more.

This article is from *Soundtracks*, Vol. II, No. 2 (October 1976). Copyright © 1976 by Southwest Iowa Learning Resources Center. Reprinted by permission.

Things to Remember, Things to Forget

This is a wonderfully complete list. Learn it by Friday! But if you want to do yourself a favor, see how many you already know, or remember, or forgot, or believe. You may not need to memorize it after all.

William C. Miller

THINGS I WISH I COULD REMEMBER

Not to volunteer to do committee work the night of my favorite TV program.

Not to applaud in assembly when they announce the principal is ill.

Not to expect facts and research findings to cause people to change.

Not to equate telling with teaching.

Not to censure students in public.

Not to be afraid to admit my mistakes.

THINGS I WISH I COULD FORGET

The face of the child who got a failing grade.

The feeling in my stomach when my supervisor is in the back of the room observing the lesson.

The fact that my name is on the hall duty roster.

The pressures brought by accountability, assessment, and standardized testing.

The sadness in the eyes of that ghetto youngster.

The idea that students are just little adults and that we should prepare them to live sometime in the future.

This article was originally published as "**Learning About Teaching,**" in *American Educator*, Winter 1977. Reprinted by permission of the American Federation of Teachers, AFL–CIO. William C. Miller is Deputy Superintendent of Schools, Wayne Co., Michigan.

THINGS I HOPE I NEVER FORGET

That the seductive blonde senior is the board president's daughter.

That each of my pupils is someone's dearest possession.

That being laughed *with* is fun; being laughed *at* is torture.

That I'm in the "people business"—and shouldn't take comfort and refuge in paper work.

That schools are for kids.

That there should be joy in learning.

That my goal is to provide the kind of program I'd like my own child to experience.

THINGS I HAVE TROUBLE REMEMBERING

What door to go out during the fire drill.

How I felt about school when I was there.

That my mail box should be checked; (by the time I get there, it's packed so tight I can't pull the stuff out!)

That many of my fellow teachers were not even born when we were fighting World War II.

That my students don't know about alleys, cellar doors, rain barrels, or even Brigitte Bardot.

That the school curriculum is what the kids *actually* learn and do, not what I think or hope they learn.

That I can't make students learn or learn for them. I can only set the climate for learning.

THINGS I WISH I'D NEVER FOUND OUT

That most administrators are busy keeping the lid on rather than doing what's good for kids.

That many faculty members are more concerned with parking places than learning spaces.

That grades are so important to some people.

That grades are so unimportant to some people.

That kids find the first and the last day of school exciting and that what comes between usually isn't.

That some kids never get a chance.

That some teachers gave up on kids years ago.

That many kids have given up on teachers.

THINGS I STILL NEED TO LEARN

To talk less and listen more.

To know the name of every kid in all my classes.

To appreciate good ideas when they aren't expressed grammatically or spelled correctly.

To not be influenced by how pretty or clean a kid is but to pay attention to what he is *inside.*

To give more attention to affective goals even though everyone's emphasizing cognitive areas.

To realize the most important thing a teacher can do is help a kid feel he's glad he is who he is.

THINGS I USED TO BELIEVE

That knowing what is in the textbook was learning.

That my students saying "Yes, Sir" and "No, Sir" was important.

That thirty kids was the best size group for any purpose.

That knowledge students got from sources other than books was somehow of less value.

That neat handwriting was the reflection of a neat mind.

That doing difficult mental work strengthened the mind like a muscle.

That report cards showed a student's progress.

That older teachers know everything.

That older teachers know nothing.

THINGS I DON'T WANT TO BELIEVE

That in many classrooms the textbook is the curriculum.

That custodians and business managers play as important a role as they do in what happens or doesn't happen in schools.

That parents aren't interested in what their children are doing in school.

That school boards and administrators are antiteacher.

That teachers are antischool board and antiadministration.

That politicians are as important to schools as they are.

That schools are mostly run for the convenience of teachers and administrators.

THINGS I'D LIKE TO BELIEVE—BUT CAN'T

That my students can get along without me.

That PTA meetings aren't deliberately planned for nights when the weather is miserable.

That higher salaries will make that ineffective teacher more effective.

That staff members with Master's degrees teach better than those who don't have them.

That decisions in schools are made on the basis of what's best for children.

That more money alone will solve education's problems.

THINGS I WISH I'D DISCOVERED SOONER

That there's no such thing as a free lunch.

That you should only take a job working with someone you can learn from and respect.

That honesty really *is* the best policy!

That all changes aren't for the better.

That the pencil sharpener is a social corner.

That socialization is necessary.

That if you want to help people change, pay less attention to what you do *to* them, or *for* them, and more attention to being a model of the behavior you want to encourage.

THINGS I STILL DON'T UNDERSTAND

How they arrange to have at least one wise guy scheduled into every class.

Why, if we believe what we say about learning, we don't have individualized instruction.

Why the school can't buy the construction paper everyone needs, but can afford expensive teaching machines nobody wants.

How the classroom desks—or their contents—get changed around over the weekend.

Where all those gloves and overshoes go that come up missing.

Where all those gloves and overshoes come from that nobody claims.

Why every time I get playground duty it rains.

THINGS I WISH WERE TRUE—BUT AREN'T

That a youngster is always better off to stay in school rather than to drop out.

That there's no such thing as a bad boy.

That I can reach every kid.

That when there is a battle between the brain and the glands—the brain would win.

That all kids can succeed if they would just try a little harder.

THINGS I CAN'T ACCEPT

Being "held accountable" for students' performance without having significant control over the goals, time, or resources involved.

That schools are so bureaucratic that *nothing* will change them.

That everyone needs to learn the same thing, the same way, at the same time.

That anyone, no matter how high his station, should determine what's best for my kids in my classroom.

That the public cares so little about having good schools that they won't tax themselves to pay for them.

That schools can't educate all kids—white and black, rich and poor.

THINGS I'M CERTAIN OF

He Scrawls Back

Steve Brody has erected some amusing defenses against the Cougher, the Snoozer, and the Scrawler, which he generously passes on.

Steve Brody

Many teachers are forced to erect defense mechanisms to cope with the erratic behavior of some of their students. I am no exception, and over the years I have developed a full repertoire of protective techniques. A few of these methods have proved successful, and so I pass them along to you for what they are worth.

One of the most persistent irritations is the *Cougher*. What makes this breed difficult to defend against is that they multiply so rapidly. I once began a session with nothing to disturb the cathedral quiet but a young miss muffling a delicate cough with a tissue. Thirty minutes later my classroom sounded like a hospital ward full of flu victims.

One year I had a chronic cougher named Marylin Runge in my class. Marylin was a cougher for all seasons. Hers was one of those low, penetrating sounds that seemed to carom off the blackboards. Marylin sat in front center, and when she cranked up to cough, I ducked behind my desk.

What does a teacher tell a cougher? Stay home? Go see the nurse? Not when the student is gunning for a perfect attendance record. So I evolved more subtle techniques. When returning Marylin's compositions, I would attach the latest bulletin from the American Medical Association on the treatment of colds. I suggested that she read *Microbe Hunters* for a nonfiction book report. Once I surreptitiously stored a package of cough drops in her desk. Somewhere along the line Marylin got the message and switched her priorities from attendance records to good health.

Another prime nemesis of teachers is the *Composition Scrawler*. This type has done more to impair the vision of teachers than the fine print in our contracts. I started out in this business as a clear-eyed 20-20, but time and theme have exacted their toll.

I have set up two separate defenses against the scrawler. In step number one, I write a critique on the scrawler's composition in the same illegible style. This prompts the offender to seek me out for a translation, at the same time expressing dismay at my lack of legibility. I respond by maintaining that

This article was originally published as **"Defense Mechanisms,"** in *Today's Education*, Vol. 64, No. 1 (Jan.–Feb. 1975). Reprinted by permission. Steve Brody teaches English at Eastchester (New York) Senior High School.

sloppy writing is contagious. Most students take the hint and make an effort to control their errant ball-points.

Occasionally, however, the message goes unheeded, and I must resort to sterner stuff. At such times I will read the scrawler's paper aloud to the class, letting the chips fall where they may. Recently I read a book report in this manner, written by scrawler Florence Packman. It came out as follows:

> The Grupes of Weath is a stony abond the Jood farily. They louse thore hume in Oklaboma becowes the deest had rooved the lard. The bunk fanced them to jive up thore horse, so thy heave and jo to Cabigarnia. . . .

Florence raised her hand and pleaded that I cease immediately. "Please," she exhorted. "I'll print my compositions from now on. I promise to be neater. I'll take more time. Only please stop reading my paper aloud."

Florence was true to her word. Her penmanship improved to the point where it is now something to write home about.

Another character who can ruffle a teacher's equanimity is the *Snoozer.* Time was when snoozers regarded my classroom as their own personal baili-wick, a refuge from the travail of compulsory education, where they might renew themselves for more arduous disciplines like math or science or jew-elry design.

I was reasonably tolerant in those days, sensitive to the rigorous regimen of healthy, active teenagers. Word soon spread that I was an easy mark, good for 40 minutes of beddy-bye. On mornings following a late basketball game or a senior hop, my classroom resembled a bivouac area after a twenty-mile march.

I have adopted stern measures to deal with the snoozer. I now keep a loaded Polaroid camera handy. When offenders doze off, I tiptoe to their desks and snap their pictures. I then wake them and confront them with the factual testimony. Unless they promise faithfully to mend their ways, I threaten to send the pictures home to their parents as proof that they are betraying their parents' trust and tax dollars.

The admonition almost invariably pays off. One day recently, however, my campaign to eradicate snoozers struck a snag. Walter Rohr, a heavy-lidded senior, fell fast asleep during a class discussion of Wordsworth's poem "Intima-tions of Immortality." Thoroughly disgusted, I reached for the camera and snapped Walter in his comatose state. Then I jarred him awake and flung the picture at him.

"That will go to your parents," I said.

Walter shook the cobwebs from his brain. He studied the picture, then looked me square in the eye.

"Can I order six extra prints?" he asked. "I want to send them to my friends."

II
FIGHTING BACK

You Gotta Fight or Switch

The Return to Fundamentals
in the Nation's Schools

Take a Good Look Back

Pressures Cited for Pupil Suicides

Students in Crisis

When "Straight A" Students Rebelled

Some Startling Research
Encourages Sweeping Change

You Gotta Fight or Switch

While discontented kids cause billions of dollars in damage, conservative adults are voting down school bond issues and tax revenues. Both groups are, at times, strident and impulsive.

Most teachers, wherever they teach and whatever the age group, are likely to be hit by budget cuts. And most school people have been cowering before the anticipated blows.

Not Thomas Sobol. One of the most articulate schoolmen we know, he is affirming the role of the schools and fighting back. Sobol administers the Scarsdale schools, one of the wealthier districts in the nation, in which he can state that "our norms are above national norms and have been increasing recently." He is an atypical administrator leading an atypical community. Yet I include him because he summarizes essential concerns of those critics who demand less spending for schools (in particular, those of Frank E. Armbruster whose article "The More We Spend the Less Children Learn" which was featured in *The New York Times Magazine*) and brilliantly answers their attacks. Let Thomas Sobol be your guide.

Thomas Sobol

What does the public think, these days, of the work of the public schools? To judge from most of what one reads, not much. In recent years we have been told that the institutions we inhabit and the work we do within them are grim, joyless, and oppressive. We have heard that we are mindless, and some believe that society, to save its soul, must become deschooled. More recently, it has been shown to us that the school and all that it attempts makes little impact on the lives of children—we have not, after all (in a capitalistic society) eliminated economic inequality, and we have not overcome the sway of family background. In short, we don't have much to show, especially for what we spend.

Some of this criticism reflects the prevalent distrust of established authority and institutions. Some is specific to us, as old claims are challenged and new aspirations unfulfilled. How general is it? It's hard to say, but it had to mean something, a week ago last Sunday, when we picked up the *New York Times Magazine* and saw the bold yellow title on the cover—"How Schools Fail Our Children." Now the *Times* does not have to publish this article unless it chooses

This article is taken from a transcript of **"Remarks to District Faculty."** Copyright 1977 by Thomas Sobol. Reprinted by permission.

to. So one must assume that either the editors wish to feed what they take to be the popular appetite, or they believe that the article makes an important statement worthy of public attention. Either way, they have helped to create the climate of public discussion as we begin the new school year.

What does the author, Mr. Armbruster, have to say?

His thesis can perhaps be summarized in four points.

1. First, scholastic achievement has declined. "Scores on academic achievement tests," he writes, "reveal that the academic ability of schoolchildren declined almost unremittingly in the second half of the 1960s and the first half of the 1970s. In a sample of school systems we compiled which contained more than half the entire primary and secondary pupil population of the United States... generally the data showed that average achievement scores for all grades above third and fourth not only fell, but fell simultaneously, and each year the same children dropped farther and farther behind the old achievement norms as they progressed through the grades. In certain cases, scores were so low that they may have reached the theoretical lower limit for multiple-choice tests. Many high-school graduates entering college these days cannot understand the textbooks that high-school graduates used to be able to read."And so on.

2. Second, this decline in achievement has been accompanied by a vast increase in spending. Indeed, the implication is left, subtly, that the decline has occurred *because* of the vast increase in spending. According to Mr. Armbruster, "Last school year, Americans spent far more on all levels of education than they spend for defense; for primary and secondary schooling the bill was $75 billion, more than four times the 1960 figure. In some expensive school districts, it now costs a taxpayer approximately $4,000 per year to send his child to high school—about as much as the tuition at an Ivy League college." And, as I say, the implication is left of a cause-and-effect relationship. "As costs go up, graphs show, scores go down... As money spent has increased at an ever-faster rate since the mid-1960s, almost without exception, achievement has consistently fallen. The districts that were holding their own during this period often spent much less per pupil than those experiencing declines."

3. Third, the sole, single, solitary, unarguable reason for this pattern is "innovative education." An alleged lack of money for education or the underprivileged circumstances of many pupils are, in Mr. Armbruster's phrase, "highly questionable excuses... If money and home environment cannot fairly be blamed for the decline," he writes, "what can? The factor that does appear to affect academic performance is the degree to which the schools sacrifice traditional disciplines and subjects for the sake of 'innovative' teaching activities." And what are these in his view? "English as a second language" programs; a failure to insist on middle-class manners of speech and deportment; the teaching of the "whole child"; efforts to "teach pupils to think" clearly; abandonment of rote teaching; the new math; open classrooms; English electives; social sciences other than history; and so on.

4. Finally, the author offers a prescription for our ills. It bears the simplicity of genius. Let us return, he says, "to a system we had about twenty years and three-quarters of a trillion tax dollars ago . . . Diagramming sentences, essay writing and correction by teachers, and the strictly enforced use of proper grammar, grade-equivalent vocabulary, and good diction at all times in school are essential. Numerical or letter-graded report cards every four weeks for elementary school, and six weeks for high school, are ways to help assure that teachers and parents will be alerted to problems . . . Many math and other primary-school problems might be reduced by a new emphasis on rote learning. For example, we know how to teach children the multiplication tables, and we know that this knowledge makes long division much easier. Children can and do learn the 'times table' by rote, chanting in unison if necessary."

What are we to make of such a statement? It ignores experience, obfuscates research, distorts data, offers isolated incidents as if they were general truths, and misleads by implication. And worst of all, infuriatingly, like all such broadsides, it does hit something, a maddening kernel of truth.

Let's look again at Mr. Armbruster's argument, point by point.

First, we must acknowledge that on certain measures academic achievement *has* declined. We should not try to explain that fact away, nor should we ignore it. We should investigate the reasons and deal with them. More about that in a moment. But first, in the spirit of intellectual honesty, let's note the fact that not all achievement scores have declined, neither in general nor for all sections of the population. An analysis of test results here in Scarsdale would take more time than we have this morning, but let me share with you a few comments from the report of the Board's Advisory Committee on Educational Planning last spring.

> Scarsdale students are significantly above the national norms in standardized tests, and the differential between Scarsdale and national norms has been increasingly modestly during the past several years . . . Much has been written about the decline in the verbal SAT scores on a national basis during the past several years, and Scarsdale has been no exception. While still way ahead of the national figures, scores of Scarsdale students have declined recently and the differential has been narrowed particularly for the girls . . . The comparison of math scores indicates that while the national average has been declining, the scores of male graduates have been increasing (+ 18 vs -9 for the national average). The female scores, while declining, have been declining less than the national average . . . The College Board also administers achievement tests in a variety of courses . . . Comparative scores indicate that both national norms and Scarsdale norms have increased and the differentials have remained about the same.

The record is spotty. All our scores are high compared to national averages, but they ought to be. Some of our scores have gone down. Some have gone up. But enough have gone down to warrant inquiry. So on Mr. Armbruster's first point, we must face the fact that if we take the tests seriously, and if we value high scores on them, we have a problem which we must address, albeit a much more complex problem than Mr. Armbruster implies.

What about Mr. Armbruster's second point, that greater spending has led to lower achievement? Here, too, we must accept a certain responsibility. Like many in the expansive, liberal 1960s, we may have believed too much that money alone could solve our problems. It was, after all, the time of the War on Poverty and of quality plus plenty for all. But once again, let's look beneath the surface of the numbers. What do we spend our money on? One of the main items is salaries. Relative to the rest of the society, teachers in the 1950s, most observers would agree, were underpaid. Today, depending on where you sit, they may or may not be. But why should it be that if teachers' salaries have been raised, that pupils' scores should improve on the SAT's? Or again, if the costs of fuel oil and electricity and gasoline and state and federally mandated expenses such as pensions and social security have skyrocketed, why should we expect pupils to get more right answers on the PEP tests? Is the food we buy in the supermarket better because it costs more than it did in 1957? I used to pay seventy-five cents for a haircut, and now I pay $7.50. Is my hair any trimmer or less gray? When I used to drive across the Kappock Street bridge in Riverdale it cost a dime; now I shell out fifty cents. Is the West Side Highway that it leads me to in any better condition?

As I have said, the decline in achievement, where it exists, is an important phenomenon to be taken seriously. The increase in costs for education, competing as it does for other public services and threatening as it does the prospect of continuing public support, is also an important problem to be confronted forthrightly. But any linking of the two demands reasoned inquiry into the relationships between cost and quality. We do not find it here. The author does refer, in passing, to student-teacher ratios and the relationship between academic achievement and specific patterns of spending. Perhaps, in another forum, he has or will pursue these and other lines of inquiry. But not here. "As costs go up, scores go down."

One more question before I leave this point. Why must we assume that a given expenditure on a child's education is valid only if it results in measurable academic achievement? "It is not obvious," he writes, "that high-school graduates who come from lower schools with full-time librarians, music, art and gym teachers in kindergarten through fourth grade show superior skills in these areas when compared with students who did not have such teachers in the lower elementary grades." So what? Might it be that the experiences these teachers provided, *whether or not* they led to higher scores, may have been good for children to have? If the child develops his body, feels wonder, paints a picture, sings a song, senses a power and stirring within, does this not count? Is all of life and young growth measured by tests? My point is not that all things that librarians, music, art, and gym teachers do are valuable. My point is that there is an endless series of value judgments to be made about what experiences we wish to provide for our children (and, in a democratic society, our neighbor's children), and that these choices are not defined by answers to multiple-choice tests some Saturday in grade 11.

Mr. Armbruster's third point is that the decline in academic achievement is the fault of the schools alone. I wonder how he knows that? The fact seems to have escaped so many others. Here, for example, is the report of the twenty-one-member panel of the College Entrance Examination Board, attempting to account for the decline of the SAT scores in recent years. "There is no single cause and we suspect no single pattern of causes," it concludes. From 1963 to 1970, the decline may have been caused in part by students taking the test who in earlier years would not have gone to college. But since 1970, "searching for the causes of the decline. . . is essentially an exercise in conjecture." The panel reported that "no clear causal relationships can be proved" but cited "circumstantial evidence" for six factors. These were:

The growth of elective courses and other educational trends that have contributed to the neglect of "critical reading and careful writing."
Diminished attention to basic skills as evidenced by trends such as grade inflation, automatic promotion, tolerance of absenteeism, and less meaty textbooks.
Widespread television viewing, which the panel said "detracts from homework" and in other ways "competes with schooling."
The "decade of distraction" from 1967 to 1975 in which events such as the war in Vietnam, political assassinations, and Watergate presumably "affected youths' motivation."
An "apparent diminution" in student motivation, at least in relation to taking tests.

The panel acknowledged, however, that it could not explain some major aspects of the decline in scores, such as why verbal scores have fallen more than math scores.

That would seem to be a pretty mixed bag.

And we did not have to wait for the SAT report to have a sense of the partnership of schooling with other influences on children's lives. In the past ten years a series of studies has shown that family background is the most powerful determinant of a child's "success," and that, for most people, the schools fail to change the patterns rooted in the family. Chief among these studies, perhaps, have been those of Coleman and of Jencks. Their work suggests that any judgment of an educational program must be made in light of what is happening elsewhere that affects that program. As President Larry Cremin of Teachers College has written, "The real message of the Coleman and Jencks studies of equal educational opportunity is not that the school is power*less* but that the family is power*ful*." As if anticipating critics who believe either that the school is all-powerful or that it has no power at all, Professor Cremin writes:

Coleman's data did indeed suggest that the effects of schooling were less potent and less uniform than had traditionally been assumed. His data did not indicate, however, that the school had no power, but rather that it was educating sequentially and synchronically along with other institutions and that its effect on different individuals was partly dependent on what happened to them in those other institutions. It is not that schooling lacks potency; it is rather that the potency of schooling must be seen in relation to the potency of other experience (some of which is educational in character) that has occurred earlier and is occurring elsewhere. The point has obvious bearing on assessments of the effects of schooling that ignore other educational factors, fail to hold them constant, or refuse to correct for them.

Nevertheless, knowing that the schools are but one important influence in children's lives does not excuse our responsibility here. After all, Scarsdale has not changed so much in fifteen years. In the past few years we have acknowledged error by reemphasizing the teaching of arithmetic skills and by reasserting writing requirements in elective English courses. We should continue to look at our students' scores and to make whatever adjustments in program or in our own effort seem indicated. But meanwhile, we don't have to believe that the scores have declined simply because we do things somewhat differently than we did in 1957.

Which brings me to Mr. Armbruster's last point, that we should turn the clock back twenty years. I find this a most extraordinary suggestion, coming from one who values history so much. Why would a man of his persuasion want to go back to such a time? I remember twenty years ago very clearly, since I was just entering the profession and everything seemed new. Public education was everywhere under attack. A host of critics led by Admiral Rickover and Arthur Bestor were telling us that we had failed to train the intelligence of our young, that we lacked academic standards, that we had fallen behind the Russians, that we had quackery in the public schools, that Johnny couldn't read. I have no doubt that if Mr. Armbruster had been active then, he would have been loud among the chorus.

But I'll tell you what, Mr. Armbruster. I'll make you a deal. We'll go back to 1957. We'll drop the Alternative School and the CHOICE program and our efforts to teach our Japanese children English and our various attempts to help the handicapped. We'll drop the new math and the new sciences and all the other curriculum reforms developed by scholars and teachers during these years. We'll give report cards every four weeks, we won't teach any of the social sciences except history and geography, we'll diagram sentences until you're blue in the face, and yes, we'll get the kids to chant the multiplication tables in unison.

But you have to meet your end of the bargain. Since we're going back twenty years, you go back too. You undo Little Rock, repeal the Civil Rights movement and its aftermath, expunge the Kennedy and King assassinations, wipe from memory the Vietnam war, make as if the baby-boom kids had never come of age and a youth culture had not been created, pretend there was no sexual revolution and no youth rebellion, and disinvent the television set. Because unlike you, Mr. Armbruster, we know from daily contact the young people whom we're talking about, and we know that what happens in our classrooms day after day, year after year is very much conditioned by what these young people do outside our schools and the attitudes and habits they bring with them when we meet them. No doubt you read that as defensive. Are you nonetheless willing to allow for the possibility that it may be true?

The truth about what we do, with all its possibilities and all its limits, is vastly richer and more complex than this kind of argument. Standards have slipped, and it is in part our responsibility to improve them. Costs have risen, and it is in part our duty to hold them down. We have been making both efforts; they must continue. But in doing so what is needed, I believe, is not a wild pendulum swing to the past but a balanced effort to combine intellectual quality with the best of progressive method. Mr. Armbruster claims that "pupils must know the history of our civilization and great literature in our language. They should be exposed to some higher mathematics, some real science, and to at least one of the major foreign languages. They simply *must* be able to transform ideas into written material in a comprehensible and grammatically correct way." I'll buy that. Meanwhile, in a passage in which he summarizes the approach of the "open schools" which Mr. Armbruster disparages, Joseph Featherstone writes:

> Good teachers start with the lives of children here and now, and proceed from their experiences toward more disciplined inquiry. Teaching is more effective if teachers can find out where learners are by watching them in action and talking with them; learning is more effective if it grows out of the interests of the learner. (And of course interests are not just there, like flowers waiting to bud: they are formed and cultivated by good teaching.) Experience and theory suggest that active learning is better than passive. Giving children choices within a planned environment helps them develop initiative, competence, and an ability to think for themselves. A good curriculum offers children knowledge worth acquiring. It is essential that children learn reading skills, for example, but they must also see the point of being literate, taking an interest in books and knowing how to use them. Teaching practice ought to reflect the enormous diversities among children, treating them as individuals, and proceeding, when possible, from their strengths, rather than from their weaknesses . . . The aim of the enterprise is to influence students to become thinking, autonomous, sensitive people.

I'll buy that too. The two ideals are not in conflict, they are complementary. Fortunately, there are other public voices who agree. In an editorial in the self-same *Times* last summer, Fred Hechinger wrote that

> It would be naive to expect the school to free itself entirely of society's pull of ideological gravity or flatly to resist the currents that are the consequence of the American character. And yet professional educators, like their counterparts in other fields, have an obligation to take a firmer stand against the absurdities of each fleeting era. It is by moderating the progressive and tradi-

tionalist extremes—indeed by fusing many of their specific practices—that the most promising pedagogical answers may be found. By resisting the call to jump on every passing sociopedagogical bandwagon, academic leaders may be able better to achieve both progress and stability.

The vital goal of keeping education relevant is not the equivalent of surrender to every popular fad; but making students once again mindful of intellectual traditions can surely be accomplished more constructively than through the imposition of such requirements as the reading of *Silas Marner* on captive young audiences—as appears to be happening in the name of reform in some suburban schools.

If quality and intellectual vigor are not to be just another short-lived phase, they ought to be viewed not as a conservative reaction to the pseudo-progressive excesses of the sixties, not as a move back, but a journey forward—reform, not retreat.

That, I believe, is how we should use our time these next three years. I look forward to working with you in this effort.

The Return to Fundamentals in the Nation's Schools

Declining achievement, alarming drops in scientific knowledge, unaccountable schools...these are worrying the American public. But should schools be blamed? Willard Wirtz, who did more than anyone else to bring the declining verbal and mathematical SAT scores to the attention of the public, thinks not. Testifying in Congress, he said that distractions in the years from the mid-sixties to the early seventies had contributed to a lowering of the motivation of students and to the drop in scores. Nevertheless, many hard-working teachers who finally devised workable and humane approaches, find now that they are being scored for their students low scores.

The back-to-basics movement is not one that can be accommodated by a mere change in your plan-book. You must sift the valid charges from the panic to decide what your response should be. Gene Maeroff's summary of the back-to-fundamentals movement will help.

Gene I. Maeroff

"Back to basics" is the slogan of the most-talked-about movement in elementary and secondary education today, a fascination with the idea that the schools have slipped in their teaching of the fundamentals and must reorder priorities to stress the three R's—reading, 'riting and 'rithmetic.

Educators and parents throughout the country are debating the merits of the push toward basics, which is influencing thinking on a wide front and resulting in scattered examples of reconstituting entire schools.

For instance, the Miami-Dade County system in Florida has established six Traditional Basic Skills Schools, and the Pasadena system in California has three new Fundamental Schools.

Almost 10 percent of Pasadena's 26,083 students have volunteered to attend the Fundamental Schools, which run from kindergarten through 12th grade, and 1,400 more are on waiting lists. The schools have dress codes, strict discipline and character education and emphasize patriotism and extensive work in the basic skills, including phonics in reading instruction and computational abilities in mathematics.

Underpinning the basics movement is a thin layer of nostalgia, a yearning for the untroubled simplicity of the so-called good old days. But there is, as well, a concern that the schools should be made more accountable and show better results for the tens of billions of dollars they receive.

THE BACKGROUND

The notion that there is a need to do a better job of teaching the basics has been nurtured by an academic climate in which achievement in the fundamentals seems to be faltering.

A steady decline in the scores on both the verbal and mathematical parts of the Scholastic Aptitude Test by college-bound students in high schools across the United States is perhaps the most notable indicator of the slippage.

Other evidence of declining achievement has been provided by the National Assessment of Educational Progress, a federally sponsored project to measure periodically the learning of America's young people.

Last month, the National Assessment reported that the writing of 13-year-old students surveyed in 1974 was less coherent and more simplistic and awkward than that of their counterparts four years earlier.

The National Assessment has also shown a drop in the scientific knowledge of young people and an alarmingly low level of sophistication in consumer mathematics. However, a recent examination of basic reading performance by the National Assessment found an improvement last year, as compared with three years earlier.

Complaints about an alleged deterioration of standards have become commonplace among college officials and employers. They say that today's

---

This article is from *The New York Times*, December 6, 1976. © 1976 by The New York Times Company. Reprinted by permission.

high school graduates often lack the basic skills necessary to handle college work or to do what is expected of them at entry-level jobs.

Young people are criticized for sloppy grammar, poor spelling, difficulty in following printed instructions and inaccuracies in computation.

The period in which achievement levels have become controversial has coincided with the relaxation of formal requirements such as the mandatory study of foreign languages. There has been a proliferation of alternative courses allowing students, especially in secondary schools, to avoid the basic courses once demanded of all.

Moreover, a general mood of what some call "permissiveness" has descended on the schools, and youngsters have been given more flexibility in running their own affairs, even at the risk of occasionally clashing with the authorities. Indeed, a recent public poll by the National Education Association found that "discipline" was identified as the main problem in the schools.

In light of the picture that is being projected of the schools, the question presenting itself is simply this: Is there a need for a return to basics?

PRO

"We think the back-to-basics trend is a good idea," said George Weber, associate director of the nonprofit Council for Basic Education in Washington. "Nobody expects the schools to turn out 100 percent Einsteins, but more and more people believe it is not unreasonable to have all children achieve a minimum level of competency."

The liberalization of the curriculum that began in the early 1960s is one of the forces blamed for the supposed de-emphasis of the basics.

Taken to the extreme, the reasoning was that many of the traditional approaches to schooling were no longer needed. Television, the telephone and hand-held calculators were cited in behalf of arguments to diminish the importance of reading, writing and arithmetic.

The advocates of back to basics point out that spelling bees, penmanship lessons and the memorization of multiplication tables and historic dates were deemed instructional anachronisms; that new attention was focused on feelings and attitudes of students, sometimes referred to as affective or humanistic education.

One of the innovations symbolizing the changed educational philosophy of the 1960s, new math, which critics maintain gave so much attention to concepts that computational skills were downplayed, is now falling into disfavor as the swing is back toward concentrating on the skills themselves.

Another of the changes, open education, a methodology that gives youngsters more control over their time and activities, is also finding itself threatened.

"Open education as it is practiced in many places does cause a move away from basics," said Dr. Paul H. Gendler, District Superintendent of Merrick, on Long Island, where the implementation of open education classes was suspended when the approach seemed to be causing a drop in the district's achievement scores.

Merrick went back to open education this year, but only after rectifying the organizational problems and other difficulties that Dr. Gendler thinks may be continuing to plague open education elsewhere.

CON

Implicit in the back-to-basics movement is the suggestion that the schools have lessened their commitment to the fundamentals, a suggestion that not everyone is ready to accept.

"I didn't know we ever left the basics," said Dr. William L. Pharis, executive director of the National Association of Elementary School Principals. "What we see in this movement is a Puritan ethic that anything that is good for you has to hurt, and that if kids are enjoying themselves in school there must be something wrong."

Open education may be a special scapegoat of the back-to-basics movement, since—its strengths or weaknesses aside—the method was never adopted by more than a small minority of the schools and can scarcely be the cause of a wholesale decline in achievement, the defenders of the system say.

The reasons for the downturn in test scores are complex, and few experts would agree that more emphasis on basics is all that is needed to turn the scores around. Adding to the confusion is the fact that some national tests have not shown declines.

What is known is that school dropout rates have declined, and that many of the youngsters who in prior years would not have been around to register low scores on achievements are now being included in the testing.

Also, there is the matter of what the tests are testing. If the emphasis in teaching is on understanding why the Battle of Gettysburg was fought, but the test wants to know when it was fought and how many people died, then the proper debate should concern itself with educational goals.

Basics is a fuzzy word that is being used to cover a wide assortment of dissatisfactions, societal as well as schooling. Mr. Weber of the Council for Basic Education is all in favor of more reading, writing and arithmetic, but he is leery of those who would use the movement "to go around measuring the length of boys' hair and girls' dresses."

THE OUTLOOK

What seems likely to emerge from the attention to basics is a new effort to get a high school diploma to represent a uniform standard. Arizona, and more recently Oregon, have set specific requirements for such a diploma.

In most states, though, there is no assurance that someone with a high school diploma reads above the sixth-grade level, can write an acceptable essay or is able to cope with certain computational tasks.

The establishment of these standards may be an objective on which both sides can agree—whether or not they think that there has been a deterioration in the teaching of the basics.

Take a Good Look Back

Conservatives love to look back at "the good-old-golden school days." Armbruster, for example, claims that back then we succeeded in teaching all children, even those who were bilingual and bicultural, by emphasizing the basics and enforcing discipline.

In truth, the children he speaks of were not in the schools—not for long. In 1906, less than 17 percent of the students in Massachusetts between the ages of fourteen and sixteen had graduated from elementary school. Only 8.8 percent nationally made it through high school.

In 1920, only 20 percent of the students who finished fifth grade completed high school. Whereas by 1960, some 60 percent of the population stayed in school long enough to graduate from high school. By 1968 it grew to 76 percent, and now the figure representing the number of children who stay long enough to graduate hovers around 75 percent.

Although the number of high-school-age children has increased by 500 percent, the number of drop-outs has remained relatively "constant since 1920, and now 60 percent of the high school graduates go on to college."

So the poor who were insufficiently motivated and who dropped out of schools because they were failing or failed to see much point in staying are now remaining in school. Yet we have not yet solved our social and economic problems. Is it any wonder, then, that many who remain do not achieve as well or behave as well as those advantaged few who did stay in school in the golden mythic days of yore? Should we return to the days when we forced these children out? In those days they went to work. What will they do now?

Thomas C. Hunt and Elmer U. Clawson

Urban education has a long history of turmoil and conflict of charge and counter-charge. Within the last decade there has been heated debate over community control, compensatory education, busing, and financing of schools, all of which bear on the topic of equal educational opportunity. Among the several other issues which faced central-city schools around 1900, and at the mid-twentieth century, is school dropouts. The fact of the matter is, dropouts have been a constant occurrence ever since American schooling, accompanied by compulsory attendance legislation, was initiated on a "mass" scale in the 19th century.

The main attention of this article will be concentrated on two periods of time. The first is the age of rapid industrialization and urbanization which occurred around the turn of the century. Accompanied by the immigration of many people from southern and eastern Europe, the enactment of child labor laws, and the growth of the high school, school dropouts became a source of some concern. The second period is that of the mid-twentieth century. It was during this era that the great migrations of southern blacks to the urban North occurred. This period was also characterized by a heavy dropout rate. In both instances, new and heavy strains were placed on the schools.

Massachusetts, in 1852, was the first state to enact a compulsory attendance law. By 1918 every state had enacted such legislation. While these school laws required attendance to the minimum age of 14, it was possible in 1918 in a number of states to avoid attending school, and in New York City in 1900 there were an estimated 40,000 children of legal school age who were not in school.

The minimum school-attendance age had been raised to 16 in a number of states by the mid-twentieth century. Reports, however, continued to record high truancy and dropout rates.

At their inception, compulsory attendance laws were believed necessary protection for society. They would insure that children of the lower classes would go to school, become literate and moral thereby, and thus be of benefit rather than a danger to society. While there was considerable opposition to paying for the education of someone else's children, the practice did become more prevalent throughout the nation as the nineteenth century progressed.

As a result of compulsory attendance laws, the schools inherited a problem. They were forced to assume the roles of caretaker and custodian. Some children did not want to go to school, but the schools were legally ordered to keep them. In spite of legislation, and the efforts of truant or attendance officers, the situation was "fluid" and has remained so.

A corollary of required schooling is dropouts. The high schools at the turn of the century had their dropouts by the "thousands," the elementary schools by the "tens of thousands." According to Susan M. Kingsbury, in 1906 there were 25,000 youngsters in Massachusetts, between the ages of 14 and 16 not attending school in that state. Five-sixths of them had not graduated from elementary school.

This article was originally published as **"Dropouts: Then and Now,"** in *The High School Journal*, LVII, March 1975. Reprinted by permission.

When surveyed, children at the turn of the century gave a number of reasons for dropping out—poor health, lack of interest, the need of their services at home. Understandably, they did not mention failure in school as a reason.

Others have found additional reasons, some of which were operative both around 1900 and at the middle of the century. School people in the early 1900s asserted that the curriculum had to be made more "practical." This contributed significantly to the rise of vocational education in secondary schools. Somewhat the same was true at mid-century.

In both periods there is evidence to refute the contention that central-city residents were not interested in academic curriculums, but there is no evidence to support the claim that, with the advent of vocational education and its implementation in secondary education, the dropout rate was curtailed or even moderately modified.

Intelligence tests have contributed to the plight of the white ethnic immigrant and the black in schools. School people in both periods thought they had "scientific" data by means of these tests. This data, having been scientifically obtained, was then used to make judgments about the intelligence of students. For instance, Arthur R. Jensen, among others, has argued for a genetic intellectual inferiority among blacks based on the results of intelligence tests. Similar arguments were advanced relative to the immigrants a half century ago. Thus the use to which these tests were put has contributed significantly to the problems lower-class minorities have faced in schools.

TEACHER ATTITUDES

Attendance at school relates to a number of items, dropouts being one. In 1911, children of native white Americans showed the largest proportion attending school at least nine-tenths of the time, while blacks showed the smallest percentage. Low achievement contributed to dropouts. Undoubtedly so did the attitudes these children encountered in school. Immigrants and their children, at the turn of the century were referred to as inferior by social and educational leaders. These attitudes could not help but affect teachers of immigrant children.

Blacks in the mid-twentieth century faced similar circumstances. Prejudice against them was rampant, not only in the South, but also in the North where discrimination was on a *de facto* rather than a *de jure* basis. Educationally, they were segregated in both South and North.

There is a plethora of information about white teacher attitudes to black children in northern metropolitan areas. The sum of these writings is that white middle-class teachers frequently regarded the lower-class black students in metropolitan schools as not having the intellectual qualities and character traits necessary to succeed in school or society. Teacher attitudes, when coupled with low scores on intelligence tests and low achievement in schools, operated to lower the self-concept of these students and accelerated their underachievement.

American schools have always had their dropouts. However, based on fifth-grade students from 1920 to 1960, high-school withdrawals declined at a rather steady rate from about 80 percent in 1920 to about 40 percent in 1960. The high-school-age population increased some 500 percent between 1920 and 1960,but the evidence shows that the number of dropouts remained relatively constant. Consequently, the likelihood of the young American's graduating from high school has increased as the twentieth century progressed.

This declining ratio should not be of comfort to American society in general and to educators in particular. For, facing an increasingly more complex technological society throughout this same time period, the young American needed to develop more skills to successfully enter the job market, if he was not going to college. High school was the place that this was supposedly to occur. The evidence for lower socioeconomic class youth, especially nonwhite youth, does not indicate this occurred.

A number of reasons have been advanced as causes of dropouts around 1900 and 1960. One which has not been mentioned as yet is the cost of attending schools which are supposed to be free. For instance, it cost $125 to attend a public high school in Milwaukee in 1942. In 1931 a group of 150 high school principals across the nation estimated that it cost their typical student from $3.00 to $15.00 annually (costs of food, clothing, shelter, and transportation were excluded). In six high schools east of the Mississippi the actual average cost was $125 per pupil. This occurred during a period when 26 percent of American families had an annual income of $750 or less (1931-37), with an average of $470. Thus 25 percent of their income would have to have been spent to keep one student "up" *and* keep him in high school.

When one considers the optional extra-curricular costs—dances, yearbooks, graduation expenses, athletic contests, etc., it is little wonder that Havighurst found in his study of dropouts that 67 percent had a strong dislike for dances, athletic contests, etc.

Havighurst found several other interesting factors related to dropouts. He noted that a majority came from low income families, with a home and neighborhood which was indifferent or even hostile to school, and that 34 percent of the parents of dropouts were indifferent to their children leaving school, 13 percent were opposed, and 6 percent had encouraged their children to quit school.

Among the arguments advanced to motivate students to get their high-school diploma was the earning power this would bring in later life. For minority group, nonwhite students, many from lower socioeconomic classes, this is not true. Hansen found, in 1962, that each additional year of schooling did contribute $60 per year in earnings, but that there was a difference of $608 per year between white and black incomes.

The dropout problem remains. Various proposals have been brought forward, including "on the job" training, career education, "relevant curriculums," abolishing compulsory schooling laws, etc., as solutions, whole or partial, to the problem. As school people confront the issue today, it would benefit them to keep in mind the fact that school is not a panacea. They might do well to consider the possibility that, at least for high-school-age pupils, school might not be the best place to be. Above all, school people should never engage in a campaign against dropouts which results in their vilification and social stigmatization. Dropping out of school may truly be said to be "a symptom of preexisting problems rather than the problem itself." And the source of that problem may well be in the fiber of society, of which our schools are an integral part, as well as in the individual and/or his family.

Pressures Cited for Pupil Suicides

The real costs of competition are rarely mentioned by supporters of rigor, but this item will remind us why we embraced informal education after the emphasis on excellence in the late fifties. Look at the effects school pressures have on the Japanese students, for they hint at what we can anticipate when *we* tighten the screws.

TOKYO—More than 800 Japanese students between the ages of 5 and 19 committed suicide last year because of school-related problems, official figures indicate.

Most of the students appeared to have become disheartened by their inability to complete a heavy homework load or by poor results in school examinations in Japan's high-pressure educational system. The students chose hanging, gas, drowning, electrocution, or jumping from high places in their suicides, reports showed.

In a recent case, a 10-year-old Tokyo girl jumped to her death from the top of a 14-story apartment building because she could not finish her homework during her summer holidays. The same day, a 17-year-old high school student hanged himself at home because his grades, though satisfactory, had dropped a little from those of the previous semester. In Yokohama, a 15-year-old girl, unable to make up her mind which college to enter, threw herself in front of a speeding train. Schooling in Japan is compulsory until ninth grade. After that, if students wish to continue their education, they must take a series of tough entrance tests. Parents, hoping to get their children into the top

This article was originally published as **"Pupil Suicides Up in Japan; Pressures Cited,"** in *Newsday, October 11, 1977. Copyright* © 1977 by Agence France-Presse. Reprinted by permission.

schools and universities, which virtually guarantees them a lifetime job in the country's major firms, start pushing their offspring as early as age 5. But chances of being accepted in the 34 most prestigious Japanese universities are only one in six. The result is often unbearable strain and competition.

In the Japanese system of education, students are forced to memorize more and more information just to beat others in competition, Prof. Kanichiro Ishii of Kyoto University said.

Vacations, even in summer, often are simply a time for Japanese students to cram for advanced-school entrance exams. Sometimes they study 18 hours a day. Even elementary school pupils are overwhelmed with work. In addition to their own language, they have to memorize more than 1,000 complicated Chinese characters and as many as 3,000 English words, plus numerous mathematical theorems.

In April, a 13-year-old student, barred by his parents from watching television, hanged himself in his room. In another case, a 9-year-old boy, forced by his parents to attend three prep schools and an English conversation class, began spitting blood on his way to school and had to be hospitalized.

The nationwide problem is so severe that the number of pupils under 14 years of age suffering from stomach ulcers has jumped every year for 10 years. The number of suicides has gone up 10 per cent in five years.

Japanese cartoonist Osamu Tezuka said recently that death ranks second, after love, as the most popular cartoon topic among Japanese students.

The suicide trend among Japanese youngsters will continue to rise unless something is done to change the nation's educational system, some sociologists say. Education ministry officials concede the current system is related to the number of children's suicides. But reform would take years, observers believe.

Students in Crisis

Were *our* children ever under this kind of pressure? Let's glance back to the student statements of the early seventies to remind ourselves.

HE ALWAYS WANTED TO EXPLAIN THINGS

He always wanted to explain things.
But no one cared.
Sometimes he would draw and it wasn't anything.
He wanted to carve it in stone or write it in the sky.
He would lie out in the grass and look up in the sky.
And it would only be him and the sky and the things inside him that needed
    saying.

And it was after that he drew the picture.
It was a beautiful picture.
He kept it under his pillow and would let no one see it.
And he would look at it every night and think about it.
And when it was dark, and his eyes were closed, he could still see it.
And it was all of him.
And he loved it.
When he started school he brought it with him.
Not to show anyone, but just to have it with him like a friend.
It was funny about school.
He sat in a square, brown desk.
Like all other square, brown desks.
And he thought it should be red.
And his room was a square, brown room.
Like all the other rooms.
And it was tight and close.
And stiff.
He hated to hold the pencil and chalk.
With his arm stiff and his feet flat on the floor,
Stiff.
With the teacher watching and watching.
The teacher came and spoke to him.
She told him to wear a tie like all the other boys.
He said he didn't like them.
And she said it didn't matter.
After that they drew.
And he drew all yellow and it was the way he felt about morning.
And it was beautiful.
The teacher came and smiled at him.
"What's this?" she said. "Why don't you draw like Ken's drawing?
Isn't that beautiful?"
After that his mother bought him a tie.
And he always drew airplanes and rocketships like everyone else.
And he threw the old picture away.
And when he lay alone looking at the sky,
It was big and blue and all of everything,
But he wasn't anymore.
He was square inside,
And brown,

The poem **"He Always Wanted to Explain Things"** was handed in to a teacher in Regina, Saskatchewan, Canada by a Grade 12 student. Although it is not known if he actually wrote the poem himself, it is known that he committed suicide a few weeks later. The poem originally appeared in *Generation*, a Saskatoon-based magazine. **"A Suicide Note"** and **"A Statement by Community School Students"** is reprinted with permission from *Education Explorer I*, produced by the Education Exploration Center.

And his hands were stiff.
And he was like everyone else.
And the things inside him that needed saying didn't need it anymore.
It had stopped pushing.
It was crushed.
Stiff.
Like everything else.

A SUICIDE NOTE

I'm sorry it had to be this way. I just couldn't take this screwed up world any longer. I tried, but I wasn't strong enough. I'm just a weakling, always ready to take the easy way out. It's just all these damn people that are as plastic as hell, always trying to be something they're not. Their main goal in life is to make money, so they can be something. I even try, that's what really bothers me. I'm not saying that all people are like that, but there isn't enough to go around. I'm such an unimportant person, there's no way I can change the world. It's taken so long to get it this way, there's no way I could change it overnight. Even if I tried my hardest to change it for the next generations, the world is going kaput anyway. It's not just society that made me decide I couldn't take it any longer. I was just in such a depressing state of mind. I'm just so lonely and instead of looking better, things are worse, with absolutely no way of them looking better. So, I don't want you feeling bad, I want you to be happy. I'm sure that the place I'm in now is very mild compared to the hell back on your world.

Darlene

A STATEMENT BY COMMUNITY SCHOOL STUDENTS

The learning that is important to individual growth can take place only when the student wants to learn. Any person in any situation has the freedom not to learn simply by closing his mind. An important step in the educational process is, then, for both student and teacher to recognize the student's unqualified prerogative to choose what he wants to learn. Learning will best take place when the student is both constantly challenged to evaluate his ideas and actions (in the light of accurate feedback) *and* secure in the knowledge that he alone can decide what is important to him.

It is no longer true that there is a body of knowledge that must be passed on to the younger generation. The body of knowledge that is usually referred to is, for the most part, a collection of fragmented pieces of information that burden instead of giving strength and bore instead of arousing enthusiasm. Knowledge is good only for the individual who appreciates its value. Education must focus on the kind of knowledge that will develop our potential to live.

When "Straight A" Students Rebelled

In the fall of 1970, Thomas Sobol addressed the teachers in our town about the state of the students: their growing alienation and their violent anger. He spoke of problems he felt teachers must face if they were to understand the student riots and the reason so many were dropping out of school and fleeing from the straight world.

It's been almost ten years since we questioned the rigors of the post-Sputnik classrooms (now again so lauded by critics) and opted for a child-centered curriculum. Remind yourself by reading Sobol's review of the times. It may strengthen your resolve to save the schools and today's children.

Thomas Sobol

Ten years ago, in 1960, when I was a teacher of English in the Newton High School, Massachusetts, I participated in a workshop on articulation. About a dozen of us met every morning and early afternoon to discuss the great issues which were dividing the junior from the senior high school departments. I remember the occasions as being pleasant, probably because I was ten years younger then, and I remember that some members of the group even felt some sense of accomplishment when the workshop ended and we all went off to enjoy the last week or two of summer before returning to the reality of school. We had all had a good time talking and we understood one another so much better, you see. The issues, by the way, had something to do with whether *Huckleberry Finn* was a seventh-grade or an eleventh-grade book and whether one should teach topic sentences beginning in the seventh grade or in the ninth. I can't remember what we decided anymore, and for all I know, I forgot it shortly after Labor Day that year. Somehow it just never seemed to matter once I got involved with the kids again.

Now that pretty well sums up my experience in the matter of articulation. So you can see what impressive credentials I bring to the task at hand today. Nevertheless, I ought to make some attempt, before I go on to what I really want to talk about, to pay some attention to the topic which the Committee has assigned. So let me summarize for you very quickly the obligatory conventional wisdom about school articulation. [At this point the speaker summarized such wisdom through the use of commentary and slides. Many smiled, and some were heard to laugh.]

This article is taken from a transcript of **"Articulation in Great Neck, 1970."** Copyright 1970 by Thomas Sobol. Reprinted by permission.

But it is not that of which I now wish to speak. I should like to turn instead to a different kind of articulation problem—the kind of articulation problem posed by what someone has called "the terrible disjunctions of our age." We live in a time of abrupt and polarizing discontinuities, gaps in perception and experience so divisive and fragmenting that it has become an open question whether our society can survive with its health and sensibilities intact. It has become cliché to talk about the society being in revolution. But that it surely is. And not only is this true on the national level, it is true here in Great Neck as well. As the revolutions continue, they produce gaps or fissures in the very foundations of what we do in schools, gaps which demand "articulation" by any human being or any school system that wishes to deal honestly with its responsibilities. I would like you to consider with me for a few minutes four such areas here in Great Neck.

ARTICULATION PROBLEM #1

Let us acknowledge, first of all, that we have here in Great Neck a deep and widening gulf between the "haves" and the "have-not's," and more specifically between whites and blacks. This is not the kind of problem it has been fashionable to talk about in Great Neck, which continues to send over 90 percent of its graduates on to higher education. But you had better believe it's there. Last spring, after the invasion of Cambodia and the deaths at Kent State, several of us stood at the flagpole on the mall in front of the South Senior High School trying to preserve some kind of order. The vast majority of the students were highly overwrought, and in their frustration wanted to take some action against any accessible symbol of authority—in this case, to lower the flag, by force if necessary. Through the good efforts of many faculty members, a peaceful solution was accomplished—the students agreed to withdraw from the mall, return to classrooms, and vote on whether they wished to lower the school's flag as a symbol of their feelings. And so the flag came down. And almost immediately another group of students, smaller in number but equally vehement in expressing their feelings, made preparations to rush the flag and restore it to full staff. This group, of course, was primarily nonJewish (though not, incidentally, nonwhite)—the so-called "Greasers" or "Hyde Park kids." Again some cool faculty heads prevailed, and the raise-the-flag group was allowed to take a flag from the gymnasium and parade upon the mall. But what emerged in the course of all of this, as shouts and threats were hurled back and forth from one group to the other, was not so much political conflict as socio-economic and ethnic conflict. A girl in one group called the others a bunch of "dumb, stinking greasers." A boy in the other group yelled that "You Jews always get what you want." And so there it is, apparently seething just below the surface, waiting only for some new issue to trigger a new explosion.

And if the alienation and active resentment among some members of the Christian minority is strong, it is as nothing as compared to the bitter estrangement of many of our black students. This is a problem about which, largely because of the color of my own skin, I must speak with less authority.

But those who know say that they cannot exaggerate the resentment which many of our black students harbor toward a school system as well as a social system which they consider to be repressive. For many of our affluent, middle-class students, school has become a giant put-on; for some of our black students, it is a giant put-down. The distrust is deep. I heard the story the other day of how the young black child who had come to love Faith Marshall said in a moment of conflicting tenderness and guilt, "Well, I like you, but I'm not supposed to." The perceptions and the actions are not always rational; but what should concern us, I believe, is the depth of the feeling, well-founded or not. Our purpose, of course, should be to help and educate such students. But if you're not predisposed to make extraordinary efforts in that regard, you might be interested to reflect on an observation made recently by Kenneth Keniston to the effect that "The frequency of protests involving black students [at predominantly white colleges] is directly related to their numbers: protests become probable once a 'critical mass' of about fifty black students is reached."

Now let me stay with this matter long enough to point out that to some students from certain socioeconomic backgrounds, the system itself can be repressive, quite apart from the conscious or inadvertent prejudices of its members. It's not entirely a question of any of us being good or bad or sensitive or insensitive; it's a question of the way in which we organize ourselves and of the values which our organization promotes. A system which values people only as academic learners, which prizes scholastic attainment almost to the exclusion of all other qualities, which almost from the very beginning sorts and labels its children as "smart" or "dumb" or "average" like so many potatoes into bins, such a system cannot help but be repressive to a group of young people whom luck has not favored for this particular kind of competition. So I ask you as you go off to your workshops to think about our special programs and our Basic Classes and our other arrangements of an academic kind and ask the extent to which these are in fact the way to meet this particular problem of articulation. And ask yourselves, what else can we do? How do we live better with our minorities? How do we help them to educate themselves?

ARTICULATION PROBLEM #2

There is a widespread feeling among our young people and among a growing number of adults that a broad gap exists between the schools and life. This has always been true to some extent. But the feeling now seems to be that because of outdated curricula and outmoded instructional practices the school has almost lost touch with the life of the world around it. Ask the students, and they will tell you: whatever life is, it's what the schools are not. But let them speak for themselves. I'd like to read to you part of a letter written within the past year by one of our own students here in Great Neck. The letter was written to the superintendent by a seventeen-year-old boy who was applying for permission to meet certain requirements for graduation in an alternate way. I'm going to alter two or three of the words that he used, out of deference to your sensibilities. But I'm bothered about doing that, because the original Anglo-Saxon makes the point more forcibly.

The act of my sitting here and writing this last scrap of nonsense of a long and tiring school career is certainly more than absurd enough to deserve the honor of being the capstone on the rest of the nonsense.

We live in a time of greater imperialist fascism and genocide than any other time in history; we are all members of a regimented and repressive system designed to create dehumanized plug-in modules for the empty niches of an oppressive society; and I sit here, a living nightmare out of Kafka, driving for no rational reason that I can discern to receive a piece of simulated parchment, a ticket to the Amerikan Dream I know I will never use.

Nevertheless, I am catering to this idiocy, and will attempt to explain my plans to Achieve Educational Experience in Lieu of the Senior Year. I am fairly certain that anyone capable of understanding my goals for intellectual development would never have asked for an exposition like this, and am absolutely certain that those who have asked will never be able to understand.

Nevertheless: After twelve years of stultifying and stagnating repression, my most imperative need is exposure, is expansion: Exposure to new ideas, new concepts, to life, to anything, to everything; expansion to adapt myself, to stretch myself, to assimilate the new—to change. I have lived seventeen years of life in a society where education serves least what is most important: How to live. How to Live includes how to relate to other people, how to create a society, how to coexist, how to love. How to assume the responsibility of knowing that Mankind's wellbeing is each person's responsibility, that the quality of life is determined by those that live it. How to grow to assume that responsibility, the responsibility to community and humanity our society ignores and degrades.

I, as a seventeen-year-old human being raised in the repression of a secluded fairyland ghetto of rich farts and cotton-candy dreams, am faced with two terrifyingly important crises: Firstly, that our times and our world demand immediate action on my part, on everyone's part, to restore humanity and justice to the ravaged and oppressed. This week more than one thousand human beings in Indochina will roast alive, writhing and screaming, their flesh charring and sizzling under Dow Chemical napalm. Sixty per cent of the world, geographically and economically, is subjected to the exploitation of Amerikan Coca-colaland. The magnitude of the crimes being committed against humanity today is incredible; it is no longer noticed by us. In a world where inhuman horror is a thrice-daily color newscast on the tube, atrocity is mundane. Any human being who would call himself such must stand up and strike out. Any who doesn't is just another German living next door to Auschwitz who just didn't know.

My second imperative is the need to equip myself to deal with the world as any decent respect for humanity compels. That is an enormous task. It means undoing the fettering disabilities seventeen years of Amerikan education has burdened me with. It means equipping myself with the necessary skills to contribute to the building of a humane society, a culture of decency and humanity.

This is my goal in lieu of the Senior Year. It means travel. It means intensive, self-conscious examination into my own attitudes, my own racist preoccupations with chauvinism and other bacteria I don't even realize infect me yet. It means talking, listening, reading, loving, watching, hearing, doing, retching. It means revolution and it means acceptance.

Now I don't ask you necessarily to agree to all of that. I know that not all students share the writer's strong convictions. But there is no gainsaying the reality that many of our students, including some fairly young ones, strongly feel that life as they know it and would like to experience it is set aside at the schoolhouse door.

Recently, we have begun to develop programs which are designed to bring the life and work of the community more into the school and to extend the life and work of the school more into the community. One thinks of the grandparents serving as aides in the Parkville School, of numbers of high school youngsters working with children at the elementary and junior high school levels, of the new School to Employment Program conducted by Mr. Ourlicht to parallel the established Cooperative Work-Study program conducted by Mr. Frank, and of course the various extramural ventures of students enrolled in the Village School. But most of these programs, thus far, represent *ways out* of the school rather than fundamental changes in the nature of the school. And so my second set of general questions is, how do we reshape that which we are doing so that school represents an intensifying or a clarifying of experience rather than a substitute for it? What needs to be done by way of curriculum or teaching or school organization to close this articulation gap?

ARTICULATION PROBLEM #3

We are becoming increasingly and painfully aware of the gap that has long existed in our schools between matters of the head and matters of the heart. We believe that our primary responsibility is the development of the intellect, and at that, an intellect defined as academic rationality. Our job is to cultivate the rational mind, and emotion and intuition and experiencing with the body can take care of themselves.

Now this idea of the purpose of education is based on a world view that has pretty much prevailed in our society since classic Greece. We have tended to conceive of the body of experiences worth teaching as being essentially rational and, in a broad sense, scientific. The "enlightened" man is the rational man who through cultivation and detachment of his intellect can transcend the darker impulses of his nature. We glorify order, system, regularity, objectivity; we prize that which can be analyzed, synthesized, explained; often it seems as if we were Platonists all, and the idea or the word is more important than the thing itself. List ten causes of the Civil War. Name the eight parts of speech. Explain why the density of salt water exceeds the density of fresh. While meanwhile the young bodies of our charges surge with wild new impulses and a yearning for the farthest star .

A great many people have been writing lately about the growing challenge to that prevailing emphasis on the rational side of man's nature. Let me read you a brief passage from Theodore Roszak's book *The Making of a Counter Culture:*

Nothing less is required than the subversion of the scientific world view, with its entrenched commitment to an egocentric and cerebral mode of consciousness. In its place, there must be a new culture in which the nonintellective capacities of the personality—those capacities that take fire from visionary splendor and the experience of human communion—become the arbiters of the good, the true, and the beautiful. I think the cultural disjuncture that generational dissent is opening out between itself and the technocracy is just this great, as great in its implications (though obviously not as yet in historical import) as the cleavage that once ran between Greco-Roman rationality and Christian mystery. What *is* new is that a radical rejection of science and technological values should appear so close to the center of our society, rather than on the negligible margins. It is the middle-class young who are conducting this politics of consciousness, and they are doing it boisterously, persistently, and aggressively—to the extent that they are invading the technocracy's citadels of academic learning and bidding fair to take them over.

Now perhaps you're going to tell me that it should be our task to defend the citadel. Okay, that's a reasonable point at which to join the argument. But since we can't conduct the argument here, let me mention two bits of evidence that may suggest that I'm not entirely all wet. Some of you may have read in yesterday's *Times* about the report of a study group commissioned by the C.E.E.B. which has proposed sweeping changes in the Board's examinations. Among the changes, the study proposes measurement not only of mathematical and verbal ability, but of musical and artistic talent; sensitivity and commitment to social responsibility; political and social leadership; athletic, political, and mechanical skills; and so on. Second, I ask you to consider how many of the major problems our society faces could be solved by improving academic training. It seems to me that our problems at Berkeley and Columbia and Harvard and all the riots did not occur because the students could not read; they occurred partly because too much of what they read no longer made sense of their experience. Our problems with the environment await much less the development of new antipollution devices than they do the economic will and political know-how to apply the knowledge already available. We can send a man to the moon, but the sky in which we seek him burns our eyes.

And so I ask you, as you go to your workshops—can we, without sacrificing intellectual rigor, find a place in our schools for the expression and development of feeling and of intuition? Or do we continue to let the kids work it out on their own, in their music and their drugs? How do we refashion educational processes to help humans become more human?

ARTICULATION PROBLEM #4

Finally, we have a problem which is probably more pervasive and ultimately troublesome than even these three. It is a problem of values—of the clash between the growing value system of the young and the established value system of the older, the clash between culture and counterculture. This problem of values is indeed so fundamental that until we confront it all our fussing about with school programs is mere tinkering.

A great deal has been written about this problem in recent years, so that I'm sure the gist of it must be familiar to you. But stop and consider for a moment how many of the values which we took for granted in our growing up and perhaps still live by are under direct challenge in the world that is developing. Most of us, for example, grew up believing that competition was the American way. You were supposed to shoot straight and play by the rules, but life was a race in which the prizes went to the swift and the enduring, with only pity for those passed by. Free Enterprise. The Open Market. Nature red in tooth and claw. But today we see among many of the young the ethic of cooperation, the placing of the well-being of the group above individual advantage. You need only to listen to their criticism of our grading system to see evidence of that.

Or consider the value of individuality in itself. For most of us freedom has been the cornerstone of our political beliefs. But I talk to the young man and he tells me that the trouble with us old-style liberals—he thinks I'm an old-style liberal—is that we're all hung up on individual freedom. One of the biggest problems that he will face in this world, he tells me, is that there will be so many people that the quality of life, if not existence itself, will be sorely threatened. In such a predicament, he asks, which right is more important: the right of an individual to decide how many children he wishes to sire or bear or the right of the collective society to restrain his freedom in order to safeguard the whole? And that for me is an old question in a new realm.

Or another—the value of hard work as an end in itself. That's surely something I grew up believing, though I may hear more about that one later. But the new ethic, and certainly an appealing one, seems to be to do only that which must be done so that life may be enjoyed in the time that's left. Or chastity—well, maybe that one hasn't changed so much.

One can cite even further value clashes. The established culture tends to be goal-oriented; the emerging culture tends to be process-oriented. We of the establishment make a great deal of aims and purposes and behavioral objectives; among the young the current hitchhiking ethic, as exemplified by films like *Five Easy Pieces*, is not to go to any particular destination, but to go anywhere with whomever promises the most interesting ride. The established culture is achievement-oriented; the emerging culture is fulfillment-oriented. Increasingly, the question among the young is not "What can I accomplish?" but "What can I become?" Not "What prize can I win?" but "What will make me feel and be better?"

And so it goes. Established culture is impersonal and objective; emerging culture is personal and subjective. Established culture is money and thing-oriented; emerging culture is person and people-oriented. Established culture is future-oriented (especially in its schools—do this now because it'll be good for you some day and besides you need it for the next level—otherwise our program won't be articulated); emerging culture is now-oriented. The schools,

Friedenberg tells us, prize neatness, obedience, accuracy, safety; the young are drawn to courage, love, and sacrifice. And on and on.

Now I admit that I'm painting all of this in very broad and sweeping strokes, but we don't have time now for the details. The hard and often appalling fact is that a growing number of young people reject outright the value system of their parents and indeed the very future for which the schools are so busy trying to prepare them. Listen:

> Dad looked at his house and car and manicured lawn, and he was proud. All of his material possessions justified his life.
> He tried to teach his kids: he told us not to do anything that would lead us from the path of Success.

> WORK, don't play
> STUDY, don't loaf
> OBEY, don't ask questions
> FIT IN, don't stand out
> BE SOBER, don't take drugs
> MAKE MONEY, don't make waves

> We were conditioned in self-denial.
> We were taught that "loving" was bad because it was immoral. Also in those pre-pill days a knocked-up chick stood in the way of Respectability and Success.
> We were warned that masturbation caused insanity and pimples.
> And we were confused. We didn't dig why we needed to work toward owning bigger houses? bigger cars? bigger manicured lawns?
> We went crazy. We couldn't hold it back any more.

One writer who has made a recent attempt to draw these strands together is a Yale law professor named Charles Reich, in his book *The Greening of America*. According to Reich, we are now experiencing a "revolution of consciousness" that may reform the entire social and cultural order. He believes that "Americans have lost control of the machinery of their society, and only new values and a new culture can restore control." Among other things, they have substituted statuses, public and private, for selfhood, "and so become the victim of a cruel deception. [They] have been persuaded that the richness, the satisfactions, the joy of life are to be found in power, success, status, acceptance, popularity, achievements, rewards, and the rational, competent mind. [They want] nothing to do with dread, awe, wonder, mystery, accidents, failure, helplessness, magic. [They have] been deprived of the search for self that only these experiences make possible. And [they have] produced a society that is the image of [their] own alienation and impoverishment."

Clearly we don't have time this morning to detail Reich's thesis fully nor to challenge some of his assumptions. But if there is any validity at all to his premise of a rise of a new level of consciousness, a new value system among the young, then this clash of values should be very much on our minds as we discuss problems of articulation. We must ask, what values do our schools in fact promote? What values do they suppress? To what extent should we seek to impress these values upon our students? To what extent should we help them to define and express their own?

PROPOSALS

So there are four problems of articulation—have's and have-not's, school and life, head and heart, and old values vs. new values. Now if I were a theoretician or a wand'ring minstrel I would leave you there and ask you to go work it out. But I am not those things; I am a teacher and a school administrator, and I work every day in the same nitty-gritty world that you do. So in the few minutes that are left to me, I'd like to suggest very quickly some of the kinds of programs we might be thinking about and promise that I won't be getting on a plane tomorrow to fly off somewhere, but will be right here to do what I can to help.

I would like to see at all levels programs that allow a great deal more scope and choice and independence to the learner—programs less tied to the text, the syllabus, the period, the classroom, even the teacher. I would like to see us depend more on their initiative, their curiosity, their energy. I don't want us to abdicate, but I want us to guide and not control. I believe that the open classroom and the integrated day and the Independent Study Programs and the Village School are just *some* of the ways to do this.

I would like to see more people from the community working in the schools and more people from the schools working in the community.

I would like to see more programs that cut across disciplinary lines—perhaps in which teachers from a number of disciplines pool their expertise to help a group of students solve a real-life problem.

I would like to see a reflorescence of the arts—of music, drama, dance, painting, sculpture, and the rest—in which these expressions do not become "subjects" or "ism-s" to be mastered and graded "75," but things to do for the sheer joy of the doing.

I would like to see a differentiation in the roles of teachers, so that we can recognize the differences among us and capitalize upon the best talents of each of us. I am not thinking of some hierarchical pattern now, though that may be useful too, but of teacher-counselors and teacher-researchers and teacher-resource persons and maybe others in addition to what we all are now, teacher-general practitioners.

I would like to see schools within schools, where a small number of teachers and pupils could get to know one another well and work out a way of living and of learning that makes sense to them.

I would especially like to see us make available a whole range of alternate programs representing a diversity of educational styles, so that a student and his parents could choose that which best fit his value system—a kind of "voucher plan" for the selection of alternatives all under the public umbrella.

And most of all, I would like to see these things *soon.* We have no right, any more, to sit and wait until eighty others do it and then maybe decide to try it here. We are not talking now about educational fashions or bandwagons. We are talking about the very palpable, flesh-and-blood reality of our students, who by and large endure each day in a condition of something more restrained than excitement. They are variously bored, estranged, apathetic, hostile. And the question is not, "Are they right?" but, "What do we do about it?"

We have a great deal going for us, you know. We have a body of potentially alert, concerned, talented students. We have parents who are educated and generally in support of our efforts. We have an able teaching faculty, one which succeeded in meeting the challenges of former decades in exemplary fashion and which has already begun to do much to meet the challenges of the new. We have a Board of Education which reflects well the divergent educational thinking of the community and which is solidly and unanimously behind our efforts to improve education. And we have a superintendent who has more intellect, more compassion, more courage, and more of the wisdom earned through suffering than any man with whom I had ever hoped to work.

We have two things against us. The first is time. We are all of us so harried that it is very difficult to rise above the day-to-day to do the kind of planning which does justice to our aspirations. Somehow we must do something to make more time available to the individuals and groups who need it in order to continue the kinds of things you'll be talking about today or that you've already started.

And finally, of course, there is one last barrier, and that is that, regrettably, for all of us change is difficult. No matter what our point of view, no matter how much zest we may have at first, the enormous day-to-day practical difficulties grind us down. And so we get tired, and there is a temptation not to care.

Yet somewhere way down in the gut and marrow there is something that will not let go. Something about us, perhaps our closeness as teachers to young life, asserts that it *is* possible to control our lives and it *is* possible to shape experience for a greener tomorrow. As I was finishing these lines yesterday, the November wind blew strong and a hard rain began to fall. And English teacher to the end, I turned again to a piece by Shelley that many of our young people find increasingly congenial. It's his *Ode to the West Wind*, in which he exhorts the wild fall wind to burst black rain, and fire, and hail, and purge us clean of the year's decay; and then he asks to become himself an instrument of purgation, and ends this way:

> Be thou, Spirit fierce,
> My Spirit! Be thou me, impetuous one!
> Drive my dead thoughts over the universe,
>   Like wither'd leaves, to quicken a new birth;
> And, by the incantation of this verse,
>   Scatter, as from an unextinguish'd hearth
> Ashes and sparks, my words among mankind!
>   Be through my lips to unawaken'd earth
> The trumpet of a prophecy! O Wind,
>   If Winter comes, can Spring be far behind?

Some Startling Research Encourages Sweeping Change

Wayne Jennings, principal of St. Paul Open School, has collected studies showing how and why education should change. He has done his homework. If you want to make a case for change, begin to collect studies as he has done, wherever you can find it.

Wayne Jennings

There are some amazing studies that add up to the statement that education must change.

One famous study in the 1930s (the 8-year study) occurred in 30 high schools all over the United States. Three hundred colleges agreed to accept their graduates no matter what courses the students took. The students were followed for four years of high school and four years of college. The students who came from the most experimental and progressive schools did far better in college grades, creativity, citizenships, etc.

One group of students from an extremely experimental high school were studied 20 years later to see how they turned out. The "guinea pigs" were found to be strikingly successful in their careers, as family members and as citizens.

A study just released (Project talent) selected 1,000 30-year-olds from a project fifteen years earlier of 400,000 talented 15-year-olds. The 30-year-olds were interviewed extensively. The results: "The evidence of these interviews suggests that high school education as a whole serves no very useful purpose."

Numerous studies have examined college students to see what difference their grades made in their success in such careers as medicine, law, engineering, and teaching. There was no difference in the success rates of students with high and low grades!

Two very important studies examined the effects of high and low scores on the ACT and SAT tests. (These are the college aptitude tests high school juniors and seniors take). Their scores told how well students would do in college but *not how well they would do in their careers.* Instead it was found that students who engaged in extra-curricular activities, hobbies and ran their own business were far more likely to be successful than those who didn't.

Numerous studies on reading suggest schools should try different approaches. Several studies have found that students taught to read at a later

From the *Southeast Alternative Newspaper,* ed. by Sally French, Minneapolis Public Schools. Copyright 1974.

age (say 7 or 8, instead of 6) caught up to the earlier ones in two years and had fewer negative attitudes about school and themselves.

Other studies show the gains from remedial reading disappear after one year.

Several studies find that by late elementary school 20% of children are "against" school and even those who are satisfied regard their classroom experiences with such adjectives as: dull, boring, uncertain, restless, and inadequate.

Obviously there is much about learning that we don't know. In areas, like Minneapolis, where there are several patterns of education to choose from the research results would be far different. This is because it is recognized that children and youth learn in far different ways and there exist several models to fit this variety of learning styles.

We must continue to support educational alternatives. There is an enormous body of research—vastly more than has been cited here—to back up the more experimental approaches. We need to encourage and develop even more effective programs. SEA [South East Alternatives] can be proud of its contributions to American education.

WHO DO THE
TESTS BENEFIT?

The Chosen People

The Calvinists believed that God smiled on his chosen people, so wealth was a sign of godliness. After exposure to antitrust suits, consumer suits, bribery trials, professional malpractice and overbilling, pork barreling and fraudulence in almost all of the wealth-amassing pursuits, we no longer hold this innocent view. We know money and power beget more money and more power. Or do we?

We no longer would argue that the wealthy are morally superior, but we do, I think, confuse wealth and intelligence. Certainly the standardized tests do assure everyone that this is a meritocracy—those who do poorly and cannot get into the best schools believe themselves inferior and therefore deserving of a life of dreary labor, while those who do well settle into "clean" jobs without guilt. All the entry ways into the world of comfort—law school, medical school, high ranking business schools—are denied to low scorers. Testing high is a key to later economic success.

Just what does a high score mean? Even ETS admits that the scores are only rough estimations of one's *testing* ability. According to Steven Brill, writing in *New York Magazine,* a high ranking executive of the College Board admitted that "there is a one-in-six chance that the student who scores a 600 one day could take another SAT the next day and get a 500 or a 700—odds which are mind-boggling when you consider that the 700 kid will get into schools where the 500 kid is doomed."

In fact, a psychology professor from City College is quoted by Brill as saying that the value of the tests in predicting how the students will fare in law school or college is "so low as to be practically meaningless."

What is not "so low as to be absolutely meaningless" is the statistical correlation of wealth to SAT scores. "High school seniors coming from wealthy families have higher median board scores than seniors from middle-income families, who in turn have higher median scores than those from low-income families," according to Brill who studied data supplied by ETS.

Many challenge the validity of the scores, the political bias and even the racism of the testers and evaluators, the appropriateness of the criteria, the clarity of the material, and so on. Always the questions and concerns are at root political considerations, sometimes petty, more often major ones that challenge our whole system of beliefs.

At any rate, we do think that no examination of the pressures teachers face can leave out the testing pressure. You are under pressure to understand the tests, to help others understand and if possible to work to change testing conditions or choose other measures, and to help the children in your care to master the skills being tested as long as they are to be judged by them.

Should these findings and explanations be shared with the public along with the scores? Teachers in Lincoln City fought to have full interpretation accompany publication of scores.

NCTE Journal

Should test scores comparing academic achievement in Lincoln City's three secondary schools be released for publication in local newspapers? Not according to a committee of high school teachers who registered a formal objection against the practice during the L.C. Board of Education meeting last night.

"Asking the public to compare the quality of education provided by three schools on the basis of test scores is like asking them to compare the nutritional factors in two families' diets on the basis of their grocery bills," said Pauline Rovere, spokeswoman for the teacher group, which also urged the board to give local citizens easier access to classrooms, where they may see and judge educational programs in action.

Criticizing last month's board decision "to create a community-wide demand for improvement in the quality of education in Lincoln City through press releases giving standardized test figures," Ms. Rovere, English department chairman at Riverwood High School, presented charts and diagrams illustrating some of the problems of interpreting such figures.

"This is an elaborate, sophisticated process," she said. "Scholars and test experts themselves often disagree on the real meanings and values derived from such scores. The general public cannot be expected to form sound opinions of local schools on the basis of newspaper headlines."

Pointing out that standardized examinations are "by definition designed to place as many students below the average as above," Ms. Rovere asserted that "these norms were never meant by test publishers to provide goals for students to reach. Yet that is exactly what too many anxious parents and other members of the community believe them to be, no matter how often school officials and test-makers both deny it.

"To report test scores without supplying complete data about the nature, validity, and reliability of the test itself and about the cultural background, the

This article was originally published as **"Teachers Protest Publication of Test Score Comparisons,"** in NCTE Journal, Feb. 29, 1975. Copyright © 1975 by the National Council of Teachers of English. Reprinted by permission of the publisher.

socioeconomic status, and the motivational level of the students taking it inevitably leads to comparisons that unjustly inflate the public estimation of one school and damage the reputations of others," she said.

Ms. Rovere cited statistics released over the four-year period 1962–66 by the College Entrance Examination Board to demonstrate "the striking differences in percentiles that can be found in using the same test with different groups of students.

"Identical raw scores achieved on the Scholastic Aptitude Test were reported as indicating a differential of no less than 95 in percentile ranking between a representative sample of all high school girls in the country (96th percentile) and all students enrolled as freshmen in one large technical training institute (1st percentile)," she said.

"A newspaper that presented those statistics without a column or two of detailed explanation would leave the impression in the public mind that the technical institute freshmen were hopelessly incompetent academically when compared with the representative sampling of high school seniors," Ms. Rovere continued. "Yet that is not what the test results indicated.

"Unless the board is ready to change its long-standing policy against hiring qualified experts in evaluation to help interpret test results for the newspapers, and unless the newspapers themselves agree to accompany all test scores published with complete interpretative data, the release of all this information can only have results exactly contrary to those the Board of Education intended," said Ms. Rovere.

"Instead of releasing test scores, the board should encourage personal visits to the schools by interested citizens who can compare for themselves when they see what is being accomplished in the educational program—sometimes in spite of such handicaps as overcrowded classrooms, outmoded and poorly maintained buildings, and inadequate equipment," she concluded.

Following Ms. Rovere's remarks, the board voted to hold in abeyance further releases of test scores to newspapers pending additional study and analysis.

Testing: A Political Football in the Profession

While the NEA suggests that teachers are doing well these days, everything considered, and testing can't but hurt the cause of good education, that's not the position Albert Shanker takes. President of the United Federation of Teachers, a group that vies with NEA for members and for national leadership, he says the NEA is "reacting in an infantile way."

Albert Shanker

The big education story that broke with the reopening of school was the report of the Advisory Panel on Score Decline. The panel was headed by Willard Wirtz, former United States secretary of labor and at present the head of the National Manpower Institute.

The Wirtz report is one which should be read and studied in the months ahead. It is not the report of one who seeks to dismantle education or reduce public commitment to our schools. On the contrary, it is the report of those who believe in American education and who realize that the recent decline in scores cannot be explained in any simplistic way. Nor do they propose easy answers.

The report does provide conclusive evidence of the decline in test scores. It also shows that the decline is real, not merely relative. Students do not do as well today as they did 15 years ago—and this is not the result of increasing the difficulty of the tests. Nor is it merely an urban or regional problem. There has been a real nationwide decline, and the decline has been big.

It would have been easy for the panel to seek scapegoats and to try to pin the blame on a single cause. But it did not. The report has no simple blame-placing. It does not jump to conclusions, and there is no naive demand for accountability or performance standards for teachers. Instead, there is a detailed set of factors set forth leading to the decline.

Most, but not all, of the reason is the fact that more students now take the SAT exam. Once the group which had hope of going to college was much smaller. As colleges opened their doors and as more and more of the previously excluded were reached, more and more average and below-average students took the exam, as against those who previously took it. This lowered scores—but simultaneously opened the doors for many who had been excluded.

But this is not the only reason for the score decline. Other reasons given by the panel are

- More elective courses which, though not bad in and of themselves, frequently do not require the same amount of exertion in developing reading and writing skills;
- Lower general standards, more absenteeism, more remedial level college work, grade inflation and automatic promotion;
- Thousands of hours spent in watching TV instead of doing homework;
- The huge increase in the number of students from broken families;

- The turmoil which resulted from the Vietnam war, Watergate, the assassination of national heroes, etc.;
- Lower student motivation.

The report must be taken seriously. The American taxpayer who spends billions on education will be looking at these results to ask how we can get improvements. And teachers are no less concerned. Most of us became teachers because during our schooling we developed a love for science, mathematics, literature, or history and wanted to pass on that love and those skills. Declining standards have led to teacher disappointment and frustration. What is needed now is serious planning to see how teachers, parents and the schools can turn this decline around. There will be broad support for such an effort.

Unfortunately, the National Education Association has reacted to the report in an infantile and disturbing way. The NEA calls tests like the SAT "wasteful, inadequate and destructive" and says that "tests of this kind don't serve students, parents or teachers; they do not measure what is being taught and what is happening to our students. They ought to be dispensed with once and for all."

Undoubtedly the NEA and its president, John Ryor, made these remarks because they are afraid that revealing the SAT test score decline will give the schools a bad reputation. They are afraid that teachers may be evaluated in terms of test scores—how well or poorly students do. They are afraid that if test scores are emphasized, teaching and curriculum may become completely hitched to test taking and test passing.

But in spite of these possible abuses of knowledge, the NEA position is dead wrong. Any information is subject to misuse and misinterpretation, whether that information is in the form of student test scores, statistics on death due to various diseases or national unemployment figures. The fact that knowledge can be used by some to suit their own needs is no reason to keep everyone ignorant as to what the facts are. To the general public and to most newspaper editorial writers, the NEA position looked suspiciously like a plea to keep giving the schools more money while keeping taxpayers in the dark as to whether the students are really learning.

The overwhelming majority of American teachers share a different view. They are proud of what American education has accomplished. It has brought a nation of immigrants—largely illiterate in our language—within a very short period of time to the wealthiest nation, one of the most advanced and the most democratic.

Standardized tests have measured our overall progress. They show that we have done very well. From time to time they will reveal temporary setbacks and problems which we must face squarely. We should not be afraid of test measurements. When they show we are not doing well, we should honestly acknowledge it and seek improvement. Of course we know that tests are fallible. They are subject to error and misinterpretation. We should seek to improve methods of testing and measurement, and to educate the public as to what the results mean. But we cannot wait until there are perfect and infallible tests. We must use the best measurements available to us. The worst possible approach would be to end all testing—to throw out the baby with the bath water—and have no guidelines for teachers, parents, students or the taxpaying public.

More Politics of Testing

A group of thoughtful colleagues developed this very useful "List of Understandings" to be circulated among teachers, media personalities, school administrators, parents, national press writers, and the like to help us all "resist unwise testing." The list is a working list and not ranked, not considered complete, and not refined. But here it is.

A LIST OF UNDERSTANDINGS

1. Tests do not necessarily measure what the profession or the public values in education; more than likely, tests in the language arts cover only a small fraction of the learnings that the school and the society value.

2. Technical excellence in preparing tests and endowing them with high reliability and statistical sophistication should not be confused with the appropriateness of the tests to given students, given schools, or given curriculums.

3. The parent's question "How's he doing?" has two meanings: How's he doing in relation to a standard, and how's he doing in relation to his own growth potential. The parent must ask whether meeting a norm is more appropriate as a value than is improving toward a goal.

4. Undue concern about tests produces harmful effects, among them: (1) it encourages teaching to the test, (2) it brings about a narrowing of the range of learning opportunities made available to youth, and (3) it reduces the capacity of students to be able to cope with circumstances in a changing world.

5. The measurable outcomes from instruction are far less important than the opportunities for learning that the school presents. Undue attention to testing in evaluating school instruction is wrong-headed.

This article was taken from a report to the Executive Committee of the National Council of Teachers of English from an Ad Hoc Committee on the Effect of External Testing, 1973. The statement does not carry the official endorsement of the NCTE. Reprinted by permission.

6. Teachers and their professional groups should have a primary role in interpreting the results of testing to the public.

7. Parents and teachers should be suspicious of tests constructed by persons whose current and recent history has taken them away from classrooms; teachers who are close to the reality of student's lives should be close to the processes of identifying test objectives and constructing test items.

8. The economics of the testing industry are such that substantial consensus about the curriculum and its topics must be attained (or guessed at) before standardized tests can be constructed and used. There is and has been very little consensus about the English language arts curriculum, and test makers have had to focus attention on a very small part of the whole language arts curriculum. Their tests, despite labels such as "English," "Language Arts," or even "Language Skills," are misnomers.

9. The public should know that this pluralistic society subscribes to a great variety of goals of learning; standardized tests touch only a few of these.

10. Similarly, the people of the society use and value a variety of learning and living styles; standardized tests gauge only a very narrow range of those styles, chiefly the analytic and rarely the expressive.

11. The public needs to know the great number and variety of tests in use, the costliness of the testing process, the lack of feasible use of the data that testing programs spin out.

12. The people should understand that certain power figures and a broad cut of the people have a blind faith in numbers which affords them a spurious comfort. This faith undergirds the testing industry.

13. The effect of standardized testing is, as often as not, to delimit opportunity for students; tests too often are used to pigeonhole students, not to help them.

14. Many, many tests are seriously dated in content, shamefully biased toward or against certain social and economic groups, and notoriously unreliable as measurement instruments. They are an embarrassment to the testing industry.

15. The public should know that colleges are depending less and less on the results of standardized tests, and that class rank is of at least equal significance in entrance decisions.

16. There *are* alternatives to standardized testing that are far closer to the reality of the curriculum and the reality of life.

17. Current attempts to use standardized test results as the vehicle for "accountability" simply exaggerate classical problems of test validity. Weak tests are the Achilles heel of the accountability movement.

18. Used with restraint and intelligence, many standardized tests can be helpful in assessing programs and even improving instruction. But the weakest aspect of testing programs in schools is guidance of teachers

in what uses to make of test results and guidance of the school power structure in intelligent planning for use of tests.

The Money in Making Tests

There's big money riding on the tests, so the conglomerates influence the profession and sell us all on the "importance" of testing. The public is now convinced that their tax dollars are spent (or misspent) on the basis of how well school systems perform on the tests.

If you feel uneasy about tests, Jerrold R. Zacharias, the famous nuclear physicist professor at MIT, might be your strongest ally. "I feel emotionally toward the testing industry as I would toward any other merchants of death....I feel that way because of what they do to the kids. I'm not saying they murder every child—only 20 percent of them..."

Sherwood Davidson Kohn

...From what scattered and incomplete data are available...it seems likely that the testing market is worth somewhere in the neighborhood of $150 million, a figure that seems small indeed when compared to the $1 billion-plus revenue of the total market in textbooks and educational materials, including tests. But the proportion is misleading. The testing industry affects such costly items as curriculum development, textbook and equipment sales, administrative and instructional time and budgets, and printing and distribution expenditures. Montgomery County, Maryland, for example, tests a minimum of 60,000 third-, fifth-, seventh-, and ninth-grade students each year, employs a full-time test administration staff at the system level, and will spend more than $55,000 on tests, testing materials, and test processing in 1976. The industry, through ETS's College Scholarship Service, also influences the dispensation of millions of dollars' worth of scholarship funds without the slightest gesture of accountability to students and parents who must reveal in their applications all manner of confidential financial information, including income tax statements. And the effect is felt even beyond the traditional bounds of academic activity. The competitive pressure of standardized, norm-referenced testing, the desperate struggle to place well in a universe of credentials that may easily affect an

This article was taken from **"The Numbers Game: How the Testing Industry Operates,"** in *The Myth of Measurability*, ed. by Paul L. Houts, copyright © 1977 Hart Publishing Company, Inc. Reprinted by permission.

entire life, has spawned a multimillion-dollar ancillary industry that involves the design, publishing, and administration of courses and instructional materials concerned exclusively with teaching students how to take tests. It seems obvious that test publishing holds within its narrow technical purview the broadest potential for bureaucratic callousness, psychological trauma, and economic control.

In any case, the major profit-making publishers of tests refused to tell me what their actual grosses are or how many students take their tests annually. Most would not even venture an estimate of the total market. Oscar K. Buros, who edits the *Mental Measurements Yearbook* and *Tests In Print*, the definitive compendiums of test reviews and available measurement instruments, told me he cannot learn the figures. The industry steadfastly shields them from view— for competitive reasons, its spokesmen say.

But it is readily apparent that the educational testing industry affects numbers of people and amounts of money far out of proportion to its size. *Tests In Print II* lists 2,585 tests on the market, 1,678 of which are published by the industry's forty-five top firms. Of these, ETS, Harcourt Brace Jovanovich, Houghton Mifflin, Science Research Associates, and the California Test Bureau publish the dominant number, both in quantity and influence.

"Test publishing," writes Buros in *TIP II*, "is even more concentrated among a few publishers than [a list of all tests] indicates. There are two large conglomerates of jointly owned or interlocking publishing organizations. Although listed separately, Educational Testing Service includes the Cooperative Tests and Services and the Educational Records Bureau. Since ETS also constructs all CEEB [College Entrance Examination Board] tests, the ETS conglomerate is represented by 315 tests, 14.3 percent of the tests published in the United States. The other publishing giant, Harcourt Brace Jovanovich with its subsidiaries, Grune and Stratton and the Psychological Corporation, has a total of 174 tests, 7.9 percent of the same total. Together these two publishing groups account for 22.2 percent of the domestic tests in *TIP II*. Their dominating positions are even greater than these statistics reflect. Their tests are among the most widely used in the country."

Test scoring is even more concentrated. ETS and SRA score their own tests and some others, and CTB does part of its own scoring, but Westinghouse Learning Corporation's Measurement Research Center is probably the leading wholesaler in the scoring business. And after visiting the ETS facilities in Princeton, New Jersey, and MRC's in Iowa City, I have the impression that scoring is concentrated in a series of bare concrete rooms where clerks and technicians, deprived of their shadows under fluorescent light, herd pencil-marked test booklets through paper cutters, wooden sorting racks, and electronic scanners in an eternal routine of shuffling and counting. It all seemed quite dehumanized, and I was relieved to find—small comfort—that at least MRC's scanner was discreet enough to refrain, as ETS's did not, from flashing each child's name on a screen as it zapped through the machine.

More wholesale, or contract, machine scoring is done by MRC than by any other firm in the world. I do not know how many test booklets are checked, placed in batches, slit apart, and scanned at the Iowa City plant, because Burdette Hansen, a vice-president of the firm and manager of its local facility, refused to release the figures. But he did say that MRC scores tests for Harcourt Brace, Houghton Mifflin, the American College Testing Program, the California Test Bureau, and even some for ETS. The numbers must be impressive, and considering the chances of misuse, even somewhat alarming.

"I feel emotionally toward the testing industry," said MIT's Jerrold R. Zacharias, "as I would toward any other merchants of death. I feel that way because of what they do to the kids. I'm not saying they murder every child—only 20 percent of them. Testing has distorted their ambitions, distorted their careers. Ninety-five percent of the American population has taken an ability test. It's not something that should be put into the hands of commercial enterprises."

A puckish, white-haired nuclear physicist of seventy, Zacharias was part of the team that worked on the Manhattan Project during World War II, was a member of the President's Science Advisory Committee, and is now professor of physics emeritus at MIT and head of Project ONE, a group at the Education Development Center in Newton, Massachusetts, that is producing a TV series about mathematics. An implacable foe of standardized, multiple-choice, norm-referenced testing, he is passionately opposed to what he feels is a mindless, secretive, stagnant, technology-obsessed business that is hopelessly prone to all manner of abuses against the human spirit.

"I think the whole psychological test business should cease and desist," he told me in his airy, book-and-apparatus-lined office at MIT. "It's an outrage. Measurement is a very important thing to me. But it implies one-dimensionality. The mind is not one dimensional."

Zacharias gave me a sharp look. "Secrecy," he said. "That's what the trouble is. It will become one of the big issues in testing within the next ten years. And there is only one way to keep the testing business honest; that is, keep it open."

The Special Vocabulary of the Testers

It may be that you have very little power to do anything at the moment but "come to terms with testing." You might be brave enough to take up the demerits of the system in teacher meetings.

But to do this you do need some tough-minded incontestable data on which to base your concerns or you'll be labeled a fuzzy thinker. And you will need some sophistication to be able to explain the meaning of the marks to parents who come, worried and perhaps silently begging to be assured that their child isn't defective or doomed to a life of manual drudgery. How will you explain to the enthusiastic testing experts that their objective tests are not so objective, and to the parents of the child that because the tests are faulty, they are not reliable indicators—regardless of how the "psychologist" has scared them.

This piece by Mitchell Lazarus is not easy reading, but it is important. Here you have a general analysis of the four most critical terms of the test-defenders: objectivity, standardization, reliability, and validity. If you find yourself writing a critique, you can use the piece as a reference. If you find yourself arguing at a school board meeting, you might need to commit some of this language to memory.

Mitchell Lazarus

FOUR TROUBLESOME WORDS

In testing, there are four words that often cause confusion: *objectivity, standardization, reliability,* and *validity.* Each of these words has at least two meanings; they mean one thing in English but something very different in testing. When a test maker says a test is "reliable," he does *not* mean it can be relied on; when he says it is "valid,", he does *not* mean its results are meaningful. In both cases, the technical uses of the words are very different from what one might expect. The test makers have a language of their own. Unfortunately, their language consists of English words used differently.

A test is *objective* if everybody takes it under more or less the same conditions, and if the papers are all graded under more or less the same conditions. Essay exams, for example, usually lack objectivity; they are difficult to grade consistently because the grading criteria tend to waver and shift as the grader works down through the pile of papers. Multiple-choice tests, however, can be objective if administered under uniform conditions. This objectivity is probably the main selling point for multiple-choice tests, although the economics of machine scoring are likely to be just as important.

This article is from **"Coming to Terms with Testing,"** published in *The Myth of Measurability,* ed. by Paul L. Houts, copyright © 1977 Hart Publishing Company, Inc. Reprinted by permission.

Note that any multiple-choice test, consistently administered and graded uniformly, can be objective—regardless of what defects it may have. The test may be ambiguous, wrongheaded, open to argument, even downright erroneous in the answers it counts as correct; it is an objective test nevertheless. For example:

How tall was Macbeth?
a) 4 gallons
b) 3 pounds
c) 6 acres
d) 2 hours

Even nonsensical items such as this are completely objective—using the word in its narrow, technical sense.

Moreover, objectivity in a test does not mean it is impartial or fair. Many objective tests discriminate against one group or another, and some discriminate against students who know the subject matter extremely well. In its technical sense, objectivity offers no protection against bias in the test.

Objectivity, in fact, is a minor virtue. It is necessary for reliability and validity, which *are* important (when these words are properly used), but objectivity in itself should not count for much, since an objective test can still be a bad test.

In one sense objectivity can even be a drawback. Some kinds of subject matter are much easier to test objectively than others. And since test makers value objectivity highly (at least in part because multiple-choice tests can be cheaply machine scored), their tests focus on certain skills and traits at the expense of others. This focus, in turn, leads educators to put an unnatural emphasis on teaching these particular skills, which can distort the whole educational process. Although imagination, creativity, a constructive sense of humor, and extremely high intelligence do not show up well on current tests, they are traits sorely needed in this society. These traits can even be a drawback in the testing situation; for example, when teachers must tell their better students before a test, "Don't think too much." That is a great loss, both for the individuals and for society.

Standardization has two very different technical meanings in testing. In one sense of the word, it can refer to making arrangements for all students to take the test under similar conditions. Typically, this includes making sure that all students receive the same instructions the same way, that they all have the same available time, and so forth.

The other meaning of standardization, which is the way we shall use the word here, concerns establishing norms for performance so that test scores come out as percentiles.* The test maker gives the test to a sample of students,

---

*The *percentile* is the percentage of students whose scores are below (or the same as) the student being reported on. The fiftieth percentile is average; percentiles ranging from twenty-five to seventy-five are roughly average. The higher the percentile, the better the score. Instead of percentiles, some tests report in stanines or other breakdowns, but the principles remain the same.

finds their percentiles among their fellows in the sample, makes a table of their scores against their percentiles, and later uses this table to translate scores into percentiles for other students.

The rationale for this practice is that a particular score in itself is not informative without information about scores from other students. For example, suppose two students receive scores of 200 and 300. Are these scores good or bad? We know one student did better. But did he do much better, or a little better? On the other hand, if we know that the percentiles corresponding to these scores are the thirtieth and the ninetieth, we are better able (supposedly) to evaluate the students: one did quite poorly, and one did very well. (Then one must add: compared with the sample group.) But the percentiles give no information at all on how each student actually performed; they report only on how he or she compared with the standardization group.

Standardization, then, has no bearing on the quality of a test; it affects only the reporting of scores. Furthermore there is nothing standard (in the ordinary English sense) about a standardized test. The test is not necessarily a recognized authority or an established basis for comparison, even though the word tends to invoke this kind of image. In fact, the word *standard* in standardized does not refer to the test at all; it applies to the sample population.

The people in the standardization group must be picked very carefully. If the test is for national use, these students must represent a fair cross section of the national population. But, although we sometimes hear otherwise, this fair representation is not a guarantee against discrimination in the test. For example, even though a standardization sample has the right number of blacks, the test can still discriminate against black culture. The presence of, say, 11 percent blacks in the standardization group has only a particular black child taking the test years later.

In general, if a test has defects, standardizing it will not uncover or correct them. Standardizing in that case will merely allow one to report the defective scores in the form of percentiles.

Reliability turns up heavily in materials promoting tests. Test makers consider it to be very important. But again, this word has two meanings, and the technical meaning is not what one might expect from the meaning of the word in everyday English.

In its technical sense, reliability simply means how well a test agrees with itself. Suppose we administer a test today and again tomorrow, somehow compensating for what the child learned the first time. The results will probably not be identical, even though the child's knowledge remains the same, for any test has built-in error. For example, think of measuring with a rubber ruler; the instrument itself gives different answers at different times. But the closer the results are, the more "reliable" the test is considered. In other words, by correlating the scores from both sessions, we can estimate the test's reliability. A reliable test tends to agree with itself more than an unreliable test does; the rubber ruler is stiffer.

In practice, the test-retest technique has its problems. Today, companies usually test two forms of the same test—one against the other—relying on the forms being equivalent. Or they divide the test into two parts and test the parts against each other. There are other techniques, too. The result is usually given as a "reliability coefficient": in achievement tests, .95 is considered excellent, .90 pretty good, and .80 not so good. The aim is always to determine how much the test is likely to be in error for any particular child.

Reliability, in its technical sense, is easy to measure, and there are established ways to make tests more reliable. (Some methods, such as shortening the time so that most students cannot finish, may artificially boost the reliability coefficient unless there are precautions in the analysis.) Test makers have good control over this kind of reliability, and they promote it as an important characteristic of their tests.

Because reliability has two very distinct meanings—technically and in ordinary English—the word lends itself to very misleading claims. Any test can be technically reliable but completely miss the mark in terms of its stated purpose.

Validity is the soul of a test; that is, the degree to which a test measures what it is supposed to measure. It is here that most discussions of testing run aground and most informed proponents of tests fall silent, because validity is extremely difficult to measure or establish. This point is crucial, because anyone who uses test results as a basis for making decisions is depending primarily on validity. To use a test score, one must believe that the score means something. Test makers claim to establish this, and they sometimes publish "validity coefficients." But their understanding of validity is unique and technical—very different from the way in which the majority of people ordinarily use the word.

Test makers assess technical validity in two ways: either by having an expert look at the test and pronounce it valid, or by comparing the test results with some other measure. (There are about ten variations on these two techniques.) The first approach, usually called "content validity" or "face validity," is validation by opinion. If a test looks like a test of addition and subtraction, then this approach makes sense; many other cases are less obvious. But when test makers say a test "possesses high content validity," they mean only that certain people have said that it looks like a good test.

The second approach is validation by comparison. For example, scores from an arithmetic achievement test are compared with actual performances in arithmetic, or scores from a French test are compared with the students' actual abilities to speak, understand, read, or write French. This approach looks more scientific on the surface, but it, too, has fundamental problems.

To validate by comparing, there must always be some second measure of the competence—some other way to measure ability that is sound enough to prove the test is working properly. The difficulty here is that this second criterion, whatever form it takes, is also a sort of test, and so it needs validation, too. It, in turn, must be validated either by opinion or by comparison; if it is validated by comparison, it will lead to a third measure that must also be validated, and so on.

For example, suppose I devise a multiple-choice test to measure creativity. To validate it, I might invent a number of problems, using real materials that students can handle, that give opportunities for creative solutions. I could have a sample of students try both the objective test and the hands-on problems. Suppose I find a good correlation—that students who do well in the hands-on situation also score high in the multiple-choice test. Does this validate the test? Not until I can establish that the hands-on problems are themselves good measures of creativity. To do that, I might take another sample of people, perhaps adults this time, and put them through the hands-on tryout. Then I could examine their life histories for evidence of creative accomplishment, trying to correlate this evidence with creative solutions in the hands-on situation. But this, in turn, assumes that the life histories are good indications of creativity, and there are several reasons to doubt this. Therefore, I must now show that my history technique is accurately identifying creative people, and so forth.

As well as being somewhat contrived, this scenario fails to mention many problems along the way. But it does show that in principle every validation points up the need for yet another validation.

There are only three ways in which such a chain of validations can end: (1) the validation may ultimately rest on an unvalidated measure; (2) the validation chain may terminate at an instrument having content validity or face validity; in other words, simply opinion; and (3) the validation chain may become circular, with the validation of A depending on B, the validation of B depending on C, and the validation of C depending on A. This may have happened to some extent in IQ testing.

In short, if we use the word *valid* in its usual dictionary sense, validation is a very uncertain business. Testing people make the problem seem less severe by redefining the word—by softening it to the point where a test can be called valid even though an informed user would put very little faith in it. The careless user, however, may take many tests far too seriously if he does not appreciate their major uncertainties and limitations. There is no way to assess validity in the sense that most people ordinarily use the word.

FURTHER TROUBLES

There are other defects in the tests, which need to be pointed out in any discussion of standardized testing. These defects take several forms, and the list that follows is in no particular order of importance. Furthermore, not every defect in the list applies to every test, but nearly all the criticisms apply to nearly all the most widely used, standardized, norm-referenced achievement tests.

- *Inappropriate content.* No test can examine "mathematics" or "reading" or any other subject area in general; a test can only sample particular content within the subject matter. Thus each test becomes a statement about what content the test maker thinks is important enough to sample. This is a matter of judgment, and sometimes the judgments are questionable. For example, mathematics tests put such a heavy stress on calculation that a child's "mathematics" score is mostly a calculation score. Yet longhand calculation is a nearly obsolete skill, far less important today than many other parts of mathematics.

• *Need for reading and linguistic skills.* Before a multiple-choice test is a test of mathematics or anything else, it is a reading test first—and beyond that, a reading test in a particular form of English, usually compact and stylized. A low score can mean low achievement in the subject under test, or it can mean poor reading. There is no way of telling which. Although indispensable in themselves, language skills are too unpredictable to become contaminating factors in tests of other subjects.

• *Frequent incorrectness.* Many existing tests, including some of the most respected, show serious mistakes in subject matter: both wrong answers counted right and perfectly good answers counted wrong. This impedes students who know the subject matter extremely well, because they must put aside their knowledge and instead figure out what the tester might want. Although it is unfair and inexcusable, this problem appears surprisingly often.

• *Ambiguity and lack of clarity.* Many items on current tests are unnecessarily obscure or frankly ambiguous, as examples quoted throughout this issue show.

• *Clerical emphasis.* Most large-scale tests are scored by machine. To accommodate the machine, students must usually mark their answers by shading in little squares on separate answer sheets. Finding the right square on the sheet is troublesome for some students, and it distracts them from the main purposes of the test. Children who are sloppy or careless in their answer sheet bookkeeping will receive low scores even if they know the answers to most of the questions.

• *Excessive time pressure.* By design, many tests are too long for most children to finish in the time allowed. This puts youngsters who tighten up under time pressure at a serious disadvantage, even though calmness under stress is not, supposedly, the trait that is being tested.

• *Inflexibility.* Different people think in different ways, but present tests make no allowances for individuality, no matter how effective. A creative answer is almost always a wrong answer, and an alert sense of humor can only lead the child into trouble. Tests force children into particular styles of thinking, styles that come more naturally to some youngsters than to others.

• *No credit for partial understanding.* On current large-scale achievement tests, answers are either right or wrong. There is no room for answers that are merely better or worse. A child will receive an item score of zero whether he or she has no idea what the question is about, or whether he or she eliminates all the wrong answers but two and then makes the wrong choice between those two. Guessing is a good tactic in the second case, but some children find it very hard to guess on a test, even if they are encouraged to.

• *Secrecy.* An atmosphere of military secrecy surrounds educational testing today. Parents have no access to the tests that play an important role in deciding their children's futures, and the public has no way of judging whether it is being well served. The testing industry has a tremendous advantage in defending itself, because only very dedicated and persistent critics can even gain access to the materials. Our society has become suspicious of secrecy lately, and this suspicion should extend to testing and to tests.

• *Lack of diagnostic value.* Standardized achievement tests are almost useless for classroom diagnosis, and so fail one of the most important testing needs altogether.

Cultural and linguistic bias. In present achievement tests, the question itself, the available answers, and information the student might use almost always appear in printed form. This means that every test is in a particular language, and that it must take certain linguistic usages for granted. Children who grow up in the same cultural environment as the test makers may have little trouble, as they share the same nuances of language and unspoken values. But other children—including many minority children—carry a different set of implicit understandings. Thus many minority children have the extra task of "decoding" each question, trying to grasp what it might mean in somebody else's language and culture. This is probably part of the reason that minority children do less well on achievement tests than majority youngsters.

Norm-referenced scores. Comparing people to one another along a single scale of ability is fundamentally demeaning and unfair. The case is even stronger with tests that fail to measure the ability well. People are different; they have different kinds of skills, abilities, and styles. It is foolish to pretend otherwise, yet the concept of norm-referenced tests assumes that people are very similar in certain kinds of ways.

This list can be broken down into two categories: those defects that arise in particular tests and can be fixed, and those that are basic to the test format and cannot be fixed. For example, incorrectness and ambiguity could be eliminated or greatly reduced through proper care in preparing the tests. Their occurrence need not reflect on the testing process as a whole. However, many of the other defects stem from the norm-referenced, content-validated, multiple-choice format itself. There is no way to correct these defects except by shifting to a different kind of test altogether.

The inescapable outcome is that we need alternative approaches to testing. The rather dry points above have been distilled from millions of youngsters sitting tensely at their school desks, shading in the little squares on which their futures depend. Competition and achievement are hard enough when the judging is fair, but when it is not, the joy of accomplishment—of proving oneself in the arena—can only turn into bitter frustration and apathy. We need tests that treat children equally, although not always identically; tests that overlook race, culture, and language to discriminate mainly on the basis of capability instead.

Under analysis, much of the apparently solid foundation on which testing rests simply disintegrates, leaving the whole testing business largely unsupported. Had testing questions been current two thousand years ago, a cynical Roman might well have observed (along with *caveat emptor*, which never goes out of date), *quis custodiet ipsos custodes?* In the end, until better tests can be developed, it is up to those who use the present tests to guard themselves.

IV
WHO DO THE
TESTS HURT?

Due Process, Human Rights, and Testing

Are you convinced that people—all people including students and children—should be aware of the danger to themselves of any procedure, medical or psychological, that they engage in *before* they agree to the procedure? Do you think they should have a say in their participation in questionable experiments? If so, perhaps you should lobby for the "due process" procedure for testing suggested by Edwin Taylor and Judah Schwartz. They suggest that a permission slip be sent home to be signed by the parent and child, which would grant or refuse permission for testing. It would include:

Description of the test to be given.
Who will be taking the test.
Who is expected to benefit and in what ways.
Who will use the results and for what purposes.
Whether or not the student's name will be known to those studying the results and what control student and parent have over dissemination of results.
Whether or not the test results will become part of the student's permanent record.
The consequences of *not* taking the test for the student, the school, and those administering the test or using the results.
Description of the report that will be made to the parent and the child (the parent must be accompanied by the child) after the test results are available.

Why exercise such caution? Because the tests have been shown to penalize children who think differently because they are creative, intelligent, or culturally different, and the penalty for them is very high indeed. José Cardenas, Superintendent of the Edgewood Independent School District in San Antonio and Robert Williams, professor of psychology at Washington University in St. Louis, describe what is meant by cultural bias of tests and what it does to test takers.

José A. Cardenas

USE OF TESTS: EDUCATIONAL ADMINISTRATION

Research indicates. . . that more is unknown than is known about intelligence and that the assumptions and methods of testing are not always valid. Performance can be based on more than the one variable of intelligence. Our assumption that all other factors are equal or are nondependent variables that have nothing to do with intelligence is false. Language facility, reading ability, and cultural compatibility all influence test scores.

Too many intelligence tests assume that all children have had common experiences—for example, that they are all familiar with snow. We haven't had a snow holiday for the last five years in the Edgewood school district, and most of the kids have never seen snow; yet some group intelligence tests ask about the use of a sled. One question on the WISC asks, "If your mother sends you to the store for a loaf of bread and there is none, what do you do?" The child who answers, "I go back home," is considered to be intellectually inferior to the child who says, "I go to another store." However, in rural areas, there is no place else to go. In some families, the parent and not the child is supposed to make such a decision. During my youth, I was sent for tortillas, and the purchase of a loaf of bread was unheard of in my house until I was fifteen years old.

Testing methods can. . . be incompatible with a culture. For example, some tests emphasize competitiveness, but Mexican-American children perform better in a cooperative situation. . .

It is simplistic to give a Puerto Rican child a Spanish translation of the WISC or the Peabody Picture Vocabulary Inventory. Some English stimulus words become Spanish paragraphs when translated properly. I have never heard a one-word translation of "cream puff," yet this word is on the Spanish version. Also, the Spanish equivalent of an English word may be on an entirely different level of difficulty. No matter how good the Spanish translation of a test, it must also take into account the regional variation of the language. When I once told a test translator that her translation must be regionalized to be valid, she protested the expense and said, "If the kids don't know this type of Spanish, that's their problem." So Spanish-language tests can be just as invalid as English-language tests for Spanish-speaking children.

These condensations are from two addresses delivered during the Tenth National Conference on Civil and Human Rights in Education, sponsored by NEA Center for Human Relations, February 18–20, 1972. Reprinted with permission of National Education Association from *Violations of Human and Civil Rights: Tests and Use of Tests.* Copyright © 1972 by National Education Association.

Robert L. Williams

MISUSE OF TESTS: SELF-CONCEPT

What do we mean by intelligence? Is it what the intelligence tests measure? Is it a global capacity to deal with one's environment? I offer the rubber band theory to illustrate my definition of intelligence. A rubber band will stay in its relaxed state unless stretched to its capacity by an outside force. Genetics or heredity determines an individual's potential stretch, and the environment determines the extent to which he reaches this potential.

Test items drawn from white culture penalize black children, whereas items drawn from black culture penalize whites. I have developed the BITCH test—Black Intelligence Test of Cultural Homogeneity—with items drawn directly from black culture. A child who knows Malcolm X's birthday or the date of his assassination shows as much intelligence as the one who knows Washington's birthday. I've never seen the word *pick* illustrated on the WISC— only *comb*, which is something I can't use.

The three criteria for a test—validity, reliability, and standardization— exclude black people. A test is valid when it measures what it intends to measure. Currently used ability tests do not measure black intelligence. If a test asks, for example, "What should you do if you find a purse with five dollars in it?" a black child will say, "Keep it"—a culturally determined response. He will say what his environment has dictated that he say, but on the standardized test, he will be marked zero.

Reliability means test consistency—i.e., a test will yield the same score, or rank an individual in the same place, each time. Since the standardized tests are scored subjectively, and since they validate only mainstream cultural responses, they cannot be reliable.

Standardization refers to the extent to which the sample on which the test is based represents the people who will take it. Several of the major ability tests excluded blacks, Mexican-Americans, and Puerto Ricans from their standardization samples. The Stanford-Binet, WISC, and Peabody systematically excluded blacks from their samples. If a test is not standardized on a particular group, it probably does not represent that particular group and should not be used on its members. Standardization is one reason for the 15-point difference in IQ between black and white kids. The discrepancy means simply that the test is biased.

Arthur Jensen's research has repeatedly shown that tests are biased—that black and chicano kids who have IQ's in the 60-to-80 range score much higher on his Learning Test than white kids with the same IQ. Jensen's interpretation is that blacks show more associative or Level I learning than whites; if you ask black and white kids to recite six digits backwards and forwards, black kids do better than whites with the same IQ. An alternative interpretation is that the biased IQ underestimates the black child's ability and indicates that he is clearly superior to the white kids who scored within the same range on the test, because the test was standardized on the whites.

Some people argue, "The tests do exactly what they are supposed to do. They predict scholastic success." Ability tests (X) predict a criterion (Y), such as a child's performance in the classroom. The hidden fallacy is variable Z, which might be unfairness, motivation, anxiety—anything that influences X (test scores). A fair test and a fair criterion will produce a high correlation between X and Y: white people who do well on tests do well in school. The unfair WISC and a fair classroom will produce a low correlation between X and Y: a black child who does poorly on the test will do well in the classroom. Another combination is a fair predictor, such as the Davis-Eels Games test, and an unfair criterion—the culturally biased classroom. This combination will also yield a low correlation: Black kids will do well on the test and poorly in the classroom. With an unfair predictor and an unfair criterion—the classic situation for the black child—the correlation is high: the black child who does poorly on the test also does poorly in the classroom.

After I administered the WISC test to about 500 black kids, I then gave the BITCH test. Of the 420 children in the low WISC group, 75 to 80 percent scored high on the BITCH. I still have to examine other criteria to see how well the BITCH scores correlate with scholastic performance, but at least I know that most of the black children who scored low on the WISC are neither educationally mentally retarded nor in the borderline defective range.

At least four court suits are now pending on the use of standardized tests in San Francisco, San Diego, Boston, and St. Louis because they violate a child's constitutional rights under the Fourteenth Amendment.

The Boehm's test of 50 basic concepts is clearly written for white folks. It asks the child to select the picture that shows "behind the couch" or "under the table." A black child does not say "behind" but "in back of"—not "under" but "up under." We are now rewriting the instructions to that test to see if children understand the concepts in black English. Black and white children can have the same cognition but communicate it differently. To the cognition "few," a black child might say, "Well, that's not a whole bunch of them." Only the vocabulary is different, and a difference is not a deficiency. You don't evaluate black people in terms of how white they are, but this is what the tests have done. They do not measure black ability.

Eliminating and inhibiting intelligence early in life is the best way to keep blacks out of the system. I would opt for talking to children in the dialect they understand. If a child can understand what you are asking of him on a test, he will probably master the task. You cannot expect an individual who has not been exposed to German or French to understand these languages. This does not mean that he lacks the capacity to learn German or French, but that he lacks that particular exposure.

Black parents should be concerned about both the predictive variable— the test—and the criterion variable—the classroom. I think whites should also be vitally concerned. Brother Charlie Mingus said, "When they came and took the Catholics, I did not complain, but I am not a Catholic. When they came and took the Unionists, I did not complain, because I am not a Unionist. When they came and took the Panthers, I did not complain, because I am not a Panther, but then one day they came and took me." I don't think we should let another generation pass in this country that knows all about extravehicular space activity, atomic physics, and all of these highfalutin things, but does not know what a human being is.

People Don't Decide, Tests Do

We all know stories of children mislabeled, misplaced, and miserable because of test results. How can it be, if each of us knows one or two such horror stories, that we still believe this is a rare occurrence?

Thomas Cottle, the superbly sensitive child psychologist affiliated with the Children's Defense Fund, tells of two children of the 20 percent whom the tests destroyed and of one who barely escaped.

Thomas Cottle

". . . I'm as smart as anybody in that school but you'll see, they'll fix it so I don't go to college. They always have their ways of stopping me. You'll see how they'll do it."

"I.Q. tests?" I asked cautiously.

"Yeah, that's one way."

"How does that work, Cornell?"

"Well, say they want you to stay where you are, they give you an I.Q. test and say you did bad. You can't argue to no one. The dude says 95, you got 95. Or like, if they want you out of their class they'll put you in some special ed class. What do they care? We got kids in our school, they've been in those special ed classes all their lives! Every year they keep going back to those classes and there's nothing in the world wrong with them. We ask the teachers, hey, what they got him in there for? What he do? Oh, he did bad things, they'll say. Or they'll say, 'Old Jonah he's a *strange* little boy. Something wrong with his brain. Been that way since he was a little tiny baby. He can't learn the right way like the rest of us. And that's a fact!' But that's a lot of stuff, man, 'cause we'll know different. Old Jonah, see, he's got a brother or sister maybe, and

This article was originally published as **"Going Up, Going Down,"** in *The National Elementary Principal,* March–April, 1975. Copyright 1975, National Association of Elementary School Principals. All rights reserved. Reprinted by permission. The last two sections that appear are from *Science for the People,* a paper published in March, 1974.

they know there's nothing wrong with him. Folks at the school just don't like him, that's all. So they shut him up in that special ed class. Teachers try to tell us kids like him will learn better in there but we know it's a prison. I don't care what they lie to us, because we always got ways of finding out the truth. But I'll go pitch a bitch when one of those high ahd mighties goes around thinking I don't know what the truth is."

Cornell was steaming mad. Audon always quieted him down when he got like this, at least she did in front of me. I suspect she did the same when I was gone. She would throw in a few words too about behaving politely in front of company while Cornell, who was already uneasy about talking to a white visitor in his home, would give her a look as if to say, I'm no child any-more. You take care of the little children and I'll take care of myself. But Audon, I could see, valued Cornell's outrage. She knew he "had it," as she said. He wouldn't "let things go on as they had all these years. Cornell and his friends will change things no matter what it takes because they keep their eyes and ears open, and know when to do the same thing with their mouths. And that's a sign that they're intelligent. It doesn't matter, see, how people answer somebody else's question. Even a teacher's. What matters is that children like Cornell and his friends understand what it's like living in the real world. They know what's happening to them at the school. They know everything there is to know about what's going on. The secrets have been told. They used to have a kind of sheet they'd throw on themselves and all their institutions," Audon said, "especially where black folks were involved. But this generation, with the help of their elders, have pulled that sheet away, and there is America, the rich and the poor, the black and the white, just laying out there naked like a woman ready for her lover to come in that front door of hers, for everyone to see. But these kids see it all in a special way. They see it and behind it too. Every last one of them. 'Cause they got it. The intelligence I mean."

" . . .I'll tell you something else—we got a boy in our school took one of them tests and scored seventy something. Everybody knows he ain't that dumb. Teacher, she was surprised to find that out too, so she asked him how come he did so bad? He told her it was because partly he got so scared he couldn't think straight and partly cause when he'd take too much time or miss something, the man giving the test would say, 'Well, if you don't know that one and it's the easiest, no sense giving you the rest.' Then another kid, he said that when he took the test the man kept telling him he was sounding like hw asn't only dumb but sick in his mind, you know. He kept saying, 'Maybe we better stop, maybe we'd better stop.' So finally the kid got so frightened they stopped and he wasn't half way through the test. But then they put down his score without anybody saying he'd only worked half the test. Everybody's got a story like that, man. Everybody.

"You know my sister Paula? She was taking the test and they came to the part where they got these blocks, you know, and you're supposed to match up the designs on these little cards. So she starts working on the first one, and the guidance counselor, Mr. Kiplinger, he's sitting there real stitch ass, you know, like he really knew his business, timing her with this big stop watch. So Paula's working away, looking at her blocks, then looking back at the little cards." Suddenly Cornell began to laugh out loud. Nothing he did could suppress his laughter. "She's working these, see," he continued, trying to catch his breath and looking over his shoulder for fear that Audon might have heard him, "putting all these blocks together only she figures out there's two blocks missing. Well, she's ready to lay her bitch on him when he says, 'Smile awhile, Pretty Paula face. You go on and do the best you can with the two blocks missing. Don't make no difference. Just go on like they were there.' So she does. Each time she finishes a design she says, 'There it is and the other two blocks would go like, here and there,' you know." Cornell poked twice in the air in front of him, as if pointing to the missing blocks. "So old stitch ass, he smiles and compliments her, but all the time he's marking on the page that she couldn't figure it out. She could see what he was writing all the time. That's why her score was low and why she stayed in the same class.

"I don't know this one boy but Derond Williamson told me about a kid who did real well on his test. Fact he did so well that when he got done the woman giving him the test stuck out her hand, you know, to shake his hand. So he just walked away. Spun around, man, dug that heel of his into the rug and departed. So she yells at him, 'Where you going, boy? I'm waiting here to shake your hand.' 'You ain't touching my hand,' he goes. 'Oh yes I am,' she goes. He goes, 'I don't know of a single rule in the Constitution of the United States that says I got to shake your hand!' 'Don't you give me stuff about the Constitution. In this school you'll do as I say!' 'I did your little whitey test,' he goes. That's what he said. 'And that's all I was supposed to do. Nobody told me about shaking no lady's hand at the end.' Now she's really screaming at him but he don't pay her no mind at all. He just goes. So she takes a whole lot of points away from him and they put him in that special ed class I was telling you about. That kid was three years older than me. He was sixteen and a whole lot smarter. He just proved that on the woman's own test, but he committed the fatal sin, man. He misbehaved. He talked back to the goddess. Nobody ever said nothing about her calling him boy. He was in that class half the year before they sprung him. Then they put him in the second year class where everybody was too young for him. I tell you, man, that dude, he was really smart. I heard him talk. He could find a word for everything, man."

"He finish school?" I wondered.

"Not a chance. He left school two weeks after they sprung him from special ed. I saw him hanging around outside a couple of times after that, but he's gone now. Maybe he's in the army." His voice had become soft. "Maybe the streets got him."

Cornell stared at me without speaking. Then he sighed deeply and his eyes closed halfway as though he could see Paula, frustrated by the absence of the two small wooden blocks. This time he didn't smile. "Hey mamma," he whispered, "look what they've done to my score. They do it to us everytime. Move us here, move us there, pushing us around all the time. It ain't what school's supposed to be. You know what you got to learn in that school, in all these schools? You got to learn where your place is. If they think you're dumb, they put you in that special ed class until you drop out of school, which is what they want you to do. If you got too many brains showing they paint over your test scores so no one will come around and ask, how come this kid ain't in a higher division? Up and down, we're a bunch of yo-yo's. If anybody'd ever stop to think what we got to do to finish they'd know where we're spending all our energy. Hell, getting out of bed ain't no easier for me than for my grandmother. What do I got to get out of bed for? What do they think I'm supposed to be doing in school that matters? I ain't learning from school, I'm learning *about* that school. They're teaching away but I see way behind their sweet asses.

"They're all hung up in these I.Q. tests. They ain't honest tests. Everybody knows that. All the advantages go to the white kids. And since they mess all over with us, why do they even bother to take time to give us the tests? I'll tell you why. So's they can convince themselves that they're doing the right thing. So's they can sleep at night. Go on home to their old lady and tell her they did the best they could that day with those nasty little black boys and girls, that evil eleven percent, but those nasty little black boys and girls just couldn't do the tests so they'll go into the special classes. Hate to do it to you little boys and girls, but you know the rules we've written here for you all. Doing the best we can." Cornell's imitation had ended. "Hell, that Kiplinger was probably spreading his fat stitch ass over Paula's blocks so to make sure she'd flunk. He got a glimpse pretty quick how smart she is and he knew there'd be no way of keeping her back after that. Folks like they got there would eat those blocks 'fore they'd be honest enough to admit black kids got what it takes to be intelligent.

"They control us with those tests, man. They got us dancing on the end of those scores. Hey mamma," he shouted out, looking upward, "they're going to break my ass just like they broke my score. 'I ain't going to give you no trouble, teach,'" he announced to an imaginary person in front of him. "'I won't try to bust out of my division. Just let me take the good courses. Let me see if I can do 'em. Let me show you what I know. You folks got to change your minds about this intelligence idea. You got to learn from us and *our* intelligence. You think, lady, we could make it this far without being super intelligent? You think we don't know what's happening? You think we're blind and stupid? . . .'"

*   *   *

This morning, I walked down the halls of a Boston area public school. The atmosphere in the school, that intangible quality that observers of education always mention, was difficult to describe. The children were in their classrooms running around or sitting at their desks. In one room there was utter chaos; in another room there was an uncanny sense of order and obedience. In still another room, a group of about ten children, perhaps eight or nine years old, huddled together on a green rug. They sat at the foot of a young man and looked up at him as though he were imparting the secrets of the world. The children obviously loved that teacher. Outside their classroom a small sign was taped to the blond oak door. It read, "Shh—we're testing in here."

It was pleasant enough in that room—unlike the atmosphere I usually find in the schoolrooms I visit. In one of Boston's city schools, where a sign also indicated that testing was going on in a classroom, I witnessed very different behavior. I watched a child sit for more than fifteen minutes—it seemed like a century—refusing to answer even one question the tester was asking. The tester, an older woman, seemed patient enough, but it was evident that this child wasn't going to speak. It was also clear that the child was terrified. She might not have been able to speak even if she had wanted to. The child stared at the tester, her eyes rarely blinking, and with each new question or request she swallowed, opened her eyes as wide as she could, and smiled—just slightly.

After fifteen minutes of this torturous routine, the tester gave in and excused the child. The girl stood up, opened her eyes wide, and walked slowly from the room. Outside in the hall she began to run, and disobeying the signs to walk at all times, she raced up the stairs at the end of the corridor and collided with a friend. She began at once to explain her testing session, and in an instant the two children were laughing hysterically and darting up the stairs together. That same day that same ten-year-old girl had the following statement entered in her official school record, "The child's IQ is so low she is not testable. Recommendation: special class work is required, probably not in this school."

Several months later the girl was out of school. Unable to find her a special class or special school, her parents let her drop out of school for a time. After several months, the child was readmitted to the same school, and a young psychologist was brought in to test the child. It was late spring, and the psychologist took the girl and the testing equipment out-of-doors. After talking together for almost an hour about all sorts of things, the psychologist explained the testing procedure and began to work with the little girl. The psychologist's final accounting showed an IQ of 115. The child's verbal ability was outstanding. Her weaknesses were in reading comprehension and arithmetic. A tutor was provided to work with the child in those weak areas. One year later she was tested by one of the school's guidance counselors, and her IQ tested 124. In the fall of the same year, the girl was admitted to a voluntary busing program, and she now attends the suburban school that I visited this morning. Her classmates say, "She's neat, except when she talks too much!"

*   *   *

In a small industrial town in the western part of Massachusetts, I heard other accounts of the effects of testing on some white, middle class juniors who attended the town's main public high school and who met with me on several occasions. On one rainy afternoon at the front entrance of their school, a young woman told me a sad story.

"Georgia Willows," she began, "had been in my class ever since kinder-garten. I never liked her too much, but I had to see her all the time 'cause our parents were friends. I remember she lived in this real large house. We used to play there. Georgia always thought she was the smartest girl in the world. God's gift, you know. By the time we were in grammar school, everybody considered her the smartest girl in the school.

"Then last year this other girl visited the school on one of these exchange programs—from Holland—and not only was she gorgeous, she was even smarter than Georgia. I think she spoke about six languages. She'd never even been in America before and she spoke better than I do. And she'd read a lot of books I hadn't even heard of, American books! So Georgia really had someone to compete with in school. She had thought she was going to be the queen all by herself, but then this Stephanie came and Georgia really got upset. One time at our house, when her parents were visiting, all of a sudden she started to cry. We were up in my room, and out of the clear blue, she began to cry. And she kept saying, 'If I'm not the smartest person in our class, if Stephanie's IQ is higher, I don't want to be alive.'

"I didn't think she was serious about it, but she was. Just before Easter she killed herself. Her mother told my mother that Georgia never got over not being the smartest. I think if IQ means that much to someone, something must be wrong. But maybe there's something wrong with testing people and making them think that how smart they are is the most important thing in their lives."

In that same school, the issue of testing was discussed by a young man who had just learned of his own performance on a set of standardized achieve-ment tests.

"I try not to compare myself with anybody," he began, "but kids talk. Everybody says they aren't going to tell anybody what they got, but in about five minutes everybody knows. Some mystery. I was thinking about tests and all that the other day, and I decided that there's only one way to get rid of them—which they should 'cause they only make people anxious. If you elimi-nate money in our society, you could eliminate tests and all these test scores. See, to be American means that you have to have a lot of money. No matter what you earn you aren't satisfied until you have more than the next guy. That's the same thing with tests. Giving us our score isn't enough. They have to give us the percentile reading as well. Nobody's supposed to get 690 and think they're really special. The guidance counselor tells them right away that 690 may sound good, but it's only the eightieth percentile. You got to have money and you got to have IQ points and PSAT points and SAT points. Americans love numbers, and quantities. Big's the name of the game. Produce and get bigger. Inches, pounds, dollars, points on tests, that's all anybody cares about—even the minority students in our school. Nobody asks them whether they're happy. All people want to know is whether their achievement scores have gone up, or how many points they scored in a basketball game."

I have experienced many pleasant incidents in grammar schools and high schools during the last few years. I remember how proud and excited a boy was as he bolted out of an assistant principal's office after being awarded an academic prize. I also remember the concerned faces of children as they were told that the results of some test indicated a problem that the school officials needed to discuss with their parents. Those children were crushed and afraid. They could barely hide their hurt from their classmates.

One of the most vivid school scenes, which usually occurred first thing on a school morning, was the look of anxiety and anticipation on the faces of students as they waited for their teacher to hand back a test. "Abrams, Adams, Briscoe, Coleman," the teacher calls out looking one last time at the test sheet as if memorizing the score. And Abrams, Adams, Briscoe, and Coleman—four children half sitting, half standing, waiting eagerly—bounce up or rise slowly and walk to the teacher to receive their grand accounting.

No one needs to announce their scores. Indeed, one doesn't even have to see their faces to know their scores; their bodies reveal everything. Abrams slinks away, careful not to touch anybody. Adams practically flies back to her seat and sits as if she rests on a cushion of clouds. Briscoe looks at the teacher and his body slouches; he actually seems to be several inches shorter than before he walked the few steps to his teacher. And Coleman seems to grow several inches as the teacher walks forward to bestow the good news on the slim girl whose eyes now seem to explode with excitement. Not only does she grow, but her step changes. She dances backward, showing the paper to her friends.

When the teacher returned last week's test to the third graders in that one class, the children were literally going up and going down in response to the numbers they read in the upper right hand corners of their papers. Going up and going down—in posture, in stature, and in spirit.

Throughout my life I have been troubled by the business of psychological and achievement testing. For years, the words *Princeton, New Jersey,* caused me to tremble with fright, for no matter how many people raved about that town and its renowned university, Princeton, New Jersey, meant the home office of school testing. I never questioned the use of testing. Few students in those days did. If adults had to reconcile themselves to death and taxes, then adolescents had to reconcile themselves to test results and acne, or something equally humiliating. It was a private and public response one had to the test-taking procedure. One might smile as if "who would care," like the girl I saw in that Boston school running out of the room and colliding with her friend. But inside, something was shattered. It is almost twenty years since I graduated from high school, and the nightmares of being tested and all that went with the testing procedures persist. They are dreams of terror that never fail to awake me.

How many billions of words have been written about education? How many thousands of articles have been written about the goals of schooling and the need for testing? But how many people know the financial aspects of testing? Do we pay close enough attention to what all this multimillion dollar testing business does to people? How many people know the reasons for testing that have nothing to do with diagnostic or intellectual inquiry? Are we aware of the hundreds of thousands of children who, on the basis of some test, will stop going to school and lead a life in which this early sense of incompetence, failure, and lack of grace will never be erased from their self-concept?

Children in this country are deeply affected for all of their lives by testing and the industry that underwrites it. They are going up and going down in a pattern that ought to frighten us. Some children do just fine. Others rise so quickly that they cannot comprehend the ascent, and they often never recover from the fall when they learn that test scores represent very little when hard work and disciplined ingenuity are required.

We ought to worry, too, about the child who goes home after learning that his test scores have earned him a place in the lowest academic track of his inadequate grammar school, and with tears in his eyes tells his parents: "They told me in school that I'm stupid. I didn't know what they were talking about. They told me there was no use talking back to them because they had it in their tests—everything they wanted to know about me. I said I should be in the other group because those kids were learning more and besides, they were getting all the best teachers in their classes. I didn't want them to put me in the class they put me in. But they said it wasn't what they *wanted* to do, it was what they *had* to do 'cause they don't decide what classes to put the student in, the tests decide that for them. People don't decide. . . . ."

Isn't the Reading Achievement Test O.K.?

Some who distrust IQ tests have no difficulty accepting the need for reading tests. After all, if you don't have some sort of test, how can we know that the school is doing its job, and that early reading difficulties are being recognized and handled?

On the face of it, these tests are different and necessary. But they are also potentially harmful, as Deborah Meier shows us.

Deborah Meier

The reading test mystique is, despite the number and respectability of its opponents, decidedly more widespread and powerful than ever before. Faced with a growing demand for "accountability," school administrators increasingly tend to exploit testing as a cheap and easy way of defining goals as well as of measuring success.

As a result, every parent and citizen is alerted to and armed with very precise test statistics. A child is no longer "a good reader," "a poor reader," or even "a nonreader." Now Johnny is a 2.7 or a 4.1 reader. Schools, too, are consistently classified by reading test scores—above grade level or below, and almost all "performance contracting" is based upon payment according to such test score results.

THE SOCIAL CONTEXT

It is not only the poor minority parent, with a history of legitimate suspicion about the good intentions of the school system, who is the "true believer" in the reading tests. It is not only 3R-conscious "middle America." The faith embraces also highly educated parents, including many advocates of open classrooms, "relevant curriculum," and free schools. At meeting after meeting, many such parents—while demanding the introduction of freer and more relevant schooling—will inquire about the comparative test scores of open vs. formal schools and use past test scores to prove the evils of traditional education. Well-educated and well-off parents have told me how they "had to" change schools or hire tutors because their nine-year-old *scored* low, or anyway insufficiently high! ("But does he read well?" I ask in vain.) Others praise John Holt and A. S. Neil as their educational gods and then tell me proudly that they have just learned that their fifth grade son is an 11.3 reader. In short, almost all parents "believe in" these tests. They "believe in" them even when the scores defy their own observations about their own child's reading ability, and despite a nearly total ignorance of test contents, scoring methods, or, certainly, their own child's actual performance on the test.

Test scores are hard to resist, given their widespread use by school systems, their utilization in reputable studies on education, their quotation in the most scholarly journals, their yearly publicity in the *New York Times*, and the passing references made to them by the best-intentioned educators when boasting of their own favorite programs. (Furthermore, the statistical exactitude of the testing lingo adds to an aura of scientific accuracy.) If this is the case with parents who know their own children and school people who presumably know their own classrooms, it is certainly understandable that the public whose taxes support the schools should accept test scores as hard data regarding the success or failure of school programs.

Yet an examination of the tests themselves, their scoring methods, and, most important, the manner in which children handle them, demonstrates that they do a grave disservice. They subject the young child to an evaluation system based on standards which neither child, parent, teacher, nor school may agree on or even be consciously aware of, and thus, often unwittingly, drive schools and teachers into adopting pressure-cooker programs to meet the needs of the tests, not children.

This article was originally published as **"What's Wrong with Reading Tests?"** in *Notes From the Workshop Center for Open Education,* New York: City College School of Education, March 1972. Copyright 1972 by the W.C.O.E. Reprinted by permission.

This combination of circumstances may account for what has become an open scandal in New York City schools: the widespread cheating done with regard to reading tests, not merely by students but by the educational establishment itself—including traditionalists, reformers, and radicals.

While teachers and administrators congratulate themselves on the fresh wind of humanism that is blowing across the nation's schools (albeit amidst an inhumane poverty of funds), they have paid too little attention to the entrenchment of a system of measurement that could serve as the excuse for the death of any reforms.

"Why such passion? What are you afraid of? Aren't such tests 'merely' a tool to measure a child's ability to read, which you also are eager to improve?" say well-intentioned colleagues. But what is reading? How do such tests measure it? And if they do not measure reading development, what is it they do? And how dangerous is their effect?

It is a cliché to note that education does not take place solely within the four walls of a school. In fact, *between* the ages of six and sixteen, children spend only about a fifth of their waking hours inside schools. But what is apparently less obvious is that it is therefore not possible to devise a standardized group test that measures only the data printed upon the mind by the school teacher.

Or, put another way, no standardized group test by its very nature can be without bias. Nor should it. It has to have a particular content of some sort. Furthermore, it has to have a style and a "jargon." It has to have a "format"—a way of getting to what it is after. And finally, it must be built in such a way that it can be "objectively" scored for right and wrong responses.

THE TROUBLE WITH THE TESTS

Two major "biases" exist in the reading tests given to young children. One that has been well publicized is the class and cultural bias regarding choice of content. As testing critics have noted, tests reward not only "the ability to read" but also knowledge of particular words, ideas, places, and experiences, commonly linked more with one socioeconomic group than another.

While one can *understand* the argument that a high school diploma (or a college degree) should indicate knowledge of a certain "common curricula territory, it is not the tester of reading who should be deciding on the territory. Furthermore, to aim for this from the primary school is absurd. Worse, it is dangerous. For the task of the teacher of the young is the very opposite one. Early childhood education seeks to emphasize words, concepts, and reading material that will help provide continuity between his preschool learning and his school learning, between the different parts of his own life and environment. It stretches out beyond the world of intimacy only slowly, as experience, interests, and needs widen.

A test that ignores the nature of childhood separates—with a tool of apparent scientific neutrality—children of one kind of background from those of another. An examination of the way children deal with the test documents this fact in a startling fashion. As one listens to bright, articulate black children from our inner city schools attempt to make sense of the bewildering array of test questions, the bias involved is painful and shocking.

The second bias, less apparent and probably more insidious because of its subtlety, is the extent to which standardized tests are rigged against the nature of the thinking of all young children. What appears to many teachers, in their effort to coach their students to success, as "immaturity" (if not stupidity) in dealing with test questions, is simply the normal developmental style of thought of any seven- or eight-year-old. Middle class children, because of their familiarity with certain key phrases and styles (conditioned responses), short-cut the process and succeed in producing "right" answers even though they do not carry out the logical thought implied by the question. They get it "right" for the "wrong" reason. The bright lower-class child, who cannot fall back upon a lifetime of familiarity with certain language, picture, or word-association patterns, is dependent upon real mental ingenuity to make the necessary "logical" connections. As a result, even if he has equal reading skill and utilizes greater intelligence in his effort to think through the particular question on the test, he is bound to answer wrong more frequently. A seven-year-old child, still engaged in "preoperational" thinking, or, at most, in what Jean Piaget has described as "early concrete operational thinking," is simply not in the same world as the adults who fashion such tests. It is for this reason that such a child's ingenuity and good judgment are not only useless to the task, but often even detrimental to it.

In labeling such children "slow," or seeking test-oriented get-rich-quick schemes, irreparable damage is done. Schemes to help such children "score better" (however well meant) invariably seek to substitute conditioned responses for good thinking. They block off the rich vein of associative thinking, imagery, spontaneity, and attendant self-confidence that the world makes sense upon which intellectual growth depends. In relying on drilled associations to link specific terms or words, they divorce language from conceptual and experiential growth. They fashion their own curriculum demands which focus not on children's interests or their developmental needs but on preknowledge of the nature of the test contents. The tendency for "school thinking" to become disassociated from "sensible thinking" is thus reinforced. In short, in order to "look good" in second grade, we risk a child's potential for later growth.

To make matters worse, the scoring methods currently in vogue lead to their own absurdities. Test scores are reported by grade level norms: a second-grader taking the test in April is "average" if he scores 2.7 (second year, seventh month). Towards the two ends of the scale the grade-level equivalents go wild. On one of the tests examined here, 77 out of 84 right scores 3.7, 4 more right jumps it to 5.2, and a mere 3 more catapults a student to 8.4. At the other end, average luck at guessing will place a second-grader taking this test at 2.0. A few bad guesses and he zooms down to 1.3. For this reason, a poor reader is best advised to take the most advanced test he can, where, assuming he skips nothing and has average luck, he will score amazingly high in terms of grade level. The test makers admit the scoring system is misleading. They argue that it is hard to find one that will better satisfy the public.

HOW CHILDREN HANDLE TESTS

Following the spring 1971 testing period in New York City, I spent two weeks talking about the tests with second and third grade children with whom I had worked for some years in a central Harlem school. All had just completed one of two tests: Primary II or Elementary I of the Metropolitan Reading Achievement tests. These tests are fairly typical, and the following comments are not intended as criticism of this particular set. For while in certain respects it has improvable qualities, this set is no worse than any others and better than some.

These tests are given to all second through fourth grade children (seven- to nine-year-olds) in New York City each spring. I met with about 15 children in small group discussions and individual sessions, taping their comments so that I could review them later with other colleagues. Most of the children had had a limited period of skillful pretest coaching, were among our best students academically, and had spent at least a year in fairly informal classrooms. These conversations led me to note at least four broad areas of competence that seemed to be involved in an ability to score high. Few of these competencies seemed necessarily connected, however, to "reading," "word knowledge," or "comprehension," the specific aims of the test.

The most startling realization was the extent of confusion in most children's minds about what they were being asked to think about or do. The test directions involved thinking skills that were inappropriate for most seven-year-olds; not only was there a poor choice of wording but also a mismatch between the test tasks and the minds of the children for whom the test was intended. For example, one part of the "word knowledge" subtest consists of simple line drawings followed by a choice of four words. The child is asked to select the one that "tells what the picture is about." Generally children had no difficulty thinking of a name for the object in question. But if that name did not work, the children were not always able to refocus in order to select the possible word association that the testmaker might have had in mind. A child in second grade looking at a drawing of a merry-go-round sought vainly for the word "merry-go-round." "The only word that begins with an 'm' is 'mile,' " she wailed. "It couldn't be right, could it?" she inquired insecurely. A few chose "run," because the horses in the picture, they said, might be running. The correct answer, incidentally, was "turn." Similarly, a few good readers were stumped by the picture of a ball! They went over and over the possible answers. Afterwards some insisted that there had been something wrong with their test! The "right answer," b-a-l-l, must certainly have been somewhere. They were unable to even consider "round" as a possible answer, although, as with "turn," most were quite able to read and use it appropriately.

Another section of the "word knowledge" subtest requires children to note the underlined word in an incomplete sentence, and then choose one of four words which "best completes the sentence." The sentences are of the type: "*Afraid* means. . ." "To *know* is to. . ." or "*Quiet* is the opposite of. . ." What the test seems to be seeking are synonyms and antonyms. But the children invented their own game of word association. A synonym is only one approach to "word definition" and involves a quite abstract notion about the replaceability of one word for another. If pressed for a "meaning," children (and adults) generally give a story example that describes the word or which uses it appropriately. When I asked what "afraid" means, children told me *when* or *why* you might be afraid, e.g., "Afraid means like when you go someplace new and you get afraid." They often selected the right answer, "scared," to complete this sentence because it was natural for them to use it in the context of "afraid." ("I get scared when I am afraid," seemed to make sense.) However, and for precisely the same reason, the children were divided more or less equally between right and wrong answers on the sentence "to *keep* means to. . ." The four choices included "carry" and "hold." The ones who got it right said, "If you want to keep *something* you got to *hold* onto it." The others, who answered it wrong, said with equal logic, "If you want to *keep* it you better *carry* it." In both cases the children were explaining the relationship in life between two words.

For some children of seven and eight, "opposites" were difficult and were confused in their minds with the concept of "very different." When I tried to explain the notion of opposites, I began to grasp how complex and abstract this "simple" idea was. Familiarity leads most children to the correct answers. But for some children, "tall" and "far" were opposites, just as clearly as "tall" and "short," and no reasoned argument in the world could demonstrate otherwise at this age. Their failure again was not due to an incapacity to read the right answer, but rather an inability to focus on the specific relationship involved. While this kind of data is of interest to a good teacher in assessing a child's mode of thinking and classifying, it tells us very little about his "word knowledge" and his ability to read. There might well be a statistical correlation between children who are "advanced" in such tasks and those who succeed in school and become good readers. However, if we are merely seeking a statistically predictive tool, one that will serve our purposes quite well already exists, one carefully documented in the Coleman Report, which proves that the best predictor of all is the income/educational background of a child's parents. Such statistical correlations are merely indicative of the degree to which schooling is too often made irrelevant—not proof of the extent to which schooling is used effectively. Statistical *correlations* are not always sufficient evidence as to whether or not we are in fact measuring a relevant cognitive skill.

For our purposes, what is vital to know is whether a child answers a question incorrectly because he cannot read, because the vocabulary is unfamiliar or confusing to him, or merely because he has interpreted it in accord with his own common sense, in a manner appropriate to his age and his own experience. Even his "right" answers should be scrutinized with these same kinds of questions.

A similar confusion over the meaning of the test directions plagues many children in handling the "reading comprehension" subtest. Despite persistent efforts during the pretest coaching to help children understand the relationship between the story paragraph above and the incomplete sentence tasks below, some children "refused" to grasp it. They stubbornly insisted upon inventing answers as though the previous paragraph did not exist, selecting answers instead based on their own personal experiences, intuition, or fantasies. They did so even when I reread the paragraph aloud to them, in order to get them to check their own answers. The very connection upon which the validity of this part of the test is based failed to make sense to them.

The language and subject matter are largely inappropriate for young children. For example, "a fair day is one that is . . ." The answer is "clear." But many children quite capable of reading the four choices offered had never had any reason to connect "fair" with weather. "Fair means," they explained to me, "when a teacher doesn't be unfair," "when you go on rides, that kind of fair." Similarly, few and far between were the children who were able to give me an example of where "point" and "place" were synonyms or went together in *any* way. Other words were often unfair in a test to be used with city children—as inappropriate as landlord, subway, crosstown, apartment, junkie, or project (meaning a big apartment building) would be for rural youngsters or comfortable suburbanites. We are so unconsciously biased in the world of schools in favor of nineteenth century America and suburban Westchester County, that we quite forget that some words have dropped out of urban usage. Nor can one see why a *reading* test for seven- and eight-year-olds should presume that any child's verbal, much less written, knowledge should include knowing that a "canoe" is a "kind of boat" rather than a "kind of ship," that "oats" are a "kind of grain," or that "clay" is a "kind of mud." And imagine the adult mentality that asks a seven-year-old child to select just one right answer to "A *giant* is . . ." "huge," "scary," "fierce" or "mean."

It is hardly worth belaboring the absurdity of testing reading by asking eight-year-olds to read and answer questions regarding Amazon ants, the discovery of penicillin in 1928 by an English scientist, Guy Fawkes Day and the Gunpowder Plot against the British government 350 years ago, or the contents and meaning of Egyptian religious art. It would be comparable to testing the average literate adult's reading ability by giving him passages to read from Einstein, Piaget, or an advanced trigonometry text. Thus the test *makers* seek to impose a curriculum on the primary grades—one that covers the terminology appropriate to a study of medical history, the geography of the world, and the history of Western civilization. To imagine such a curriculum actually being covered in an average school day is patently absurd; to attempt it would be educationally criminal. All good early childhood education begins with the language of the child, values his own life and experiences, and emphasizes reading and writing as natural extensions of this verbal communication.

Even the narrowest skills of reading—phonetic decoding ability and the possession of a good basic sight vocabulary—are poorly measured. Every attempt is made to "trick" readers into betraying phonetic lapses and sight-word confusions. For example, among the four choices offered alongside a drawing of a human mouth are both "mouth" and "month." A majority of our good readers selected "month" because it came first. The u-n reversal is, we know, common up until fourth grade even among many fluent readers.

Reading experts almost universally urge a casual approach to such reversals unless they are also associated with other reading problems. Yet the test had a number of such pitfalls which, to be avoided, would require a cautiousness toward reading (a word-for-word vocalization) that would indicate poor reading habits. *Month* and *mouth* and *log* and *leg*, for example, are hardly likely to be confused in a real reading situation.

Despite good sight word knowledge, strong decoding skill and a substantial verbal sophistication, some children still get into serious trouble over their interpretations of pictures or stories. For example, when shown a picture of a little boy at the beach with his hand on a girl's shoulder, almost everyone interviewed selected "push" as the best answer. While many did not understand the word "wade" (which was the "right" answer), they did not change their minds even when I explained what it meant. The word "push" seemed good enough and closer to their own experience with such a situation. Similarly, every second-grader and all but one of the third-graders misinterpreted a picture showing birds flying above and below some trees. Those birds, they insisted, were "flying many ways." Only one boy chose the correct answer, "flying in a flock." While this indicates that many of these seven- and eight-year-olds were unfamiliar with the word "flock," it also means that most of them had an interpretation of the phrase "flying in many ways" that was different from the test maker's.

In another drawing, a boy is waving toward three boys talking together in the distance. Most children incorrectly and empathetically thought the boy by himself in the foreground was "lonely because he does not have any friends." While I found the children's answer sensible, I had spontaneously answered it "correctly" by selecting "John and some boys belong to a club." Apparently I had unconsciously responded to a small suburban-type clubhouse in the background, because afterward I had a hard time defending my answer to the children or to myself! In still another drawing, bright and imaginative Karen worked out a very skillful interpretation of a picture that stumped many children. The picture showed a man in the foreground painting a wall, and some other men in firemen's uniforms in the background carrying some small objects. "The man up front is painting," Karen explained proudly to our group. "But the answer isn't this one about painting, because how would we know he was a fireman? He hasn't a fireman hat on. So they must be talking about those men back there who are carrying things, especially see this man in the fireman's hat and that must be stuff for putting out fires." So she selected, "The fireman has the tools for putting out a fire." She convinced most of the children, including those who had correctly answered, "The fireman is doing some painting," and others who had said, "A fireman works by himself." Her mistake was not recognizing a fireman's uniform minus the hat and/or being too suspicious of the test. The children who were right generally had not bothered to read all the answers, but had simply noticed the word "painting" in the first answer given, and on that basis alone picked the right answer. Two children engaged in a charming verbal battle over a drawing of a lady shopping. "The man weighs the fruit before Mother buys it" just didn't seem right to one girl. "Where will Mother put the fruit he's weighing, since she's already carrying one bag that is too full?" "Well," said her classmate, "she could carry two bags." Her own mother does that sometimes, and she demonstrated how it could be done. The first little girl remained dubious.

Another picture puzzled many children, who could not see the logical connection between any of the sentences and the picture. The right answer was dependent on first noticing the detail of rain streaks outside the window, connecting these streaks to the idea of a rainstorm, then linking a rainstorm to a power failure and finally, all of this to the candle on the table! In still another scene, we see a smiling well-dressed girl in raincoat and rain hat. Surely she was not going to let her books get wet, was the general consensus. She must have covered them, although it was hard to tell from the picture. Most children selected one of two wrong answers: "The rain will not hurt the books" or "Mary is taking good care of the books." I arrived at the right answer by following deviously deductive logic: if Mary had been conscientious and covered her books there would be two equally correct answers. This cannot happen on a standardized test. Therefore, "Mary's books will get wet in the rain" must be the preferred answer. Yet all three answers were equally easy to read and equally defensible as descriptions of the picture.

So convincing did I find the children's arguments in support of many of their wrong answers, that I often had to seek verification and counterarguments from other adults. One might claim that some of their explanations were too labored, too imaginative, or relied on a very limited personal experience. But in only a few of the cases would greater reading skill, no matter how we defined it, have helped this group of children avoid their mistakes.

For all these reasons it should not be surprising that the second-graders scored best on the last and most obtuse reading comprehension paragraph. The topic was sound vibrations and a technical description of how they are made. I "dishonestly" told the children not to bother to read it for "understanding." Instead, I suggested they start with the incomplete sentence tasks and go back then to find phrases that coincided with the possible answers. Almost every child, using this backward strategy, managed to get two out of four right, and many answered all four correctly. In the easier paragraphs, in other words, they were penalized precisely for having sought to comprehend what was written. As a result, for example, some children thought Bill was "handsome," rather than "kind," to teach his brother to ride a bike. (Ugly was equated with meanness, and handsome with generosity.) Several insisted Mike must have had "wise parents" rather than "courage" to learn to ride a bike. And virtually all the children capable of reading the story about the architect thought his most important tools were his "paper and pencil" rather than his "ideas."

For most seven-year-olds, who have just begun the reading process, reading is still a laborious word-for-word activity in which so much energy goes into decoding and recalling that precious little is left over for genuine comprehension of any sort. This situation is intensified when the subject and vocabulary are unfamiliar and require dealing with new ideas. For most children there are simply too many intellectual tasks to perform at one time, and the test is thus merely a huge miserable confidence-shattering experience. Yet they often did no worse, if we were able to hold them together long enough to answer every question, than those described here who have mastered the first stages of real reading and who were therefore in a position to bring their "living" intelligence into the test situation.

CONCLUSION

Schools can make a difference. But neither educational equality nor educational quality can be demonstrated or measured through standardized group tests for young children. The mistaken set of assumptions that underlie these tests are not merely absurd. They lead to disappointment, misplaced bitterness, understandable paranoia, frantic parents, educators, and public rushing from one educational panacea to another, and finally, despair about the utility of school reform altogether.

Learning is a complex process and much remains to be understood about it. But an evaluation system must, at the very least, take into account what has been painstakingly learned from years of careful research and observation about a child's mode of thinking, growing, and learning. To use a tool to measure a child's growth that ignores the personal, individual, and often idiosyncratic nature of a young child's language cannot help us evaluate either his language or his reading skill. Finally, and perhaps most important of all, it is essential that we demand that testing devices become the tool—and not the shaper—of our educational objectives.

Suggested Readings

Carini, Patricia, "**Productive Thinking and Achievement**," Material presented at Follow-Through workshop, Lebanon, New Hampshire, January 1968.

Carini, P., Blake, J., Carini, L., *A Methodology for Evaluating Innovative Programs*, from the Prospect School, Title 3, Project 825. Bennington, Vermont: Supervisory Union, June 1969.

Chittenden, E., and Bussis, A., *Research and Assessment Strategies*, NAEYC, Minneapolis, Minnesota, November, 6, 1971.

Chittenden, Edward A., "**What is Learned and What is Taught**," *Young Children*, Vol. 25, No. 1, October 1969.

Cole, Michael, and Bruner, Jerome, "**Cultural Differences and Inferences about Psychological Processes**," *American Teacher*, October 1971.

Feldman, Shirley, and Weiner, Max, "**The Use of a Standardized Reading Achievement Test with Two Levels of Socioeconomic Status Pupils**," *Journal of Experimental Education*, Vol. 32, No. 3, Spring 1964.

Natchez, Gladys, and Roswell, Florence, *Reading Disability*, Basic Books, 1971.

Voyat, Gilbert, "**Minimizing the Problems of Functional Illiteracy**," *The Teacher's College Record*, December 1970.

Wasserman, Miriam, "**Testing Reading in New York City: A Critique**," *The Urban Review*, January 1969.

To Avoid the Dangers of Testing...

What is *your* purpose in giving a specific test? Does the test give you the kind of information you need to change what you will be doing with the child? What sophistication of analysis accompanies the results?

If you can't answer these questions, who can? Who is responsible for choosing the test and releasing the data? Are they released only when accompanied by proper background information and interpretation?

If your purpose in giving tests is to help you help the child, then you should be able, after getting the results of the test, to pinpoint the child's problems and strengths. Does he need a larger vocabulary to understand the work at this level, or is it that his comprehension is good but his word attack skills are in need of sharpening? Is he having trouble with reversals, or is the size of the print too small?

Knowing the problem, you should be able to develop a plan to remedy it and tell the parents what they can do to help. Of what use is it to tell his mother that "Brian is reading four months behind grade level?"

On the other hand, if these tests are really incapable of contributing to specific decisions, then they are only good for public relations. Richard Stiggins of the American College Testing Program suggests that we send only sample children in to be given sample tests, saving thousands of dollars and thousands of hours a year.

Richard J. Stiggins

It is common practice among some public school districts to have a committee of teachers and administrators annually review the district testing procedures. The committee usually discusses what standardized achievement test battery and/or aptitude or intelligence tests should be used at what grade levels. And the result is generally a rubber stamp on previously used procedures.

Recently, however, a number of innovations in testing procedures have emerged which may make rubber stamping inappropriate. They include the

This article was originally published as **"An Alternative to Blanket Standardized Testing,"** in *Today's Education*, March–April, 1975. Reprinted by permission. Richard Stiggins is Assistant Director of Test Development, American College Testing Program.

use of sampling procedures and such innovations as criterion- and domain-referenced testing.

For a number of reasons, however, these innovations are not frequently part of the test review committee's deliberations. One reason may be the committee members' limited knowledge about testing, which is a highly technical subject and does not lend itself easily to simple explanation, understanding, and application.

The institutionalization of testing procedures has also contributed to the lack of knowledge and applications of innovation in educational testing. Or as Samuel Superintendent might put it, "The board of education will never let us give up standardized testing."

A third and final reason for the lack of impact of educational measurement innovation on public education is the minor role that tests play in educational decision making. Because of their general nature, standardized tests are limited in their ability to contribute to district, school, or classroom level decisions. Many educators may recognize this fact and yet continue to give the tests because their use satisfies the board and the public.

In brief, a lack of technical knowledge of testing has given rise to the three factors stated above, each of which in turn prevents the gaining of new knowledge of testing. The result is a closed system of development in educational testing which resists the implementation of practices and procedures common to other fields.

One such practice is sampling, a procedure for increasing the efficiency of data collection that is gaining prominence in educational testing as a result of recent large-scale testing programs, such as the National Assessment of Educational Progress.

Random sampling is a statistical procedure which allows such social scientists as Gallup, Harris, and other pollsters to draw general conclusions about the attitudes of an entire population on the basis of a very few scientifically selected respondents. Survey participants are randomly selected to be representative of larger groups, thus allowing for efficient, less expensive, and quite accurate conclusions.

And so it can be with achievement test scores. In situations where testers want to draw general conclusions about large groups of students, such as an entire grade level for a district, a properly selected sample can yield very accurate estimates of "typical student" performance.

Another innovation in educational testing situations, matrix sampling, takes advantage of just such a random sampling procedure to increase efficiency by reducing the number of students involved in testing. But there is another sampling dimension. Not only is it unnecessary for each student to be tested to generate accurate group estimates of academic performance, but it is unnecessary for every student to respond to every test item.

Matrix sampling involves the simultaneous random sampling of both students and test items. It involves, however, different, nonoverlapping samples of students taking nonoverlapping samples of items so that each matrix sample is a sample of students taking a sample of items.

This requires a set of items to be partitioned randomly into several subsets and each subset given to a different sample of students. For example, if there are 50 items, they could be partitioned into 10 samples of 5 items each and each sample randomly assigned to 1 of 10 samples of students.

The procedure reduces the number of students and the amount of class time required to generate the desired data. When responses to items are summarized, the results may be generalized to both the entire test from which the items were derived and the entire population of students from which the sample was selected. It is important to note, however, that no information is gathered on individual pupil performance. A matrix sample provides only group estimates.

Let me illustrate why matrix sampling might be useful and appropriate for an annual district-wide standardized testing program.

I will argue that the only truly legitimate concerns of standardized testing in any district are general conclusions about the entire student body. Testing is one process of gathering information for decision making. In education, decisions have to be made at a number of levels.

First, we must make diagnostic and prescriptive decisions regarding individual students. Second, we must make decisions regarding the viability of specific educational programs. (This is the newly emerging concern for program evaluation.) In addition, building administrators must make general school-level decisions. Finally, superintendents, boards of education, and the public must make district-level decisions.

In most districts, the information on educational outcomes required for many of these multilevel decisions is typically generated from the annual administration of a standardized achievement battery. The computer scoring service is then able to return individual pupil scores, class averages, building averages, and district summaries, all for about 75¢ to $1 per student. This seems most economical until one considers what actually happens to these test scores and summaries.

First of all, at the classroom level, these scores are designed to discriminate among students "to help with diagnosis." However, I challenge anyone to diagnose and prescribe from a grade equivalent of 3.2 in a general gross construct called "total reading." Most teachers recognize that such transformed scores contain too little information to be diagnostic or prescriptive.

The test publishers argue that teachers can do individual item analysis to reveal specific weaknesses, but any teacher who has attempted to do this realizes how tedious this task can be.

At the specific program level of decision making, standardized achievement batteries also fall somewhat short of necessary data requirements. The qualities of items selected to allow the test to discriminate among students make it very difficult for them to detect specific educational program impacts.

The items are simply too short, too general, and too individualized to be sensitive to local instructional interventions.

For example, correct responses to four additional test items represent a year's growth in grade equivalent terms between grades five and six on the *Iowa Test of Basic Skills*, Form 5, Level 12, Arithmetic Concepts. Not only is it totally unfair to characterize an individual learner's year of growth so narrowly, but as a program developer, I would be quick to challenge an evaluator who selected such an imprecise tool to demonstrate the viability of my newly developed instructional sequence. From a program evaluation point of view, instruments more sensitive to local program objectives are much more desirable for program decision making than are any national standardized examinations.

Many of the problems which arise from using standardized tests as criteria for judging specific program quality also arise when one attempts to differentiate among general program elements, such as classes, teachers, departments, or buildings. Because of the lack of sensitivity of these tools, there is little or no educational research delineating any causal line between program elements and standardized outcome measures.

To say that one school's learning environment is better than another's or one principal is more competent than another on the basis of standardized test data is a total misuse of the data. Yet the summaries returned to districts by scoring services and comments of educators would suggest that this is the intent.

To date, educational research can establish no significant stable links between any teacher, administrator, or building characteristics and differential standardized achievement test scores. Therefore, it is quite apparent that standardized test scores are incapable of contributing to specific and general program-related decisions.

What, then, are these tests capable of doing? Very simply, they are useful as gross indicators which can best serve as information for communication to the public on the state of achievement in a given district. In fact, it may be that this is the only real use they are put to in most districts anyway.

If these tests are really incapable of contributing to important specific decisions, then their use for public relations is their only appropriate use. In that case, a testing system which yields only the district average data would be sufficient. Such a system can be created by using sampling procedures. An investment of hundreds of dollars for sample data can provide information of the same value as that previously gathered for thousands. The dollar savings can be used to gather other types of outcome data which are prescriptive and appropriate for program-related decisions.

How to Pass Without Actually Cheating

Question: If you are not sure of the answer would you pick the longest answer or the shortest answer to a multiple-choice question?

Answer: The longest—because chances are it's been made long to avoid ambiguity.

We gave that one away. Bernard Feder gives away a number of other test-taking techniques which you and your class will find helpful in mastering the important skill of outguessing the test makers.

Bernard Feder

It's surprising that some enterprising person hasn't taken the information and turned it into an underground campus bestseller, maybe calling it something like *The Compleat Guide to Taking Tests*. As it is, some of the guidelines are shared in late-night bull sessions and hurried whispers before the start of an exam. Understanding this "hidden curriculum"—the testing program—means that a student can earn higher grades throughout his or her career. And those grades are, of course, the key to advanced education, better jobs, and power in general.

The hidden curriculum, generally based on the assumption that knowledge and understanding are synonymous, exerts far more influence on the lives of students than do the professed objectives and formal curriculums of the school program. And because of the reluctance of many educators to acknowledge the discrepancies between the open and hidden curriculums, most testing programs in schools are poorly designed and badly implemented. As a result, whole sets of extracurricular skills have been developed by good test takers to cope with the exams—skills that generally have been ignored, if not unrecognized, by teachers.

Imagine two students in the same history class. Both are intelligent, interested, and conscientious. They can participate with equal ability in classroom discussions, and yet one will be likely to find an *A* on his final report while the other will receive a *B*.

Let's follow them into the classroom as they prepare to take a test. Both of them, like virtually all students, are aware of the importance of the hidden

This article is from *Human Behavior*, June 1977. Copyright © 1977 *Human Behavior* Magazine. Reprinted by permission. Bernard Feder is a writer on education and social issues and an educational consultant.

curriculum. However, because most schools pretend that tests measure only what has actually been learned in the classroom, one of the pair has never been taught how to take tests. Each question is a new challenge—a measure of his ability to recall or recognize a fact, a definition, a date, a quantity, a formula, or a relationship.

The testwise student, on the other hand, is systematic. Even before he walked into the room, he had formulated a set of probabilities about the nature of the test, based on previous experience with the school, the subject and the teacher. He doesn't begin to answer questions until he has skimmed the test to check out his internal model. He may not even be aware of the specific steps, but he will do the following:

- *Find the modus operandi.* Are the questions designed to trap?—if so, he will be careful about apparently simple statements, probing for booby traps. Does the test seem to ask for a knowledge or application of basic principles?—in this case, the apparent oversimplification is probably the correct answer.

- *Play the odds.* For example, there are usually more *true* responses on a true-false test than *false* ones.

- *Check scoring procedures.* Are only correct answers counted?—if so, he will guess when he is not certain. Is there a penalty for wrong answers? Can he beat the penalty (usually a fraction of the weight of the question) by eliminating enough wrong answers to bring the odds to 50-50? Are the responses "weighted"?—if a blank draws a zero, he will guess rather than leave blanks.

- *Find the verbal clues.* Is there a repetition of words in stem and response, or the use of synonyms? Can the responses be narrowed to mutually exclusive items—choices where, if one is wrong, another must be right? Are specific determiners, such as "never" or "always" used?—they are seldom found in the correct answers.

- *Recognize rankings and orderings.* Are there questions that involve dates, rankings, or quantities? He knows that there is usually a spread on each side of the correct answer, and that the correct answer is likely to be neither extreme.

- *Look for mechanical clues.* Are there interlocking items?—do some questions contain answers or clues to others? Are some responses in multiple-choice items significantly longer than others?—to avoid ambiguity, the testmaker may have been overprecise in phrasing the correct response.

In short, he has learned not only that the test may be irrelevant to the stated objectives of the course, but that the skills necessary to pass the test may be completely unrelated to the skills that are taught in the classroom. Teachers themselves are uncomfortably aware of the tenuous connection between a mastery of subject matter and the ability to do well on tests—the instruments that purport to measure such mastery.

"What would happen at Harvard or Yale," John Holt asked in his book *How Children Fail*, "if a prof gave a surprise test in March on work covered in October?" Everybody knows what would happen, Holt answers, and that's why they don't do it. That is also why teachers announce tests in advance, "prepare" classes for tests, "review" for tests and drop hints about the nature of forthcoming tests.

By the same token, most students have learned through experience to ignore the rhetoric and professed objectives of schools and teachers and to focus on the real—albeit disguised—curriculum. They have learned that their major task, normally, is to memorize a good deal of information and that recall or recognition are the highest forms of intellectual achievement. Tests, of course, determine what students think is *worth* learning. Picture a classroom of notetakers when a teacher announces, "This won't be on the test."

From the tests, students have learned, quite reasonably, that one can display his or her achievement by retaining for limited periods a great amount of data until the moment that the test is over and the "vaccination theory of education" (a term coined by Neil Postman and Charles Weingartner in their *Teaching as a Subversive Activity*) becomes operative. Because once a student has "had" a course and passed the test, he or she is immune and need rarely demonstrate—in school or outside—that there has been any real learning.

And, despite the proliferation of curriculum offerings in schools to meet the needs of citizens in our increasingly complex society, test taking—a major survival skill—has largely been ignored as a subject. The reason may be that most tests are so poorly designed that a viable test-taking program would focus largely on "beating" the system.

Part of the fuzziness surrounding the purposes of test programs is manifested by the fact that most tests are *norm-referenced*. They are used to compare a student's achievement in math or English or history or biology against a norm or standard based on the average achievement of a group—a class population, a school population, or a national population. An *A*, therefore, means that that student did better on the test than the student who received a *C*. It really doesn't tell much about what the *A* student understands about math or English or history or biology. *Criterion-referenced* tests, on the other hand, may tell us whether a student can perform specific operations in math, can analyze a passage according to specific standards, or can interpret laboratory findings. Among students who can do these feats, a criterion-referenced test will not tell us who is "better." And the need to rank students seems to take precedence in our schools over the need to measure what has actually been learned—even if we are not sure just what the student may be "better" at.

While the Debate Goes On, Teach How to Take the Tests

For lazy students who are good test takers, a day spent finding the next letter in a series or deciding which figure is most different is a joy. There are no notes to remember to study, no red-circled words to be "written, correctly, ten times," no responsibility to recall the names and formulas of minerals.

For others, these are tests of frustration endurance. Some students can't intuit the peculiar kind of thinking required for the IQ-type test, and even if they care enough to try, they lack the patterning needed in this particular kind of analysis.

These students often need to be reassured that in certain tests guessing is good, that it's okay to mouth words when the material is difficult and they are under pressure. "Even college professors were found to read out loud or subvocally when they got to tough stuff, so put your fingers in your ears and say the words subvocally and you'll find you can concentrate better."[1]

Is this kind of training really cheating? We think not, since the tests themselves were designed to reward a kind of precious analytic thinking and game playing which bears little relation to broad, functional intelligence. You will be properly helping your students acquire the tools they need, tools which others acquired early and brought to school from home. As a teacher you can do no less than equalize the opportunity to do well. Whatever your attitude towards the validity of the IQ tests, as long as they are used, someone will judge your students now or in the future on the basis of their ratings. Even if you refuse to administer them, you should, we think, demystify them.

Arthur Whimbey

IQ tests may not measure innate intelligence, but they can make the difference between getting a good job and a poor one. While the debate over what IQ scores actually mean goes on, no one can ignore the fact that school administrators and businessmen believe in tests and continue to give them. A job, a scholarship, or college admittance often hinges on the score.

[1]Arthur Whimbey with Linda Shaw Whimbey, *Intelligence Can Be Taught*, New York: E. P. Dutton, Inc., 1975.

This article was originally published as "**Getting Ready for the Tester: You Can Learn to Raise Your IQ Score**," reprinted from *Psychology Today Magazine*, January 1976. Copyright © 1976 Ziff–Davis Publishing Company.

Many intelligent people score poorly on IQ and similar tests, not because they're stupid, but because they don't know how to use the intelligence they have. The evidence is mounting that scoring well on such tests is a skill that can be taught and learned.

We've learned why people test poorly by asking them to think aloud as they solve typical problems, or to explain their solutions after they've worked them silently. Alfred Binet, the creator of the first IQ test, used this method extensively. Jean Piaget, the Swiss developmental psychologist, worked out his theory of intellectual development by asking children to think aloud. Recently, Benjamin Bloom of the University of Chicago has used the method to study the way college students solve problems.

The approach really amounts to analyzing the task of reasoning by a method similar to that which industrial psychologists use to design vocational-training programs. They watch seasoned employees at work and contrast their expert techniques with the errors of novices.

Effective and ineffective ways to tackle the job soon become apparent, and the psychologists can tailor training programs to actual job requirements. Task analysis of IQ-test items gives us a similarly detailed account of how reasoning should proceed during a test problem.

Figural-reasoning problems make up a good part of most common IQ tests. They minimize the effects of a person's vocabulary and demand little formal education. This figural-reasoning problem is typical:

INSTRUCTIONS. The first four figures below change in a systematic manner according to some rule. Your task is to discover the rule and choose from among the alternatives the figure which should occur next in the series.

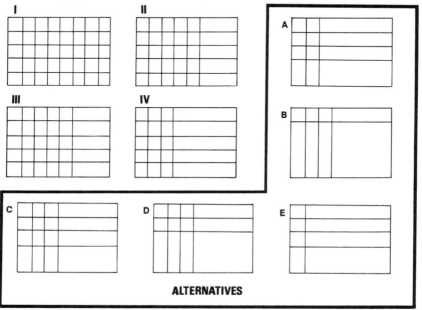

Consider the steps leading to a correct solution. First, one must compare the four figures. Each figure has fewer lines than the one preceding it, so counting the lines appears to be the next step. By comparing the number of lines in each figure, one finds that they change in the following sequence: delete two vertical lines, delete one horizontal line, delete two vertical lines. If this is a consistent rule, the next change should be to delete one horizontal line. Alternative "D" is the correct answer.

Although this is not a difficult problem, college students with IQ scores below the normal 100 miss it regularly. Their errors might seem to result from a limited memory, which would prevent them from following the details of the problem. But research has clearly demonstrated that memory is not a factor in the IQ of healthy adults.

The response of one low-aptitude student showed clearly that her weakness had nothing to do with an inability to remember or to form abstractions. She simply did not use the abstractions she had formed.

SOME MISSING LINES

This student, a college sophomore with an IQ of 95, said she couldn't solve the problem. I asked her to compare the first two figures and describe any differences she noticed between them. She said that some of the lines going up and down were missing. I asked her to compare the next two figures, and she said that some of the lines going the other way were missing. In comparing the third and fourth figures, she again noticed that up-and-down lines were missing.

When I asked her how many lines were deleted in moving from the first figure to the second, she paused for some time, and then answered, "Three." I asked her to count the lines again, and after what seemed like an inordinate delay, she said, "Two." Then I asked her how many lines were deleted in moving from the second figure to the third, and, again after much delay, she answered, "Two." I asked her to point to the lines with her pencil and count them out loud, and watched her count both the vertical and horizontal lines to arrive at a total of nine lines.

Although this stage of the problem required her to count only the horizontal lines, in each of her comparisons she counted all of the lines in both directions, as she had with the first figure. No wonder she became confused.

This student's earlier replies showed that she fully recognized that the problem involved the deletion of both horizontal and vertical lines. She had formed the proper abstraction that would solve the problem, but she failed to use it.

The response of another student to this same item illustrates why others do poorly on these tests. He worked the problem silently and then chose alternative "E." When I asked him to explain how he selected his answer, he replied, "First there are some lines taken away. Then there are more lines taken away going the other way. Then there are more lines taken away going up and down. So I guess the answer should be take away more lines. I guess answer 'E'."

I asked him whether he had counted the lines to see exactly how many were deleted in each figure and he answered that he had not. I told him to point to the lines with his pencil and count them out loud. He did, and concluded that first two lines were deleted from one direction, then one line from the other, and finally two again from the first direction. I asked him what the next step should be, and he answered that one line should be deleted. But when I asked him to pick an answer, he neglected to count lines, quickly skimmed the alternatives, and picked "B."

ONE-SHOT THINKING

Many other researchers have seen low-IQ people make similar mistakes. It appears that when they face questions that require formal reasoning, they lack the patience to isolate the correct answer. Carl Bereiter and Benjamin Bloom have called this approach "one-shot thinking." Their studies show that low-aptitude students don't seem to carry on an internal monologue, nor do they proceed through a step-by-step sequence of deductions. If they can't see the answer immediately, they feel lost. In fact, a study by Bereiter and Siegfried Engelmann reported that low-aptitude four-year-olds believe that questions should be answered immediately rather than after a certain amount of thinking.

Consider another IQ-test item:

If you have three boxes, and inside each box there are two smaller boxes, and inside each of these boxes there are four even smaller boxes, how many boxes, how many boxes are there altogether?
(A) 24   (B) 12   (C) 13   (D) 21   (E) 33   (F) 36

The solution to this problem, "E," is also straightforward, involving no high-level abstractions or feats of memory. Yet most college students with IQs below 100 miss it. Their errors show that they fail to spell out ideas fully and accurately.

One low-aptitude student chose "C," explaining, "I pictured the three boxes and the two smaller boxes inside the three boxes. . .I added three plus two, which is five, and counted the four other boxes twice. Five plus eight gave me 13." Another student chose "D, 21 boxes," saying she mentally pictured the following diagram:

| +2 | | +2 | | +2 | = 21
| +4 | | +4 | | +4 |

Many adult-level IQ tests contain basic mathematical-reasoning problems of the following sort:

During a special sale, eight spark plugs cost $2.40 uninstalled and $4.00 installed. How much is charged for labor in installing each plug?
(A) $1.60   (B) $.50   (C) $.30   (D) $.20   (E) $.40   (F) $1.20

This question requires no advanced knowledge of algebra or geometry. Almost all American adults can perform the simple computations needed to come up with the correct answer, "D." But persons with IQs below 100 often fail to analyze the problem correctly. They do not set up the computations that must be performed.

IQ AND SCHOOL GRADES

The spark-plug problem shows why IQ tests have been so successful in predicting whether a person will succeed in school, even though they have never been able to predict whether a person will be a good doctor, engineer, artist, plumber, or parent. It tests the kind of reasoning required in scholastic areas such as mathematics, physics, chemistry, accounting, or statistics. Just as the previous item involved building an entire picture by placing boxes within boxes, this one requires building an entire picture by subdividing costs. The total cost must be separated into labor and materials. Then the labor cost must be broken down into the cost of each individual plug. Once this has been done, the arithmetic becomes relatively easy. As we might expect, low-IQ students often answer "B," because they neglect to separate materials from labor; "C," because they confuse the cost of materials and labor; or "A," because they forgot to reckon the labor cost of each plug. These errors once again show their failure to seek out and use all the information of the problem.

The same students also frequently miss the next example, although it relies even more on simply following directions:

> Cross out the letter after the letter in the word *seldom* which is in the same position in the word as it is in the alphabet.

One frequent error on this item is to cross out the letter *d* in *seldom*. This reflects a failure to utilize all the information given. Another is to cross out the *d* in *word* as shown below:

> Cross out the letter after the letter in the word *seldom* which is in the same position in the word as it is in the alphabet.

The student who makes this error does not follow the exact meaning of the sentence. He fails to analyze the materials as follows: *"Cross out the letter after the letter* (so I have to cross out a letter) *in the word* (cross out a letter in some word) *seldom* (so seldom must be the word). The letter *d* is in the same position in the word *seldom* as it is in the alphabet (so I cross out *o*, the letter after *d*)."

AUTOMATIC ANALYSIS

As simple as this problem may seem to a high-aptitude student, it does require step-by-step analysis. The high-aptitude reader carries out the analysis so automatically that he is hardly aware of his own mental activities. Only when he meets with an especially intricate or confusing series of ideas does his sequential sorting become intentional and conscious. However, to the low-aptitude reader, the pattern of gradual, sequential reconstruction of the text's meaning is a foreign mode of thought.

Another popular item in IQ tests involves relationships:

Elephant is to small
as_____is to_____.
(A) large: little
(B) turtle: slow
(C) hippopotamus: mouse
(D) lion: timid

Low-aptitude students frequently select "A." They fail to ask themselves, "What is the relationship between elephant and small?" and then search for another pair of words having the same relationship. If they had analyzed the problem carefully, they would see that the problem presents an animal and an adjective not characteristic of it, and that the correct answer is "D."

BAD HABITS

Benjamin Bloom and Lois Broder have documented these departures from correct reasoning, showing that each student tends to be consistent in the way he approaches and solves problems. This consistency is so strong that they regard it as the student's habitual mode of thinking. Further, they found that the problem-solving habits of low-aptitude college students differ in two important ways from those of high-aptitude students.

First, the low-IQ student tends to engage in one-shot thinking, rather than in extended, sequential construction of understanding. Second, he seems willing to allow gaps of knowledge to exist, as if he didn't care about accurate understanding.

Bloom and Broder also found that low-aptitude students seem mentally careless and superficial. They often rush through the instructions or even skip them. They select wrong answers because they fail to comprehend what is required. When asked to reread the instructions more carefully, they frequently understand them and proceed correctly.

In actual problem solving, low-IQ students are almost completely passive in their thinking. They spend little time considering a question, but choose an answer on the basis of a few clues, a feeling, an impression, or a guess. High-IQ students, in contrast, actively attack a problem. If at first they are confused, they go at it again with a lengthy sequential analysis to get the right answer.

Significantly, low-IQ students tend to place little value on reasoning as a method of solving problems. While they may take a more active approach to other kinds of problems, they do not see academic problems as susceptible to analysis. They fail to break each problem into subproblems; either they know the answer or they do not know it, and if they do not, they guess.

Bloom and Broder developed a pilot training program to remedy these deficiencies. They had low-aptitude college students attempt to solve problems aloud. After talking over student solutions, right or wrong, they would read the ideal solution aloud, and the student would explain how his solution differed from the ideal.

Students found the task tough at first. The instructors had to help them understand how their problem-solving approach differed from the ideal example. But once a student recognized the differences, he began to apply the principles of the ideal technique and increased his accuracy.

While Bloom and Broder did not use IQ tests to measure their program's effectiveness, the students they worked with began to get higher grades. Many of them had been flunking out of school, but the training raised their grades enough to let them remain.

In a more recent study, the U.S. Military Academy at West Point examined the success of several preparatory schools at raising SAT scores and later academic performance. (The SAT is an aptitude test that many colleges use to decide whom they will admit. People who get high scores on the SAT also score high on IQ tests.) These prep schools draw students whose scores are too low to get them into the colleges of their choice. The military runs some, others are private.

After six months of intensive, full-time study, the 714 students surveyed showed an average increase of 136 points on the test (a total of 1,600 is possible). Once they got into college, students from four of the six schools lived up to their promise of higher academic performance.

PILOT PROJECT

I worked with one student in a pilot project aimed at increasing his scores on the Law School Admissions Test (LSAT) and the Graduate Record Exam (GRE), a test used to select students for admission to graduate school. Most graduate schools limit admissions to students who score over 900. This student initially scored 385 on the LSAT, ranking him in the bottom 10 percent. He also scored 750, quite low, on the combined GRE.

I designed a training program that focused on reading comprehension, verbal analogy, and figural-reasoning problems. My main tactic was to have him think out loud while he carefully examined abstract relationships. Then we talked over his errors. It's vital, I believe, that a person get immediate feedback on each step of his thinking process so he can learn to reason in the way demanded by most tests.

For example, in reading-comprehension training, I had the student read passages aloud. After each sentence or two, he stopped and interpreted them, thinking aloud as he worked through the ideas. Whenever he had difficulty with an idea or a relationship, I probed with questions. We'd discuss the topic at length, and he'd try to reason out the interpretation. I encouraged him to understand each sentence by placing it in the context of the entire article, and to combine and contrast ideas to attain fuller comprehension.

We began the program, two hours a day, four days a week, in March. At the end of April, he took the LSAT and his score went up 50 points. We continued training, and by June his GRE score had climbed to 820. The training ended. That fall his grades in an algebra course, his biggest problem area, went to B + 's and then A's. In December, he took the GRE again and scored 890, a gain of 140 points over his original score.

Our training program was neither a cram course nor a short cut to raising test scores. I believe there are no short cuts or miracle cures. The methods I used with him closely resemble the methods middle-class parents use with their children: it has long been noted that middle-class children do better both in school and on IQ tests than children from lower socioeconomic groups. The student I tutored was learning how to learn.

Psychologists are only now themselves learning how to teach learning. We know that one of the secrets is to make thought processes that are usually hidden visible, so we can teach each small step involved in problem solving.

RAISING YOUR SCORE

If you want to improve your own chances on an IQ, SAT, GRE or similar test, the time to start is now. The most important thing is to begin your preparation far in advance. IQ tests measure your skill in analyzing and mentally reconstructing relationships. Developing such information-processing skills calls for steady practice, just as you would expect to practice regularly to develop a perfect tennis serve. Therefore, the person who crams madly for a week by working typical reasoning problems is sure to fail.

Because finding out immediately whether your responses are right is essential to improving any skill, you'll do much better if you work with a small group or with a tutor. If you can't find a group or a patient instructor, there are some things you can do on your own. Get old tests and puzzle books from the library and practice. Read the questions carefully and don't jump to any conclusions. Think out loud as you work a problem, then check your answer. If you are wrong, stop and figure out how one might reach the correct answer. Ask yourself questions, lots of questions, and even when you think you have the answer, ask some more.

Read books, magazines and newspapers. When a writer makes an assertion, ask yourself how he came to that conclusion. Try to reconstruct his reasoning.

Finally, analyze your own thinking. Just as a tennis player can learn from watching videotapes of his serve, you can learn from recognizing the errors you make in reasoning. Careful application of these methods will never move your IQ score into the genius category, but it might raise it enough to open a door that the IQ test would otherwise have slammed in your face.

V
COLLABORATION AND EVALUATION

Success and the Gentleman "C"
Out of Step at the Point
Duets Excel Solos
Instead of Tests—Trust
Are 87 Percent of the Russians Feebleminded?
A Wide-angle View of Intelligence

Success and the Gentleman "C"

Obsessive concern with scores won't help kids in later life. In fact, the highest scorers on the SAT's are, on the whole, less effective as adults than their lower-scoring classmates. This is the finding of Douglas H. Heath who noted that most honor students were "tense and distant in their relationships" and lacked insight into themselves.

This is a most important finding at a time when loud critics, who insist they can reverse the general scholastic decline, are suggesting a return to school practices which, less than ten years ago, were reformed. Our rules were revised and the pressure reduced because we found that "traditional" school practices were conducive to cheating, dope taking, conformity, "turning-off and turning-on."

We believe that this generation of students is more tolerant and cooperative than those who came of age in the sixties because they have been treated as people, given choices, allowed to find themselves, think, play, create, and breathe deeply.

Do we really want to revive practices that provoked student rebellion?

Edward B. Fiske

A fifteen-year study of graduates of a small men's liberal arts college has suggested that good grades and other usual measures of academic success do not correlate with personal maturity and competence in later life.

To the contrary, Douglas H. Heath, a professor of psychology at Haverford College, near Philadelphia, reports that honor students he studied were on the whole less "effective" as adults than their less academically accomplished classmates. They tended, he said, to have an "inaccurate understanding" of themselves, to be "tense and distant" in their relationships with colleagues at work and to have "fewer close, warm relationships with their wives."

On the other hand, he stated, maturity and competence in later life seem to be positively correlated with "nonacademic" factors such as character development, moral values and "the empathetic skills necessary for understanding and relating to others."

As one implication of his findings, Professor Heath suggested: "Admissions officers and faculties, particularly of highly selective colleges, might well reconsider the types of persons that they wish to select to educate."

He urged colleges to resist the current trends toward specialization and relatively narrow vocational training and to return to "our historic understanding of the liberally educating process."

"If we continue to educate too narrowly, too technically, too reductively;" he said, "if we continue to ignore a student's character, the skills and values of adaptability, and the contextuality of our survival problems, then our colleges do not deserve to survive as liberally educating institutions."

The psychologist warned against using his data to conclude that persons of low scholastic aptitude were likely to become mature and competent adults. "They may be, but the conclusion does not follow from our findings," he said.

FOLLOWED FRESHMEN SINCE '50'S

Likewise, he said, the findings do not mean that honor students cannot become effective adults. The point, he said, is this: Adult maturity and competence require a much fuller range of talents, values, interpersonal skills than what our rather narrow measures of academic excellence tap.

Professor Heath's findings, which he emphasized were "suggestive" and not confirmed by more general research, are based on a study of 68 Haverford College men whose progress he has followed since they were freshmen in the late 1950's and early 1960's. Though well above average academically by national standards, they constituted a cross section of students at the selective Quaker men's college in suburban Philadelphia. Ninety percent went on to some form of graduate or professional study.

Results of the research, which was supported by the National Institute of Mental Health, the W. Clement and Jessie Stone Foundation and the Spencer Foundation, have been reported periodically at scholarly meetings and in various scholarly journals, including the current issue of "Liberal Education." Updated findings are scheduled to be published next fall in the "Journal of Higher Education."

The psychologist gave each subject an academic rating based on high school, college and graduate school grades, College Board aptitude and achievement scores, academic honors and evaluations by their professors. He also assembled more than 400 measures of the men's "maturity and competence" both as students and in later life. This was based on standard psychological tests such as the Minnesota Multiphasic Personality Inventory, questionnaires and interviews with fellow students, close friends, co-workers, wives, lovers, and the subjects themselves.

ACADEMICS WERE MORE 'ABSTRACT'

When he compared the academic and psychological profiles, Professor Heath found that, by the time they reached their early thirties, the academically superior students had published more articles and had received "more post-college honors" than their less academically superior classmates.

On the other hand, he also found that as adults they were "more abstract and conceptual than men who had not received honors" and that "their thought was less practical and realistic."

The honor students, he said, were less concerned about money. Their wives took the initiative sexually more often. They were less involved with their children. They were also more depressed, less aggressively energetic, and rated themselves as less psychologically healthy than they were in college, a rating not confirmed by others, however.

On the specific quality of verbal ability, Professor Heath said that the man with "higher verbal aptitude" tended to have an "inaccurate understanding of himself." As adolescents, such men "tended to be self-centered, wrapped up in themselves," and as adults they "had not learned the empathic skills necessary for accurately understanding and relating to others."

In short, he wrote, "Increasing scholastic aptitude in adolescence may be related to increasing interpersonal immaturity in adulthood."

By contrast, the psychologist found that students of more modest academic achievement were, on the average, more mature and competent, and that this pattern was evident from the beginning of their college careers. "The more mature a student was entering and graduating from college, the more well adapted he was as an adult to his vocation," he said. "He had a happier relationship with his spouse, with whom he was more sexually compatible, and he had more mature interpersonal relationships."

Professor Heath acknowledged that his sample of 68 Haverford men was "not typical of college men generally." It more nearly resembled college men in the upper 10 to 20 percent of academic talent, he said. Even this limitation, however, he said, cannot be used to "explain away the almost total failure of every academic measure to predict a variety of adult competencies."

Professor Heath concluded that, both in their admissions policies and in academic planning, colleges such as Haverford should give more attention than they now do to character development, values, interpersonal relations and other qualities that contribute to later maturity.

Out of Step at the Point

Periodically, cheating scandals make the front page. In 1976, it was West Point's turn. The situation was not unique to the Academy, but due to the relaxation of standards elsewhere, it hadn't been in the news much lately.

The last time I recall a major scandal attributed to the competitive spirit gone wild, was at a prestigious, Ivy League college. Law students systematically cut out and destroyed important pages of library law texts, so competing classmates couldn't study the required material. They were doing "defensive" studying.

West Point graduate Frederick C. Thayer shares his provocative ideas about this problem.

Frederick C. Thayer

...The heart of the West Point system is competitive struggle for survival and class ranking.... The system, in other words, is based upon educational assumptions that are increasingly discredited.

One is that individual students cannot, do not, and should not, learn anything from each other. A second is that instructors never learn anything from students, because the instructors "know" what is "right." The likelihood is that a number of cadets involved in the scandal learned more about the engineering problem from talking with their colleagues than they otherwise would have learned. It is a peculiar system that defines learning as cheating. Even worse, the system is totally at odds with the lives cadets lead after graduation.

Whether in the Army or in civilian life, West Point graduates will spend their working lives in organizational situations. Even in times of crisis, battlefield, or office, decisions will be made only after as much interaction and discussion as time will allow.

It is absurd to teach students that the way to "pass the test" is to shut one's self completely off from colleagues, make an isolated and solitary decision, then present it for "grading." The task at hand is always to discover the best solution to the problem, and the environment of the loner is not the one to be inculcated in students. The honor system is educationally and operationally insane, a relic of the assembly-line approach to education that has outlived whatever usefulness it might once have had. A system (at West Point or anywhere else) that punishes students for learning from each other is hardly worth retaining.

Duets Excel Solos

An experiment in collaborative learning with an eye to increasing the student's involvement while precluding a race for grades led to an extraordinary finding—two "C" students together do better work than "A" students alone.

From *The New York Times*, June 16, 1976. © 1976 by The New York Times Company. Reprinted by permission. Frederick C. Thayer is associate professor of public administration at the University of Pittsburgh.

James J. Berry and Wilbert M. Leonard, II

In two sociology classes at the Illinois State University at Normal, we structured the courses in a traditional fashion except that we tried a different approach to testing in one of the classes. At the beginning of the semester, we assigned students in that group partners with whom to take examinations, all of which were open-book tests. The other class took open-book examinations, too, but students worked independently. In both classes, exams were the same, the book was the same, and the lectures were based on the same materials.

Partners had similar accumulated grade point averages (within one-half a GPA unit). Partnerships could be broken if either party felt the other was not cooperating or not doing adequate preparation for the class. Only three of the thirty pairs eventually broke up.

The result of this matching process was a situation in which each student was able to confer with a partner throughout the examination. They could exchange ideas and make decisions about answers. Then, the students recorded their joint answers on the test paper.

Interaction between pair members was not continuous, and students usually carried on their discussions in an undertone. Occasionally, a student raised a voice in disagreement, but no one complained of the noise level.

What were the results? The paired students performed significantly better than those who took examinations alone. On all three exams, the paired group averaged 6 percent higher scores than the unpaired group. Also, 85 percent of the paired students indicated that pairing reduced their test anxiety, and 69 percent felt that the paired setting was a better learning one than the singles setting.

We would not have been surprised to find that two A students would do better on an exam working together than working alone and that two C students working together would show some improvement. What was not expected, however, was that two C students working together would do as well as or better than two A students working independently. The two students with the lowest grade point averages in the paired group obtained the second highest grade on the first exam and the fifth highest grade on the final. Interestingly, they earned the lowest grades on the second exam, which was taken in singles style.

On the basis of this one small experiment, we believe that—with a relatively small investment of money and/or time—improvements for many students can be made in the classroom. Students respond well to social settings where cooperation in problem solving is possible. They also react well to challenging situations that are not too threatening.

This article was originally published as **"A Different Approach To Classroom Testing,"** in *Today's Education*, vol. 63, no. 4 (Nov.–Dec. 1974). Reprinted by permission. James Berry is assistant professor of sociology at Western State College in Colorado, and Wilbert Leonard is assistant professor of sociology at Illinois State University.

There is no reason to suspect that this approach would not work in any of the traditional teaching-learning situations. High school or junior high school classes might benefit even more than college groups from this method.

Instead of Tests—Trust

J. Parker Damon estimates that it takes fifty-nine hours of staff time and costs a school with twenty classrooms and 525 students, (kindergarten through sixth grade), $1,155.00 to test each year.* Are the tests worth this time and money?

Also, since the tests may contain inaccuracies, foster harmful attitudes, and encourage inappropriate interpretations, he wonders if parents shouldn't be given the necessary consumer information about the dangers of testing, offered alternatives, and asked if they have a preference in the matter.

Parents are consulted at the Cambridge Alternative Public School. Although the larger Cambridge School Committee mandates that all children be given tests, most children at the Cambridge Alternative School do not take them. Parents there have elected to learn about each child's progress through a complex record-keeping and reporting system that they find more satisfactory.

Would these parents be as satisfied if the CAPS students hadn't scored more than three grades above the norm a few years back when achievement tests were given? Are parents who choose to send their children to an alternative school also those most likely to reject tests as the best way of assessing their child's progress? Or is the answer, as Principal Leonard Solo suggests, an example of mutual trust?

---

*J. Parker Damon, "**Questions You Should Ask About Your Testing Program,**" *National Elementary Principal*, vol. 56, no. 1 (September/October 1976).

Leonard Solo

This article is about how we document children's learning at the Cambridge Alternative Public School and how we report their progress to parents. Our evaluation processes are necessary because we are convinced that standardized tests do not tell us anything of importance about a child's learning and are even, in the main, destructive.

I do not propose to elaborate here on the pointlessness of standardized tests, an issue that has been debated at length in many books and articles.[1] Instead, I will describe the evaluation processes that we use in the hope that other school principals will realize that there are, indeed, better ways to evaluate student progress than by depending on standardized testing.

First, however, I should outline briefly the basic features of our school and explain how we came to be an alternative within the public school system. The Cambridge Alternative Public School (CAPS) was founded in 1972 when a group of parents presented the School Committee with an elaborate, detailed proposal for the establishment of an alternative school, a proposal that had evolved over two years of meetings, visits to other schools, and discussions with teachers, parents, administrators, and educational consultants. After much hassle, including a sit-in at the School Committee's offices, the committee agreed to establish such a school.

CAPS is run cooperatively by the staff and parents. There is an extensive system of committees made up of equal numbers of staff members and parents, all under the control of a parent-staff Policy Board, which is, in turn, under the auspices of the Cambridge School Department and the School Committee.

Now in its fifth year, CAPS has 200 students in ten multigraded classrooms, K-8, all of which are self-contained, open classrooms. We are not a neighborhood school, but a school of choice for parents and their children, 90 percent of whom are voluntarily bused. Students are admitted by lottery from all districts in Cambridge. Our admissions policy includes quotas that emphasize racial balance (about 30 percent black, 60 percent white, 8 percent Hispanic, and 2 percent other minorities); social and economic balance in terms of the parents' occupations; and an equal balance of boys and girls in the student body. There is no predetermined, standardized curriculum at CAPS, although we place a strong emphasis on basic skills and knowledge.

The original proposal for the school contained statements about evaluation and noted that parents were opposed to standardized tests as a way of assessing a child's progress in reading, math, self-confidence, problem-solving ability, independence, social consciousness, or any other aspect of the child's total being. The parents rejected standardized tests—or just about rejected them.

The Cambridge School Committee, on the other hand, mandates that all children in the public schools be given IQ, achievement, and reading tests.* When we receive announcements from the School Department that such tests are to be administered, we send a memo to parents explaining the tests and asking them to sign and return the memo if they do not want their child tested.

---

*At the time this issue went to press, hearings were being held before the Massachusetts State Legislature on the Advisability of banning the use of group IQ tests in the state's public schools.

This article was originally published as "**What We Do Because Testing Doesn't Work**," in *The National Elementary Principal*, vol. 56, no. 5 (May–June 1977). Copyright 1977, National Association of Elementary School Principals. All rights reserved. Reprinted by permission.

We have held parent meetings and called in outside experts to explain how the tests are constructed, what they are about, and especially their racial and social class bias.

Nevertheless, two years ago about 30 percent of the parents of students in grades three through six wanted their children's achievement levels tested. The results, as quoted from a local newspaper, were nothing to be ashamed of:

> The CAPS students' results showed them to be far superior to their counterparts on similar grade levels throughout the system. For example, in the third-grade testing, CAPS students produced total reading scores of 7.8 and total math scores of 6.7, more than three grades above the norm. Results were comparable in grades [four], five, and six.[2]

I do not quote these scores to show off, but to indicate that we do not reject standardized testing out of weakness.

Since this article is really about the alternative methods we have developed to assess each child's progress and to report that progress to parents, I would like to focus on how one of our K-1 teachers, Lynne Stinson Crosby, handles evaluation.

Assessment and reporting are dependent on a good record-keeping system. Lynne Crosby has a loose-leaf notebook in which she keeps detailed daily records under eleven different categories: (1) a list of the name, address, telephone number, and birthdate of each child in the class; (2) a school calendar with special days marked off; (3) a floor plan of her K-1 open classroom; (4) a daily schedule; (5) monthly curriculum plans in summary form; (6) weekly curriculum plans, in more detail; (7) detailed plans for each day; (8) anecdotal notes on what happened each day, with a space for weekly summaries in the areas of math, art, cooking, science, social studies, reading, and other activities; (9) anecdotal records on each child; (10) notes from staff meetings and team meetings (both held weekly); and (11) copies of each memo sent to the staff and each memo sent home to parents (usually one a day).

Here are some excerpts from her anecdotal records on one child, Chris Jones, at the beginning of the school year:

4 September. Chris entered shyly with entire family: father, mother, baby, and brother Len, who played big brother, showing Chris things in the room. Immediately joined Helen and clung to her. Later played with clay, looked at books, but showed little interest in other activities in the room. As we cooked, he began to get very whiney and held on tightly to me. He wanted to go home to Mommy and was on the verge of tears several times, but gradually got more cheerful during story time and pudding eating. Outside, he came to me twice for help getting on the climbing bars. Once up, he climbed very agilely and hung up by his feet. He was proud of being able to walk home on his own.

5 September. Much better day—more independent, less clinging. I spoke with his mother, who said Chris was anxious to come to school today.

9 September. Played on loft. Can be very boisterous and physical, but inclined to cling to get attention.

19 September. Chris joins into more activities and does them well. Plays at block building and woodworking each day. Is "tough" with other boys, but inclined to whine at times.

23 September. Very upset when Helen said she didn't like him—finally Jason, Helen, Chris, and I got it settled. Has a very nice sense of softness and love.

In addition to the anecdotal records, the teacher keeps individual folders for each child's daily work in the language arts, math, and art. This past year, the children in Lynne Crosby's room were responsible for stamping their work with the correct date and putting it in their own folders on the teacher's desk.

We have also developed our own detailed language arts and math checklists for all levels.* The teacher records on the checklist the date each child masters a particular skill and adds any pertinent comments. The primary level (K-2) language arts checklist is broken down into the following categories:

Visual skills, such as left-to-right eye movements and the ability to discriminate shapes and letters.

Perceptual motor skills, such as the ability to hold a pencil correctly and to manipulate puzzles and games.

Phonetic skills, including auditory skills, such as hearing similarities and differences in the sounds of words; and sound-letter correspondence, such as blending letters together to sound out one- and two-syllable words.

Language development, including the ability to enunciate clearly and to present ideas in complete sentences.

Study skills, such as the ability to follow oral directions and use a dictionary.

Structural analysis, including the ability to find root words, form possessives, and understand compound words and contractions.

Oral reading, including the ability to read expressively, correctly, and with proper emphasis.

Vocabulary development, including the ability to learn new words and use them creatively to describe events or tell a story.

Comprehension, including the ability to make inferences, to select the main idea from a paragraph, and to know the difference between fantasy and reality in literature.

The math checklist is structured sequentially. A child may follow the sequence through and then go back and work more intensively in a particular area. While some of the skills are obviously prerequisites for others, many—such as telling time or graphing—can be tackled as part of another project or whenever the child shows an interest in them.

---

*Copies of these checklists, and of our other evaluation instruments, can be sent to readers on request. Please write to Leonard Solo, Principal, Cambridge Alternative Public School, 54 Essex Street, Cambridge, Massachusetts 02139.

Some of the categories on the math checklist are: sets, Cuisenaire rods, counting, number lines, fractions, equalities and inequalities using symbols, geometric shapes, measurement, telling time, odd and even numbers, place value, and factoring. The basic computational skills—addition, subtraction, multiplication, and division—are approached conceptually, beginning at the simplest level and increasing in difficulty. Many other math skills in logic, spatial awareness, and problem solving are not included on the checklist but are part of everyday games and activities in the classroom.

The outcome of all this extensive documentation is a twice-yearly written progress report on each child. Instead of describing these reports, I will quote extensively from the June progress report on David, a second grader:

Social and emotional development. David has shown a great deal of growth this school year. He has become very well liked and respected in our class and has made close friends. He is honest and open with them, able to tell his own feelings and understand the feelings of others. At times when there are differences among the children (including David), he is willing to talk them through and reach a resolution without hard feelings.

David has a good self-image and lots of confidence in his own abilities. He enjoys the challenge of learning something new and difficult. He is developing the ability to stick with things until he is satisfied that they are done well.

David has responded well to having firm guidelines for classroom and playground behavior. I think he needs to know the "rules" and that they will be enforced fairly for all. I have been very pleased with David's behavior during the past term. He has been very cooperative with me and has shown many times that gentle, caring part of his personality that is appealing to both children and adults.

Language arts. David has done a great deal of story writing and book making this term. He did it reluctantly at first, but seemed to enjoy writing his own experiences and thoughts as he realized that he could do it well. He is able to use his own dictionary to record the words he needs to spell and can sound out many words on his own. These words he spells phonetically and not always "properly"; however, I have encouraged him to write this way in order not to hinder fluency.

David has also made progress this year learning to read. He has a sound phonics approach and is able to sound out the words that he is reading. He has difficulty remembering sight words and benefits from the repetition of reading stories over again. He needs lots of encouragement to read materials that are appropriate for his level. He can be easily discouraged when he tries material that is too difficult or frustrating for him.

Math. David has enjoyed his math work this year and has made good progress. He is able to reason logically, can see patterns, and is able to use numbers to figure out solutions to problems. He has skill in basic operations of addition, subtraction, and beginning multiplication. He understands place value and is able to regroup numbers to the tens place. He enjoyed the work we did with geometrical shapes and solids. He also enjoyed learning about how to write and add fractions. He knows about money and was very good at making change during our school fair. In the kinds of projects that David likes to do, such as building and making things, he is able to measure the things he needs to figure out. He has also made many good graphs this year.

Under both language arts and math, the teacher goes on to indicate the texts and supplementary workbooks David has completed. The report also includes similar descriptions of his progress in classroom activities and projects and in arts and crafts, plus concluding general comments.

These written progress reports are followed by individual parent conferences at which the teacher and parents (and sometimes the child) discuss the report and go over examples of work from the child's daily folder. These conferences usually last about an hour, and between conferences, the teachers get in touch with the parents at least once a month.

This year, we began keeping a file for each child that contains copies of every written report and samples from the child's classroom folders. This file will be passed on at the end of the year to the child's new teacher. After seven or eight years, we should have an excellent record of every child's growth through the school years—for our own information, for the parents' information, and eventually, we hope, for the child's information.

This year, we also instituted the practice of having all the children write about (or dictate) what they have learned and how they feel about their class. This report is mailed home with the teacher's progress report. Last year, a few CAPS teachers had their children write weekly contracts. At the end of the week, the contracts were reviewed and the children's activities assessed.

Our evaluation procedures require teachers to pay very close attention to what they are planning and doing, as well as to what each child is doing. Most teachers write down their comments about the children at the end of the day. Others, like Lynne Crosby, keep note cards constantly handy—even when they go to the playground—so that they can take notes throughout the day.

The basic idea behind all of these practices should be the basic idea behind any evaluation: to help each child and parent and teacher see what the child is doing and to help the child develop his or her own evaluative processes. CAPS is committed to helping children become self-learners, and we believe that self-learning must be accompanied by self-evaluation.

In spite of the wealth of data provided by our evaluation processes, some parents react negatively and ask for more "objective" proof of what their children are doing. CAPS is a new kind of school for most parents. Few of them have had any experience with open classrooms, and so they are already into unknown territory when they see no desks in rows, no teacher up front lecturing, but learning centers, movement, noise, and integrated-day curricula instead. And then parents have to contend with an unfamiliar kind of report, describing the teacher's observations of their child.

Some of the parents' anxieties, then, are quite understandable. That's why we give them a choice about standardized testing, although it's a choice that we actively discourage. That's also why we ask an outside evaluator to document our entire program every year, if possible. We try to show parents that standardized tests have many flaws, one of which is the myth that they are objective. We also work hard to help them see that they should place a large trust in the teacher, that no one knows better than the teacher—and the child—what that child is learning in the classroom. Our evaluation process is a way of formalizing that basic trust.

Notes

[1] Those who are interested in the topic are referred, for starters, to my article, **"She Knows Too Much To Argue or To Judge: Evaluation in Innovative and Alternative Schools,"** *New Schools Exchange Newsletter*, issue 20, November 1974; and to the March/April and July/August 1975 issues of *National Elementary Principal*, which are devoted to IQ and standardized achievement testing. I also recommend Banesh Hoffmann's *The Tyranny of Testing* (New York: Collier Books, 1964); and the monographs on alternative philosophies and practices of evaluation published by the North Dakota Study Group on Evaluation, Center for Teaching and Learning, University of North Dakota, Grand Forks.

[2] Cambridge Chronicle, 17 July 1975.

Are 87 Percent of Russians Feebleminded?

How would you rate tests that proved that 87 percent of Russians, 83 percent of Jews, 80 percent of Hungarians, and 79 percent of Italians were feebleminded? These were the results of tests taken by immigrants in 1913 at the receiving station on Ellis Island.

The tests haven't changed much but our attitude has—somewhat.

In a final report to the NEA Representative Assembly, the NEA Task Force on Testing recommended that alternatives to group standardized testing be developed and described some of those alternatives.

NEA

ANECDOTAL RECORDS

Recording the behaviors of individual students reveals more about a student than do test results. A teacher can develop a composite picture of a student by observing and recording behavior such as interaction with others, motivational patterns, and independent work habits.

Teachers who have set about keeping anecdotal records report that not only is the experience satisfying for them, but that they improve with practice and constantly get new insights into a student that either support or explain other evaluation results.

ORAL PRESENTATIONS BY STUDENTS

Students' oral presentations have long been accepted as one way to evaluate student progress. For example, skilled reading teachers use them both in evaluating student progress and in diagnosing specific difficulties. Subject matter teachers can assess both depth of knowledge and personal capabilities using this mode of performance.

In assigning oral presentations to students, teachers must state clearly beforehand what is expected of the students and what are the criteria for a good performance. The structure offers the opportunity for self- and peer evaluation, particularly when oral presentations are recorded.

CONTRACTS WITH STUDENTS

A contract or agreement between student and instructor specifies tasks that both parties must complete within a given period of time. An instructor carefully poses problems with varying degrees of difficulty, and students, with teacher guidance, select both the problems they will work on and the amount of time they will spend on them. Ability to perform the tasks is measured by promptness and accuracy in completing the contract items. Requiring students to work alone, as contracts generally do, adds to an instructor's understanding of a student's academic and personal development.

STUDENT SELF- AND PEER EVALUATION

Students can be, and ought to be, involved in evaluating their own work. The ability to assess one's performance is useful in ways that transcend school learning. Students can become more insightful about themselves and their approach to work.

Self- and peer assessment is complex, particularly when more than simple student products are being judged. When expressing subjective judgments, students tend to underrate rather than overrate their own abilities and achievements. Because of this, some background and skill on the part of teachers is required in dealing with sensitive affective areas and development of self-concepts. Many well-developed approaches exist for such purposes.

This article was originally published as "**A Summary of Alternatives,**" from *What's Wrong with Standardized Testing?* © 1977 National Education Association. Reprinted by permission.

PARENT-TEACHER CONFERENCES

The purpose of most parent-teacher conferences are for the parties to exchange information about a student that will help to guide him or her into productive channels and to find ways in which he or she can secure satisfaction and growth. These conferences are valuable when there is thoughtful preparation and when they are used as a supplement to written evaluations. They also offer an excellent opportunity to relate schooling to the home—a necessary adjunct for a vast majority of students.

OBJECTIVES-REFERENCED (CRITERION-REFERENCED) TESTS

The potential advantage of these tests over standardized tests is that students are judged on their mastery of objectives rather than on their standing in relation to others. In this way, they serve some diagnostic purposes. At this time, these tests have not had wide enough use to confirm fully their value, particularly when broad subject areas must be considered. If the original intention of criterion-referenced tests is not distorted, they have great potential as an alternative to standardized tests.

INDIVIDUAL DIAGNOSTIC TESTS

These sophisticated evaluation devices are reliable and valid for specific purposes. They are underused because administering them is frequently time-consuming and expensive. Also applying, scoring, and analyzing individual diagnostic tests often requires special training that is generally not available to teachers.

Nevertheless, these tests have the potential of providing additional information the teacher can use in prescribing learning strategies for a student.

TEACHER-MADE TESTS

Good examples of objectives-referenced tests are those constructed by teachers for their own use. These can closely reflect the content and emphasis of classroom subject matter, and teachers can use the results in making decisions that are as diverse as the pace of instruction; prescriptive assignments; reporting to or conferring with parents; and promoting or retaining a student. This broad range of decisions requires that teachers be familiar with methods of constructing classroom tests which will measure both factual knowledge and higher levels of thinking.

SCHOOL LETTER GRADES

Conventional grading systems of A, B, C, D, or E or equivalent designations (percentages/averages) are, for the most part, understandable to parents and acceptable to students. Giving grades can be particularly valuable when teachers use descriptions to expand and to clarify the meaning of the grades. Even such limited descriptors as *excellent, satisfactory,* and *needs improvement* may be more useful to parents and students than the standardized test statistic of "10 standard score points above the mean."

OPEN ADMISSIONS

In a strict sense, the policy of open admissions is not an alternative to testing but a practice that indicates change in college requirements. It could eliminate the need for standardized tests.

Many institutions of higher education now accept all students who have completed high school; they give no consideration to scholastic-aptitude or achievement tests. Some universities admit fourth year high school students into their freshmen classes upon the recommendation of high school teachers. Adult education and life-long learning programs provide access to degree-granting programs for working people. Combinations and variations of the above offer opportunities which in the past would have been highly unusual if not totally unacceptable.

The criterion for admission to these schools is the desire to be educated rather than the score achieved on a standardized test.

The full story is not yet in on the success of these programs, but the concept of openness provides for more equitable educational opportunities for all. This holds true for other levels of schooling.

A Wide-angle View of Intelligence

Newer research emphasizes cognitive style and perseverance as the most important aspect of success in various fields. Here are some of the more interesting kinds of specific assessments that can clue you in as to how to build on the strengths of the children in your class. Here you might also find tests you might like to take yourself to gain insight into your own talents.

Do you conceptualize in an analytic style or a relational style? For example, looking at pictures of a house with smoke coming out of the chimney, a book of matches, and a smoking pipe, which ones "go together" in your mind? If you pick the house and pipe because they both have smoke coming out, you think differently than the person who picks the matches and pipe because "matches light the pipe." Which is *right?*

Evelyn Sharp

As the IQ cult has lost its grip on the public, a broader view of intelligence is emerging. Much of the current experimentation is on cognitive style, a shadowy area that lies between the old narrow IQ concept and personality.

Research on cognitive style coalesces around the way our minds process information—an intriguing subject. Most people are almost totally unaware that others are processing information in different ways from themselves. When they know this, it may give them a more accurate—and more reassuring—self-estimate.

One of the first experimenters in this area was David Witkin. He is a critic of conventional IQ tests because of their heavy emphasis on verbal skills. In an article in *Child Development* he said that their use tended to "route children through life" on the basis of verbal competence.

He added that "Children who show a deficit in the verbal area, whatever other cognitive strengths they may have . . . are therefore likely to be referred for special testing. Moreover, these children are particularly penalized on standard intelligence tests. . . . Thus, the verbally handicapped child is not only more likely to be referred for testing than children with other cognitive deficits but, when tested, is more likely to earn a low IQ, with the prospect of being classified as retarded."

Beginning at Brooklyn College in 1944 and later moving to the Downstate Medical Center of the State University of New York, Witkin and his associates established the existence of a mental faculty that he called field dependence. It concerns the ability to separate an object from its background when there are competing cues.

In his early experiments he used very elaborate equipment—a small room that could be tilted to the left or right and a chair that could also be tilted left or right. The subject sits in the tilted chair inside the tilted room and the experimenter moves the chair until the subject says he thinks he is sitting up straight.

The point is that we judge which way is up by two standards. One is the feeling within ourselves caused by the pull of gravity; the other is by the appearance of our surroundings—the walls, doors, corners, etc., of a room, if we are indoors. If these are tilted, as they were in Witkin's room, the two standards conflict. Which is dominant? Do you rely on the sensations from within, or do you align yourself to conform to the slanted room, as one child did who answered yes to the question, "Is this the way you sit when you eat your dinner?" when actually she was tilted at an angle of 35 degrees.

Anybody can straighten himself when he is blindfolded; the test comes from the conflict between the visual cues and the inward feeling. Those who are influenced by the slanted room Witkin called field dependent; those who aligned themselves nearly upright in spite of what they saw, he called field independent.

He then devised a simpler test for the same ability. The subject sits in a darkened room and looks at what appears to be a luminous frame for a picture, except that instead of a picture, there is a movable luminous rod inside it. Both are tilted. The experimenter moves the rod around until the subject says that he thinks it is upright. The people who line the rod up according to the slanted sides of the frame are the same people who are seduced by the slanting walls of the tilting room. Those who can straighten themselves up in the tilted chair can also adjust the rod so it is upright.

The ability improves with age, especially between the ages of eight and thirteen, then it levels off and even regresses slightly in the late teens. But for a given individual it is remarkably stable. Those at the top of their group when they are eight are usually still at the top of their group when they are sixteen.

Both of these tests correlate with the Embedded Figure Test, which is something like those newspaper puzzles showing a drawing of a landscape with hidden faces in the clouds, trees, etc. Witkin used geometric drawings with a simple figure, like a hexagon or a cube, hidden in a large complex figure. Other versions, especially for little children, may show a cat embedded in a maze of intertwined lines and other figures. The experimenter says, "Find the kitty. Touch the kitty."

Each of these three tests requires the individual to separate some item— his own body, a rod, or a drawing—from its background. Results suggest that field dependence, or independence, tends to be established early in life and to remain relatively stable.

Field independent people excel at problems where the different components have to be taken apart and reassembled. Socially, they are better able to resist group pressures than are the field dependent people, who tend to be more passive. In Witkin's experiment, more boys than girls were field independent.

The ability is partly due to constitutional characteristics and partly due to environment. Boys with overprotective mothers tended to be field dependent; boys whose mothers were not overprotective were more often field independent. (Might not this account for the difference in the showing of the sexes, since girls are commonly brought up in a more sheltered way?)

Another center of research on cognitive style is at the Menninger Foundation, an outgrowth of the famous Menninger Clinic in Topeka, Kansas. For some fifteen years, psychologist Riley Gardner and others, working within a framework drawn from several sources, including Piaget, have been seeking new ways to measure and identify dimensions of the mind.

The subjects who take their tests are volunteers paid for their time. They represent a wide range of occupations—college students, farmers, housewives, secretaries, teachers, etc. Church and fraternal groups sometimes come in a body, as a way of raising funds for their organizations. On at least one occasion, their test group was made up of twenty-eight pairs of husbands and wives, chosen partly as a way of getting people with the same social and economic background but also to get some information about comparative cognitive styles of married couples.

Just what is cognitive style? To illustrate, suppose you volunteer to take the Stroop Color Word Test. First you are handed a page of color names—red, green, blue, yellow—all printed in ordinary black and repeated over and over in varied order. You are asked to read it aloud as fast as you can, and your time is recorded. Next you are given a page of red, green, blue, and yellow asterisks and asked to call off the colors as fast as you can. Again your time is recorded.

Last—and here's the payoff—you are shown a page of those same four names printed in color, but it's always the wrong color. The word "red" might be printed in green ink, and so on. You are asked to call off the actual colors you see—never mind what the word says. How much are you slowed down by the conflict between the name you read and the color you see? If only a little, then your mind works in a flexible fashion and you will probably do well on intellectual tasks where there is stress or distraction. If a lot, then your style of thinking is more constructed and you are more interference prone.

It is interesting to note that one of Binet's early tests, when he was trying a variety of things and ten years before he developed his test for the Parisian school system, touched on this same point. First the subject read ten lines aloud and his time was recorded. Then he read ten similar lines while simultaneously writing the letters of the alphabet, and the two times were compared. Binet called this a test for "scope of attention" and did not include it in the famous Binet-Simon.

The Stroop Color Word Test, individually given, is not new, but at Menninger's they have developed a way of using it with groups by projecting the pages onto a screen, letting each person read silently and time himself by a large clock marked in seconds. The examiner cautions the assembled volunteers, "Your data will be of no help to us if you do not follow the instructions exactly." After showing a few practice lines on the screen, he says, "Now we will show you the page of words. Read the entire page as fast and accurately as you can, correcting all errors as you go. When you are finished with the page, record your reading time in seconds in the correct box and look up at me while sitting quietly so as not to distract any others who may still be reading. Ready. Watch the screen."

They do the same for the other two pages. On the last part, the page where the words and the colors conflict, the examiner says, "This part of the test is more difficult than Parts I and II. Try to remain still in spite of any tendency you may feel to move in your chair. Please do not sigh, laugh, or make any other audible sound."

The results of giving the test in this way to groups of thirty or so at a time were reasonably valid and reliable for experimental purposes and speeded up the collection of data enormously.

Another dimension of the mind that influences cognitive style concerns the way you spontaneously put things into categories, working under free conditions. Do you make few groups, or many? This seemingly trivial trait has far-reaching implications and is measured by the Gardner Object Sorting Test. You are given seventy-three common objects—a bar of soap, a hammer, and the like—and told to "Group the items in the way that seems most logical, most natural, and most comfortable." When you have finished, you are asked your reason for putting the things in each group.

The reasons can be anything. "They are all tools," "They are all in a kitchen," "All belong to a child," "All have to do with smoking" are common examples given for categories. But it is essential to the test that the reason is asked for. Otherwise many people, after having made some groups, put all the leftovers together into a pseudo group not because of any similarity that they see in them but just because they don't fit any of the other categories. In such a "wastebasket" collection each item is counted as a separate group.

Your score is the total number of categories you arrange the objects into. The range is amazingly wide—from as many as thirty to as few as three. The trait proved to be remarkably stable and consistent. Whether they are sorting household objects, pictures of people cut out of magazines, or blocks with Chinese symbols on them, some individuals just naturally divide things into many small groups and other people make fewer groups encompassing more items. The same thing held true for a pencil-and-paper group test where fifty names of objects were to be sorted.

It isn't that people who make few groups lack the ability to see differences among objects, but they are more oriented to look for similarities. Others are more impressed by distinctions among things.

This raises some interesting questions for further research. One is that since learning new material often hinges on looking for similarities between the new and what you already know, might not this tendency to look for similarities have something to do with the ease with which new material is learned?

Another has to do with creativity. Writing in the *Bulletin of the Menninger Clinic, 1970*, Gardner said that, among children at least, those who arrange an assortment of heterogeneous objects into a few large groups are more explorative and more creative than those who sort the same objects into a number of small groups.

The whole thrust of the Menninger project is to identify different traits, each independent of the others but all contributing to individuality. For example, a person who is slowed down on the Color Word Test, is field dependent (Gardner and his associates accept Witkin's findings), and who makes a high score on the Object Sorting Test would have a very different learning style from one who has a different combination of highs and lows.

Another trait concerns the degree to which new experiences are infiltrated or colored by memories. It is measured by Gardner's Schematizing Test.

If you volunteer for this one, you are seated in a darkened room, and a square of white light is projected on the wall. You are given two seconds to look at it and six seconds to record your estimate of its size. Then other squares of white light are projected, one after another, and the same procedure is repeated each time. Unknown to you, the squares are getting bigger and bigger. How well can you keep up with the increases in size? Some people are pretty good at it. With others, the memory of the size the square was a few seconds ago mixes in with what they see now, and they lag behind, consistently estimating the square to be smaller than it actually is. This test, like a number of others, is plainly on perception.

When Piaget was guest lecturer at the Menninger School of Psychiatry for three weeks in March, 1961, it was perception that Gardner and his team of researchers wanted to discuss with him. Although Piaget is best known for his work on the way intelligence develops, he characterizes himself as an epistemologist—an investigator of the processes of human knowing. He has done experiments in many different areas, including perception.

He thinks that perception, being biased and subject to certain illusions, is inferior to the higher mental processes. Specifically, it is relative. For example, take a big chair and a little chair, identical except for size. If you look at them together, paying equal attention to each, the little one will appear smaller than it really is, the big one larger. That phrase "paying equal attention to each" is important. Piaget regards attention as the major link between perception and the higher mental operations.

A third body of experimental work on cognitive style is that of Harvard's Jerome Kagan and his colleagues. Kagan is one of the most outspoken critics of present IQ tests, which he considers seriously biased. In an article in the *Saturday Review*, December 4, 1971, he referred to "two similarly constructed standardized IQ tests invented by Caucasian middle-class Western men to rank-order everyone." He didn't call the tests by name but gave examples of six categories of questions from them—vocabulary, analogies, drawings with something missing, arithmetic, questions that ask the child what he would do in a given situation, and memory for strings of digits.

In his own experimental work, Kagan takes a different tack. He points out that problem-solving involves three distinct steps, in this order: First, the information is classified; second, it is stored in code form; third, it is transformed.

He feels that the importance of the first step has been underestimated in the past. Children presented with the same problem pay attention to different parts of it, then base their solution on the parts that caught their attention in the first place. (Note that this emphasis on attention fits what Piaget said on his visit to the Menninger Foundation about attention being the major link between perception and the higher mental operations.) They come out with different end results, not because of a difference in ability but because of a different way of choosing the initial information.

To find out more about this first step, Kagan used a Conceptual Style Test. He showed the child a card with three drawings of familiar objects on it—for example, a house with smoke coming out of the chimney, a book of matches, and a smoking pipe. He said, "Pick out two pictures that are alike or go together in some way."

The types of answers that children gave tended to fall into two groups, with clear differences between them. If the child said something like "The house and pipe both have smoke coming out," he was using an analytic style. If he said something like "The matches light the pipe," he was using a relational style.

Basically what the analytic child did was to mentally take the pictures apart and look for likenesses among the parts. If the card showed a watch, a man, and a ruler, he might say, "The watch and the ruler both have numbers." A child with a relational style of classifying information would be likely to say, "The man wears the watch," or, "The man uses the ruler."

In contrast to an IQ test, there are no right or wrong answers to the questions on Kagan's test. The objects can be paired in any way, and one style is no better than another. But the child's reasons reveal something important about his natural way of classifying and coding information. Kagan gave his test to 800 students in the elementary grades. He found that the relational answer was the most popular among little children and that the analytic style increased with age. For first-graders, the average was four analytic responses per student (out of thirty cards on the test). Sixth-graders average about ten analytic responses.

Research on cognitive style may also help to explain some still unsolved puzzles about conventional IQ tests. All teachers know children who consistently make high IQ squares but the only way you would know it is to go down to the principal's office and look up their records. Nothing in their performance indicates high ability.

Why don't they do as well as their tests indicate they should? If there are no apparent reasons—emotional disturbances or the like—the easy, all-purpose explanation is that they are lazy. Millions of words have been expended, rewards promised, and punishments meted out in an effort to get them to do better.

I don't think that it is always a case of laziness. Might not the fact that traditional tests are made up of fragments, coupled with the fact that the child may have an unusual cognitive style, produce misleading scores? I got the germ of this idea from a girl who seemed to fit that category. She said: "In those tests, the questions are all separate. Number two doesn't have anything to do with number one. I can do pages of those." But when it came to one long, organized task, she was no better than average.

When Galton first originated his mental tests, he said that he was "sinking shafts." This is what we're still doing in the present IQ tests. Then we take our collection of shallow core samples and, if they appear to show the same thing, we say, "Aha! There's an underlying stratum connecting them."

Maybe there is. But in the unknown and shifting terrain of the mind is this *always* true? How do we know that what we have tapped isn't a series of isolated pockets? And how about all the areas that present tests don't tap?

To sum up, IQ tests were oversold in the beginning and capabilities were attributed to them that they never had. For years they held undisputed sway in the schools—an article of faith second only to the Pledge of Allegiance. In the 1960's their power started to wane, and attention has turned to other approaches where, in some cases, experimentation has been quietly going on for a long time.

There are signs of possible convergences among views put forward quite separately by Piaget, Witkin, Gardner, Kagan, and others whose work I have not mentioned. It is possible that we may be near a breakthrough in the construction of new and better types of tests of mental ability.

VI
IT MAY BE ENGLISH
BUT IT'S GREEK TO ME!

Do Your Books Put Your Readers to Sleep?
For Reluctant Readers
Mistakes Show Progress
Children Teach Children
Basics in a Bean-Bag Chair
To Help Them Write, Right
Welcome Back Writing
All Spooko and Quiet
Hate Makes Good Copy—
Conflict, Great Drama
A Mirror for Jellyroll Jones
Why Jessie Hates English

Do Your Books Put Your Readers to Sleep?

We're all so used to the deadliness of the materials we use to teach kids to read, we hardly notice them any more. Are these materials well thought-out? Well constructed? Interesting to children?

They're a bit livelier than the saga of Dick and Jane, but are they the work of people who understand the importance of the written word, the impact of the word on the audience?

If we considered how meaningful are the books we use, we might actually rebel and substitute texts that can be taken more seriously by us and by our students. Bruno Bettelheim writes that the material we use thoughtlessly is our most dreadful adversary in the teaching of reading. Judged as we are by our successes in this field, we should not be at the mercy of our judges when the fault for failure lies not in the stars, nor in ourselves, but in the tests themselves.

Bettelheim makes an implicit case for a violation of the separation of church and state in reevaluating the desirability of the Scriptures as a beginning text, not because he wishes to link schools and church, but because he recognizes the importance of engaging the child's deepest emotions in establishing literacy.

Bruno Bettelheim

With the declining impact of the family on shaping the child's personality, primary education becomes ever more important in its formative influence on the child, and learning to read is its centerpiece. We have made tremendous progress in the technique of teaching reading.... As in the technological exploitation of our natural resources—where we have neglected to pay sufficient attention to how technological progress may rob us of much that the environment could mean to us—so in our concentration on the technique of teaching reading, we have neglected the importance of meaningful reading. As a consequence, it rarely enters the life of the child before the third grade, if

This article was originally published as "**On Learning to Read,**" in *The National Elementary Principal*, Vol. 56, No. 1 (Sept.–Oct. 1976). Copyright 1976, National Association of Elementary School Principals. All rights reserved. Reprinted by permission. Dr. Bettelheim is the author of many books, the latest of which is *The Uses of Enchantment*. From 1944 until 1973 he directed the Orthogenic School, which successfully pioneered in the education and treatment of psychotic and autistic children.

then. But the third grade is, of course, much too late; by that time, a child's basic reading attitudes are fully established. My plea, then, is that we place meaning at the very beginning of reading instruction, for the purpose of reading, after all, is to find meaning.

In saying this, I do not for a moment suggest a return to the so-called basics with their deadly drill. On the contrary, when we introduce, at the outset, what is deeply meaningful to a young child, we can dispense with much of the drill; fascination and enthusiasm make it less necessary.

Sadly, our primers offer no meaning to children. Moreover, when children, on their own, project personal meaning into their reading of primers, teachers reject it and thus further alienate children from reading.

I make these comments on the basis of direct observation and study. During the past years, I have spent a considerable amount of time with children in schools that are considered unusually good, vastly superior to the average school, and where quite a few of the children came from families with better-than-average incomes. I have concentrated on the early grades, since it is in these grades that overall patterns are formed, particularly the psychological attitudes toward school and learning.

Let me begin reporting some of my experiences by citing some spontaneous reactions of a group of bright fourth and fifth graders when I discussed with them their recollections of how they reacted to being taught reading in first grade.

One child readily admitted that though he now liked reading, he still had a hard time reading aloud. When he was asked to read aloud in the first grade, he was ashamed to say such stupid things. He simply could not do it; he blocked, and from then on, he resented reading, preferring to do anything else in class.

Another student hated the stories he had to read because they were neither realistic nor fantastic. Stories, he thought, should either give a picture of what life was really like or not pretend to do so. He would have had a much easier time learning to read, and enjoying it, had the stories been either true to life, describing how people really are, or truly fantastic, like fairy tales. He finally overcame his resentment of reading when he became acquainted with fairy tales. After he had read one, he would contemplate its content "for a long while." These were meaningful experiences for him; what he had to read in class was not.

When I asked in what sense the stories read in class were not "true to life," every child in the group was eager to talk, and each had a different objection. One criticism was that these stories portray only two age-groups: children of their own age and adults—mostly parents; furthermore, both children and parents are depicted as being insipid. The children in the group wanted to see and read stories about teenagers and old people as well. Another universal objection was that nobody in these stories shows his or her true feelings—anger, for instance. Other complaints were that they could see no reason to learn to read: in the early grades they never learned anything through reading that they didn't already know—and know much better and in greater detail than was set out in the books from which they were supposed to learn great things.

To these recollections, I would like to juxtapose the early memories of a famous scholar who felt that his first experiences with learning to read had helped to form his life. The book from which he was taught to read, at five years of age, was the Bible. He soon realized that the meaning of the first words he learned to read—the opening sentences of the Bible—was so great and varied, so inexhaustible, that even his teacher, who had read the same text innumerable times, always found something new in the words. Through the text and his teacher's attitude toward it, the magic of reading and literature was opened up to this boy in his first reading lessons. I do not need to pose the question of what vistas are opened up to the child who first learns to read, "See Spot run; see Spot jump."

Again, by way of contrast, let me quote the first sentences of the New England Primer of 1727. In those olden days, the first words a child learned to read were: "In Adam's fall—We sinned all—Thy life to mend—This book attend." There could be no doubt in the child's mind that learning to read had to do with the first and last things—with our human condition, as symbolized by the fall from grace and the hope for salvation. If only we learned to read this book, we could mend our lives and earn eternal bliss. With such promises held out to the child, learning to read, despite difficulties, surely appeared to be the most worthwhile thing anybody could do.

To many modern educators, it may seem farfetched that learning to read, which they view as a most rational undertaking, a typical cognitive task, can be mastered well only if at first and for quite some time to come, it is experienced as a most powerful magic. However, only if learning to read is viewed as the best way to gain access to this magic power, does the child's unconscious support his conscious efforts; does the id lend its great sources of energy to the as yet weak ego, so that it becomes able to master this difficult task from which it expects immediate gains for its magic and wishful fantasies. This magic interpretation of the power reading confers is further supported by the superego. For as this particular magic becomes effective, it also serves a superior power (in my examples, that of religion, which controls human existence). Hence the magic interpretation of reading is lent further credence by the superego's support, with its strength and approbation of efforts at learning to read. Without such unconscious support on the part of the id and superego, learning to read remains a most difficult task, one that gives little pleasure, and a skill that is apt to soon fall into disuse.

Much of education is a repetition of the history of the race. Literacy, man's great achievement, began as sheer magic; it was not created to serve utilitarian purposes. But modern education stresses utility and "getting ahead," thus robbing learning to read of the greatest incentive that could support it. When script developed, it served religious and magical needs; for example, "it is written that the word was with God, and the word was God." But for millennia before this was uttered, writing and reading were arcane arts that conferred special powers and privileges. Consider the long struggle about whether the average man should be permitted to read scriptures, and consider, too, that it was from the Good Book that children learned to read. Furthermore, only after man was permitted to read scriptures did reading instruction become universal.

All children are fascinated by secret language, and the beginning of school age is the time when the child most desires to share the secrets of adults. The close connection between id-motivated fascination with magic and secret language, superego-motivated interest in religion, and ego-motivated book learning creates a devotion to reading and learning in general, which can then be easily transferred to all learning.

Even today, we can see how much reading must be supported by superego representations and id desires by the fact that when parents value reading highly, it becomes more attractive to the child. This attractiveness, however, does not come from the rational and utilitarian purposes out of which parents may devote themselves to reading. What the child responds to is the parents' emotional absorption in reading. What makes it attractive to the child is that it seems to fascinate the parents. It is their secret knowledge that the child wants to be able to share. The more the parents' devotion to reading and the child's belief in its magic propensities coincide, the easier a time the child will have in learning to read.

True, later on the irrational aspects of this magic support need to be reduced, and the rational ones must gain ascendancy. But if such divestment of magic occurs too soon and too radically, reading will not be strongly invested emotionally.

What psychological constellation, then, is necessary for the intellect and the emotions to work together to promote an interest in learning (in this case, learning to read)? To put it in the simplest possible way, I suggest that learning, particularly learning to read, must make a powerful appeal to our unconscious, both the id and the superego, so that the energy of these two institutions of the mind can empower the ego to meet successfully the cognitive tasks presented to it.

Unfortunately, modern education, wishing to start out with the end product, believing it can do away with slow and tortuous development, ends up producing an ego so depleted of its natural resources in meeting its tasks that it remains weak for the rest of its life.

All superego appeals have been eliminated from our educational readers —quite contrary to what is true of the readers in Communist countries, for example, which abound with superego appeals. In our own readers, appeals to the id are to the most basic and unstructured instinctive tendencies. In fact, most of these appeals are of a locomotive nature, which inevitably causes problems for young children in a classroom. It is difficult enough for first graders to sit still and pay attention. But it becomes an insult to their feelings if they are asked to sit still when at the same time they are required to think only of romping, running, jumping, and all other varieties of active play.

It is unfair to use only one basic American reader as an example, because all those that are widely used in the USA are equally bad in this respect. Therefore, since I am not able to make my point without examples, I shall present two. *Janet and Mark,* which is the first primer in the Harper and Row Basic Reading Program, begins as follows:

> Janet and Mark.—Come Mark. Come, Mark come—Come here, Mark.—Come here, come here, Mark.—Come and jump. Come and jump, jump, jump.—Here I come, Janet. Here I come. I can ride my bike. I can, I can. I can ride and ride.—Here I go, Janet, here I go.

The verbs predominately used are those signifying a vigorous motor activity. In addition, the most frequently used admonition is the one children of primary age hate with a vengeance. They hate the parent's familiar order: "Come here." Yet, this is what the stories in these readers ask them to do. Not only school, but all of life is depicted as a row of tedious and senseless activities. Just how tedious is made clear in another of these basic readers, the ITA (Initial Teaching Alphabet) series. It goes as follows:

> In the morning you get up. You get dressed. You get breakfast. Even if you get wet you go to school on time. Then you get out of school and you go home again. After a day of getting up and getting dressed and getting breakfast, and getting wet, and getting to school, and getting out of school, and getting hot, and getting home, and getting dinner, you get very tired and get into bed, so that you can get up the next morning and start all over again.

I cannot imagine a more depressing view of life than is depicted in this passage; nor does it contain a single suggestion that something meaningful may go on in school. In fact, our readers abound in stories that deliberately and consistently direct the child's attention away from school toward after-school activities. An example from the ITA series called *School Days* illustrates well this point. (I sense a certain irony in the title, since it has nothing at all favorable to tell about days in school.) It begins:

> Bill lives in this house. Today is Monday. It is a hot sunny day. [I suppose the day is hot and sunny in order to make going to school even less attractive.] Bill goes to school. Bill rides to school on the bus. What can Bill do after school? After school Bill can fish. Bess lives here. Today is Tuesday. It is a sunny day. Bess goes to this school. What can Bess do after school? After school Bess can ride. [The picture shows her riding a horse.] Al lives in this apartment house. Today is Wednesday. It is a windy day. Al goes to school. Al rides a bike to school. What can Al do after school? After school Al can run and play. Pat lives in this apartment house. Liz lives here, too. Today is Thursday. Pat and Liz go to school here. What can Pat and Liz do after school? After school today Pat and Liz can play house. This is Ted's house. Today is Friday. It is cold and windy. It is snowing today. Ted goes to school. Ted rides on the school bus. After school today Ted can ride a sled. What can you do after school today?

Psychoanalytic studies of the so-called double bind have shown that nothing is more confusing and disturbing to children, and has more far-reaching detrimental consequences for their later attitudes, than when adults expose them to contradictory communications on important issues.[1] Our primers contain many such contradictory messages. The first message is that the educational system that requires children to go to school—and presents them with books so that they may learn to read from them—considers school and learning most necessary and important. The other message—and it directly contradicts the first—is that going to school and learning there is so unattractive that the only ways to induce children to go to school are through enjoyable nonacademic events that happen to take place there.

The Bank Street Readers at least mention reading and school, but they fail to make an appeal to id, ego, or superego. The primer of this series, *Around the City*, begins instead with an appeal to "fun":

All around the city,
All around the town,
Boys and girls run up the street,
Boys and girls run down.

Boys come out into the sun.
Boys come out to play and run.
Girls come out to run and play,
Around the city, all the day.

All around the city,
All around town,
Boys and girls run up the street,
Boys and girls run down.

It would be difficult to describe a more aimless way to spend the day, not to mention the assertion that children run up and down the street "all the day," thereby leaving neither time nor place for school or learning. Furthermore, since most stories in our primers suggest that children on their own act aimlessly, it is hardly surprising that children are turned off when they are asked to learn to read such content.

At this point, I want to discuss the meanings children project into their reading. Many years ago, Douglas Waples wrote, "What reading does to people is not nearly as important as what people do to reading." It is an insight that remains neglected, much to the detriment of the children who are being taught to read. For example, a boy was reading the story "From Hill to Sea" from the Bank Street Readers. It contains the sentence "As it runs down, the brook makes a noisy little song." The boy substituted *nice* for *noisy*, probably because he felt that noisy was not an appropriate adjective to apply when the intention is to convey the song-like quality of what one hears as one listens to a brook. We intended to tell him that the sentence as printed didn't make much sense since songs are not generally thought of as noisy. But we did not get beyond saying, "This sentence doesn't make much sense," when he interrupted us by reading "a noisy little song." The message that the way he had read it was an improvement, was all the boy needed in order to read the word as printed.

Maybe it was this experience that encouraged him to continue to improve on the text, or he might have done it anyway. But after this first incident a much more innocuous remark on our part was sufficient for the boy to correct his misreading. He read the sentence "The little brook runs and splashes down the hill" as "The little brook runs downstream." We said merely, "That sounds pretty!" But at that, he reread the sentence as printed.

While our first remark indicated that something might be wrong with the sentence, the second comment gave no such hint. By rereading the sentence as printed, the boy demonstrated that he had known all along that he had changed it in his original reading.

Both examples show that the substitutions were not the result of an inability to read the words of the text. While in the first example, the boy may have been led astray by *nice* and *noisy* beginning with the same letter, and having recognized the *n*, he may have jumped to the conclusion that the word was *nice*, such reasoning cannot apply to the second misreading, which was much more extensive in that one word was substituted for five. Moreover, the alacrity with which he reread the words as printed was a clear sign of his pleasure in our recognition that he had not misread words because he was unable to read them, but because he was dissatisfied with being a passive repeater and wanted to be an active improver.

Similar experiences suggested that the more repetitive the sentences are in the basal readers, the greater is the child's propensity to escape such passive repetition by introducing spontaneous variations. These variations make it easier for the child to pay attention. Consequently, when the child's variations are accepted positively, it not only facilitates learning to read but makes it more interesting, as passive taking-in is coupled with active manipulation.

Let me here introduce a word of caution. As can be seen from these examples, I think it would be erroneous to accept the clever things a child does to reading as a correct reading of the text. If we were to simply accept a "misreading" of the text without any reaction, we would neglect our task of teaching reading. It would confuse the child in regard to word recognition and to what are our purposes. But it is, I believe, equally neglectful not to recognize the clever things the child has done to reading. When we show children our appreciation that they have been able, all on their own, to do clever things to reading, we promote their interest in reading and their confidence in their ability to do so.

To cite another example, a rather mature black third grader was reading "Ann Visits the Roundabouts," a story in *Programmed Reading*, a Sullivan workbook about a country where people say the opposite of what they really mean. The girl in the story talks with an elderly gentleman who understands that everyone is saying the opposite of what they mean. He proceeds, like an indulgent father, to help the girl figure out what's going on and to come up with solutions to their various dilemmas in the strange land.

The girl had correctly read the word *castles* many times during the reading lesson. Thus it was not lack of familiarity that made her at one place read *castless* instead of *castles*. The passage of the story in which the error was made had the fatherly figure say: "But I have a feeling for castles, my dear. I'm quite sure this is the right way." The girl read it: "But I have a feeling for castless, my dear. I'm quite sure this is the right way."

Far from suggesting poor reading ability, this error demonstrates the girl's superior reading. Since she had read *castles* correctly several times, changing *castles* to *castless* must have been the consequence of, in her mind's eye, having read ahead, to what is (or ought to be) "the right way." To her the right way referred to the right way of ordering society. That is why only in this passage, where certainty is expressed about which is the right way, *castles* became changed to *castless*. A castless society is the opposite of one in which the castle dominates the life of the inhabitants. That the story was telling about a country in which people say the opposite of what they mean may have had some impact on the girl's changing *castles* to something that signifies a society opposite to one in which castles are all important.

That the girl had read ahead in her mind, although she was behind in her voice, is also hardly remarkable. On the contrary, it is normal in oral reading where the existence of an eye-voice span is a well-known phenomenon. In adults, the eye is often a full line ahead of what the voice is saying, which is how it must be. Otherwise, we could not read with the right emotional emphasis, which is possible only if we know what is to follow. While the eye-voice span in children who are learning to read is smaller than in adults, the print of basal readers is much larger and stands out more clearly on the page, which facilitates seeing what lies ahead of what one is reading.

As it turned out, in this case, the girl's error, in addition to its social meaning, also had a very personal one: her brother had a cast on his leg. Thus *castless* might also have expressed the wish that her brother be rid of his cast. But this would not explain why the misreading took place in the context of this passage. The wish that the brother should be free of his cast could equally well have been expressed in all other passages in which the word *castles* appeared. The explanation, however, might again be found in the particular context of this passage, referring to knowing what is the right way. A cast restricts movements in space, as racial discrimination restricts a person's moves in society. In times and places where castles are important, their rulers restrict the moves of their inferiors, as a cast restricts the moves of a person. In the imagination of a third grader, freedom of movement is very much physical and social, and the girl expressed the desire for this double freedom in her ingenious misreading.

That misreadings are based on a preceding correct understanding of what is being distorted has been known since the beginning of this century. In 1901 Freud wrote:

In a second group of cases the part which the text contributes to the misreading is a much larger one. [When compared with a series of misreadings Freud had discussed previously.] It contains something which rouses the reader's defences—some information or imputation distressing to him—and which is therefore corrected by being misread so as to fit in with a repudiation or with the fulfillment of a wish. In such cases we are of course obliged to assume that the text was first correctly understood and judged by the reader before it underwent correction, although his consciousness learnt nothing of this first reading.[2]

Children replace words or phrases of a text because, as they see it, what they are reading is not as sensible, common, or familiar as it should be. In such cases, children understand very well the word in the text. But, to put it in Piaget's terms, they see no reason to accommodate their thinking to it, because their view cleaves more closely to what the text should say than to what is printed.

A girl read that "raccoons raid garbages" instead of *garages* because in her experience (she lived near wooded hills where there are raccoons) these animals do raid the garbage. True, raccoons enter garages for that is where they find the garbage pail; however, what they are after is garbage. The child transformed one word into another because it made what was said closer to her experience. When we asked the girl why she preferred to read the word as garbage, implying that we knew it was a deliberate act, her immediate answer was, "Raccoons are after food."

If the teacher had concentrated more on the correct reading of the printed word than on what the sentence asserts; if she had corrected the child's reading, regardless of whether she believed that the "misreading" was due to inattention or to an inability to decode correctly; then the teacher would have conveyed to the child that the school did not wish her to apply her intelligence to what she reads. Given such an experience, a child may wonder why she should read; or she may come to think that what reading conveys, if not erroneous, is incomplete information. The correction also gives the child the impression that the school sees her as less intelligent than she is. If she accepts this view, it is damaging to her self-respect. If she rejects it, she may also reject school as unfair. Whatever the case, the result is to turn the child off reading.

In considering basic readers, we encounter another problem. The desire of the writers of primers to use only simple words, and to use them repeatedly, often leads them to use words inappropriately. For example, to the child who knows better, knows how the text should read, being asked to read it as printed makes all reading seem futile. It becomes an exercise in decoding without a purpose, a following of instructions that run counter to the child's intelligence.

In a study of the errors that first graders make in reading, it was found that of 1,943 ascertainable errors, 1,674, or 86 percent, were substitutions that made equal or better sense than the original text. A good example to illustrate this point is to hear a child reading "Spot can *hear* me," when the text is "Spot can *help* me." Spot is a dog, and it makes little sense to a first grader to be told in a story that the animal can be of any help, since it hardly can. But it can indeed not only hear the child, but also respond appropriately—for example, to the child's command.

Next in frequency were omissions, which made up over 6 percent of errors. For instance, the child would skip a word that was part of the text, such as reading "the umbrella" for "the *black* umbrella." Insertions—for example, reading "down *to* the creek" when the text was "down the creek"— were encountered with the same frequency. All other errors accounted for 1.4 percent.[3]

Thus most errors in the reading of the beginner—whether the child substitutes, omits, or inserts a word—either make the sentence more colloquial, less stilted, or have more common sense, or they are the result of important psychological needs.

The texts of the preprimers and primers most widely used to introduce kindergarten and first-grade children to reading consist of words that are supposed to be "easy" for the child who is just learning to read. It is ironic, therefore, that while the intent is to make the task easy for the child by using only words that can readily be sounded out, by repeating them frequently, and by combining only these easy words, reading is actually made harder for the child. The text just doesn't sound like anything anyone would ever say.

Misreading, then, for most children is a compromise between the demands of reality and those of inner pressures. If nothing in a word or a story's content offers a chance for such compromise, then they read a word that does not contain any similarity to the printed one, or they block because they are able neither to form a new word nor to read the word as printed.

In conclusion, I would like to relate an example from my experience with the reading difficulties of severely emotionally disturbed children at the University of Chicago's Orthogenic School. This last example may illustrate the importance of being able to understand that what the child does to reading is commensurate to what the reading—that is, the text—does to the child.

A child had been given up at birth by his unmarried mother. From then until the age of eleven he had been shifted from foster home to foster home, from institution to institution, and he proved completely unmanageable in all settings. Finally, he was placed at the Orthogenic School. After a couple of years' work there, he was able to go to class. He was completely unable to recognize printed words, however, and so was unable to do any academic work.

One day, as his teacher observed the boy's angry reactions when he heard other children in class read stories aloud in which parents were mentioned, she thought the time was ripe for some academic work. She sat down with him as he aimlessly played with some simple toys. She told the boy how angry it must make a child who never had a father or mother to take care of him, to listen to other children reading from books in which mothers and fathers were mentioned as lovely people. She told the boy that this need not be so; that he could do something about these annoying books, such as correct them.

When the boy did not respond, she took one of the readers and proceeded to correct it by blocking out with a heavy black marker the words *mother* and *father* whenever they appeared in the text, which was several times on the first page. The boy remained sullenly uninterested at first, but by the fifth page, he began to look at what she was doing with just the slightest, carefully hidden amusement. Two pages later, the teacher asked him whether he might like to continue to get even with what the book did to him by relating all these nice things about fathers and mothers. He allowed that he might try, and he proceeded to completely blot out the two offending words on the remaining twenty-odd pages of the book, without a single error. When he was done, the teacher asked whether now that he had corrected the book and made it acceptable to him, he might try reading it. This child, who for years had been diagnosed as hopelessly and permanently suffering from alexia, then proceeded to read the book with hardly a mistake.

Our basic readers, with their frequent references to good parents, had indeed done something very powerful to this child: they had made him a nonreader. When he could finally do something equally powerful to the books, by changing them so that they no longer contained any word that aroused unmanageable anger in him, he could read. The boy's overpowering the book was commensurate to how books had overpowered him.

This is a most unusual and extremely rare example of what reading can do to a child, and what a child can do to reading. But a child can perform only with the teacher's help. If teachers would be as ready to help children to do important things to what they read, as they are to impress on children the importance of doing what reading wants them to do, then the story of children who suffer from reading difficulties might be quite different. If we would give children the right primers to learn to read from, and if we viewed their misreading positively rather than critically, children would not be turned off reading. Instead, they would approach it with that enthusiasm for learning to read that as educators we desire to inculcate in them.

Notes

[1] G. Bateson, J. Ruesch, and others, **"Toward a Theory of Schizophrenia,"** *Behavioral Science* 1 (October 1956): 251–64.

[2] Sigmund Freud. *The Psychopathology of Everyday Life* was first published in German in 1901. The first English translation appeared in 1914.

[3] Rose-Marie Weber, **"First Graders' Use of Grammatical Context in Reading,"** in *Basic Studies of Reading,* ed. Harry Levin and Joanna P. Williams (New York: Basic Books, 1970).

For Reluctant Readers

If the children are too old or too sophisticated for fairy tales, where does that leave the teacher who wants to use powerful mythic material? The Bible is out—you can't teach it as literature or as the word of God without incurring someone's wrath. Older kids who can't read well might have trouble with classics, but for them you can use tantalizing news stories, the gossipy Ann Landers column, health columns, reports of consumer frauds, sports columns, reviews of popular TV shows, scripts of TV programs which can be acted out. And Roald Dahl, Agatha Christie, Ira Levin,...

Gloria Chantland

Increased reading rates, better reading comprehension, and improved listening skills—a big order. But that's what my twelfth grade, below-average, high school students needed and that's what Roald Dahl, Daphne du Maurier, Agatha Christie, Sir Arthur Conan Doyle, and I gave them.

I led off with Dahl's short story "Man from the South," which is a great little suspense story that's a natural for oral reading. It's about an old man who bets an American sailor that his lighter won't light ten consecutive times without faltering. The stakes are the old man's Cadillac and the little finger of the sailor's left hand. The old man holds a meat cleaver over the finger, ready to chop, as they count to ten.

I read the story aloud to the class up to the count of nine, calmly closed the book, and told my students if they wanted to know what happened, they would have to read the ending of the story from the ditto sheets on my desk. There was a race to the front of the room and then silence as they read—reading because they wanted to and reading quickly because they wanted to find out what happened to that finger.

I gave them a short quiz based partially on the portion of the story they had listened to and partially on what they had read themselves. Then I followed up with two other Dahl stories, "Lamb to the Slaughter" and "Taste," using the same technique of reading to them and then letting them finish the story. They were hooked. They wanted more. And I decided to give them more. (I had given them short quizzes after each of these stories and noted a gradual improvement.)

This article was originally published as **"The Case of the Reluctant Readers,"** in *Today's Education*, Vol. 65, No. 4 (Nov.–Dec. 1976). Reprinted by permission. Gloria Chantland is a freelance writer and former high school English teacher.

Next I moved to Daphne du Maurier's "No Motive," which opens with these lines: "Mary Farren went into the gun room one morning about half-past eleven and took her husband's revolver and loaded it, then shot herself." Detective Black is called in. He digs for clues and finds them as he wends his way along an interesting path, finally discovering the real reason for Mary Farren's death. (Incidentally, the butler was indirectly responsible, and consequently "the butler did it" became a real in-joke with us for the rest of the semester.)

"No Motive" was longer than the other stories, so I serialized it, allowing time during class for the students to jot down evidence as it was revealed. I provided clue sheets on which they listed the evidence and possible motives for Mary Farren's suicide. At the start of each class, we had fun discussing their "possible motives." Du Maurier would have enjoyed hearing some of them, I'm sure.

When they finished reading the final part of the story, I had them write a report to John Farren based on the evidence they had collected on their sheets. The results showed they were getting better at catching clues. They were really learning to listen.

It was now time, I felt, to introduce them to a couple of major detective fiction writers. First, Agatha Christie. I found a copy of *Witness for the Prosecution* in story form and started reading it aloud in class one day. At frequent intervals, I would stop reading and ask the students to assume that they were jurors and to vote "guilty" or "not guilty." Needless to say, considering the story, most of them changed their votes several times during the reading.

Afterward, I asked them in a short quiz to explain Romaine Heilger's scheme and to pick out the clue that enabled the lawyer to realize that the woman, "bent in figure, with a mass of untidy gray hair," was really Romaine Heilger. Most of them were able to do so. They were learning to listen carefully in order to catch clues and were now going one step further by figuring out how those clues fit together.

The English Department budget did not allow for the purchase of multiple copies of a Christie novel that year (I think I would have picked *The Murder of Roger Ackroyd* if it had), but we did luck out on films. *Murder on the Orient Express*, based on Christie's book *Murder in the Calais Coach*, was playing in a local theater, and I was able to rent *Ten Little Indians* for $25 and run it in two 45-minute sessions at school.

So although we did not tackle a full-length novel, I did at least manage to give the class a fairly good introduction to a major detective-story writer whose name they will remember and possibly look up for further reading after graduation.

Next, I took them to Sir Arthur Conan Doyle. (They had heard of Sherlock Holmes, but not Doyle.) I found a very simplified version of "The Red-Headed League" in play form. The students chose parts and read them aloud in class in about 20 minutes. This introduced them to Sherlock Holmes, his methods, and his sidekick, Watson. Then we dived right into "The Adventure of the Speckled Band." I read the beginning of the story, pointing out elements that it had in common with "The Red-Headed League" and helping them get acquainted with the English setting and characters.

I left them to read on their own at the point where Holmes and Watson ensconce themselves in a dark room at midnight to wait for the appearance of the deadly speckled band. Once again, they read because they wanted to read and they read quickly because they wanted to find out what happened.

But they had to read closely and accurately, too, because when they finished, I asked them to list twenty-five clues that led to the solution of the mystery. They gasped. Twenty-five! I assured them that they had heard me correctly, that twenty-five clues were right there in front of them, and I gave them copies of the story to work with. And they found the clues—by reading closely and carefully.

In fact, they were really getting good at it now. So I decided to give them a Sherlock Holmes mystery that with a little concentration they could actually solve themselves. I chose "The Man with the Twisted Lip." As I read aloud, they listened with pencil in hand and paper in front of them. I had told them to write down and hand in the solution the instant they thought of it. Several students got the solution as soon as the vital clue was given, and almost everyone had it before the end of the story. With that little success under their belts, the class felt quite friendly toward another major detective fiction writer.

Other writers helped further my objectives with these so-called reluctant readers. Ira Levin made his contribution with *Dr. Cook's Garden*, a good suspense play in which a young doctor plays amateur detective and almost becomes one of Dr. Cook's victims. And there was Melville Davisson Post's classic locked-room detective story, "The Doomdorf Mystery." We also read Patrick Quentin's "Puzzle for Poppy," the story of a wealthy, pregnant St. Bernard dog in danger of being done in for her money. The class had fun listing suspects and evidence in an effort to solve the mystery.

There were, of course, other activities interspersed along the way. We used a rate-building program for measuring and improving reading rates, which took about four minutes at the beginning of each class. We made up grid puzzles containing clues from various stories. Once I took them into an unfamiliar room and had them list fifty observations in twenty-five minutes. I also handed them pictures and had them list observations. Then I gave them copies of stories we had already read and asked for observations about characters, thus leading them to think about the people they had read about.

We looked at a copy of *Who Done It? An Encyclopedic Guide to Detective, Mystery, and Suspense Fiction* in the reference section of the library and tried to talk the librarian into putting identifying stickers on the mystery and detective fiction. Some days I loaded a cart with appealing mystery and detective stories and gave the class free reading time during the period. Many kids got hooked on books they started reading in these sessions, and I eventually had to set up an arrangement with the librarian so that I could check out library books from my own room. A few students even tried writing mysteries, and one story about a woman who hated lawnmowers was really pretty good.

Using mystery and detective fiction in the classroom was a new experience for me. The idea has my enthusiastic endorsement, for, with my reluctant readers, it worked very well indeed.

Mistakes Show Progress

When I taught children who were beginning to read, I was very sensitive to the need to support their reading efforts, even by encouraging them to "pretend read" simple twenty-five cent books, the kind then sold in groceries. They would get up, proud and teacherly in front of the class, and proceed to "read" or retell *Snow White and the Seven Dwarfs* or *Little Red Riding Hood.* I wanted to give them confidence and the feeling that being in first grade was "about" learning to read. This was successful.

But, when we got into the primers, I faced a new decision. I didn't really want to slow the children up by correcting every other word. How would they ever learn that "come on" and "come here" were not the same? I usually decided to correct or not to correct depending on the ego of the child I was working with.

However, Dr. Kenneth S. Goodman's research indicates that if the substituting word is similar in meaning, the child is in fact really learning to read. He or she is picking up the cues, predicting what is to come, engaging in the necessary thoughtful guessing. And this will make a good reader in the long run.

It will not make a good proofreader, but the fill-in reader is developing skills that will be beneficial to quick comprehension in the future, and she is being encouraged by the teacher to think of herself as competent. The child's needs and your style of teaching must determine your "druthers" in this decision, but if you choose this way, here is supportive evidence that you are not alone and that the method is "verified" by research.

Edward B. Fiske

A student learning to read comes upon the sentence, "The boy jumped on the horse and rode off." But instead of saying "horse," the student substitutes "pony." Should the teacher correct him?

As far as Kenneth S. Goodman is concerned, the answer is a firm "No."

"The child clearly understands the meaning," Dr. Goodman said in an interview this week. "This is what reading is all about."

To Dr. Goodman, a professor of education at Wayne State University, changes such as substituting one word for another with similar meaning are not mistakes at all but perfectly healthy "miscues."

For more than a decade the 47-year-old professor has made "miscues" the focus of his research, and out of it has come a new theory of how children learn to read and new teaching methods that are beginning to make themselves felt in classrooms across the country.

HOW CONCEPT FORMED

The concept of "miscues" developed when Dr. Goodman, interested in figuring out how reading skills develop, began asking beginning readers to read unfamiliar materials aloud.

He noticed that many of the "mistakes" made by the young subjects were quite logical and reflective of sophisticated reasoning. "When a first-grader substitutes 'the' for 'a' but not for other words, you realize there is a cause," he explained. He decided that such slips could be used as a "window" to the reading process, and he coined the term "miscue" to describe them.

On the basis of his observations, Dr. Goodman . . . began challenging a number of generally accepted notions about how children learn to read.

First, he rejects the assumption that reading is a process of looking at words and sentences and then deciding afterwards what they mean. Instead, he argues, reading is a process of taking in data, making informed "predictions" about what will follow, checking these predictions as the reader goes along and, if necessary, making revisions.

Thus, in the example above, the student "predicted" on the basis of the words "jumped on" that "pony" might follow and, when he got to the verb "rode" saw no reason to change it.

"There is no way to process verbal data fast enough without making 'predictions,' " said Dr. Goodman. "The difference between a good reader and a poor one is that the good reader makes good predictions and checks them quickly."

This article was originally published as **"About Education: Approach to Reading Rethought,"** in *The New York Times*, Nov. 9, 1975. © 1975 by The New York Times Company. Reprinted by permission.

READING DEFINED

Secondly, Dr. Goodman argues that reading is not the passive receipt of meaning from the printed page but rather an active process in which the reader actually constructs meaning. He thus rejects the traditional distinction that most teachers make between "decoding"—or learning to translate letters into sounds—and the subsequent gaining of meaning from written words.

"The two processes are inseparable and dependent on the fundamental search for meaning," he declared.

Finally, he argues that children can learn to read in exactly the same way they learned to talk. "By the time they are ready to read, children have already rediscovered for themselves the rules of grammar," he said. "After all, 95 percent of speech is arranging words in ways you haven't heard before. And kids can do this, so why not teach reading the same way?"

For teaching, the consequences of Dr. Goodman's ideas are far-reaching. The basic rule, he said, is to begin with what the child has already taught himself and to continue to use materials that have "meaning" for his or her world.

"Use materials that interest them," he said. "Write instructions for them on blackboards. Get them to write short notes to each other or to read stories they have dictated themselves."

Dr. Goodman cited the case of a 3-year-old who, while supposedly not able to read, could read the word "Bonneville" on a hub cap. "When he was shown 'Buick' he wasn't fooled," he said. "Clearly it was something important to his world."

A second principle, according to Dr. Goodman, is to avoid correcting mistakes—such as the substitution of "pony" for "horse"—that do not interfere with the conveying of meaning.

"The usual concern for technical accuracy gets teachers up-tight, interferes with the development of good predicting skills and discourages risk-taking," he said. "Accuracy will come with practice. It is the result of good reading, not the cause of it."

On the other hand, in the above example, Dr. Goodman said he would question a child who substituted "house" for "horse." "I'd say that doesn't make sense," he declared.

TIPS FOR PARENTS

The professor also has some tips for parents in helping their children to learn to read. The first is to encourage them to read everything they can—starting with cereal boxes and peanut-butter jars. Another is to avoid pushing precocious children too fast.

"A lot of parents like to show off their children by having them read adult material," he said. But kids can become very good at reading stuff that they don't understand. When you do this, you suggest that reading is an end in itself, not a means of communication."

Children Teach Children

When I was teaching reading, I thought I had invented the method of children teaching other children. I hadn't. It was old hat. What is startling about the program, thoroughly written up by Alan Gartner and Frank Reisman in *Children Teach Children*, is that it is the kids who teach who gain the most. In the program reported here those tutored didn't change much. In other studies of this method there was considerable improvement. Is this kind of teaching a threat to teachers? Not at all. Who should monitor the project and instruct the tutors if not the teachers?

Judith Cummings

The classic tutoring technique has traditionally called upon the brightest students to help the slowest. But a reading program in the Bronx has turned this concept around to use youngsters who are at least a year and a half behind in reading to tutor younger children, and both are said to be making gains.

It is a direct application of the theory that the best way to learn something is to teach it, and at the same time to help poor-achieving pupils improve their attitudes toward themselves and school work by giving them something important to do.

"It helps me read better and understand," Milta Rivera, a sixth-grader at Public School 25, said one recent morning as she guided Roberto Martinez through a lesson. "I have to go over it before I can help him."

Roberto, a third-grader, chimed in his own reason for Milta's diligence. "She knows that she's working with me," he said proudly jerking his thumb toward his chest.

"THE BILINGUAL SCHOOL"

P.S. 25 on East 149th Street, also known as "the Bilingual School," is one of seven schools in Community School District 7 that offer the program, and other principals are asking for it in their schools, according to the district superintendent, Carman Rodriguez. Four hundred pupils are involved in the program, called Youth Tutoring Youth, now in its second year.

"We consider the program rather exceptional, especially for the tutors," said Dr. Joseph A. Bosco, a curriculum specialist at the State University at Albany, who did an evaluation of first-year results for the district.

That evaluation indicated that the tutors achieved reading gains surpassing those of the second, third, and fourth graders receiving tutoring. Adjusting for the progress the students could be expected to make without the program, the evaluation indicated results ranging from virtually no change for third graders being tutored, to a gain of more than two years for sixth-grader tutors. The sixth graders, according to the data, were raised to their grade level.

The tutors' larger gains were anticipated when the program was designed, according to Howard Adelman, a consultant at the Bank Street College of Education here who helped create the program. He said the plan was being used on a smaller scale in Stamford, Hartford, Albany, and in Districts 3 and 10 in the city.

"The tutors gain more because there is such a tremendous impact on their self-image," in addition to the learning-reinforcement they experience, he said.

BASIS OF SELECTION

And the director of the program for District 7, David Salembier, added that the tutors were deliberately selected because they had other school problems, such as disruptive behavior or poor attendance.

At P. S. 25, young Milta Rivera and Andres Roman worked quietly with a small group in a corner while the classroom teacher, Fran Wiesenfelder, took the rest of the class through its regular reading lesson. Using sight-reading cards reinforced with phonograph recordings, the youngsters drilled their small charges through the day's lesson, which is worked out in advance by a specially trained paraprofessional.

Luis Cartagena, the principal there, said parents told him they like the program because it helped children who are having academic difficulties to feel an active and important part of the school community. He encourages this by holding a recognition ceremony for tutors at the end of each semester.

"We had one boy who got so that he didn't want to do anything but tutor. I had to have a talk with him," he said with a smile.

Basics in a Bean-Bag Chair

Not all the programs that are emphasizing "basics" disregard comfort and the pleasurable aspects of learning. In Adams County, Colorado, students in one of the most successful reading programs are found "lounging on a king-sized bean-bag chair near a sunny window that accommodates assorted hanging plants."

Judith Wagner

Snuggled among large, fluffy pillows in an old bathtub that's been lined with fur and set in the school library, a ten-year-old boy is absorbed in a mystery book. In a classroom down the hall a girl is writing and illustrating her own story in a telephone booth which has been transformed into a whimsical "alone" place. Nearby, another child and his teacher are reading to each other while lounging on a king-sized bean-bag chair near a sunny window that accommodates assorted hanging plants. Still another child carefully prints the name of the book she has just read on a circle cut from construction paper. "I'm going to feed it to the 'bookie monster,'" she explains, pointing to a fuzzy blue creature which bears more than a passing resemblance to the "cookie monster" of *Sesame Street* fame.

Quite different from the sitting-in-a-row, rote and drill reading of yesteryear, these are but a few of the practices brought on by a system-wide commitment to reading improvement in School District No. 12, Adams County, near Denver, Colorado. They're part of one of the most successful of the district's several efforts, a program called Pupils Advancing in Learning—appropriately nicknamed PAL. The project, funded under Title I of the Elementary and Secondary Education Act, aims at improving reading skills, attitude, and self-concept and at involving parents in their children's learning. . . .

Carolyn Tennant, special programs consultant and director of PAL, remarks on the need for cooperation and sharing of ideas on which the program depends. "No one is trying to corner the market on helping children improve their reading skills, and no one is suggesting that any one program or approach is the end and all of it," she says. "We seem to have avoided those apprehensions that sometimes build barriers between 'regular' teachers and the staff of a special project."

Mrs. Tennant attributes the cooperative spirit that pervades the program and has become a sort of hallmark of its participants to frequent inservice training for teachers and parents, scheduled and impromptu idea exchanges, inclusion of "regular" teachers in the PAL pupil evaluation process, and an open-door policy that amounts to a standing invitation to classroom teachers, administrators, and parents to observe the program in operation.

PAL's ultimate goals are twofold: to develop reading skills and to improve student attitudes toward self and school. Mrs. Tennant believes that these goals are not discrete, but rather, that they are functions of each other. "As students feel more capable in their reading skills," she says, "their attitudes about themselves and their surroundings improve. When their attitudes and self-concepts improve, they become capable of further success in their learning experiences. The effect is helical—full circle and always up. It's a marvelous thing to see happening with youngsters."

This article was originally published as **"Where PAL Means Better Reading,"** in *American Education* 12:7 (Aug.–Sept. 1976). Reprinted by permission. Judith Wagner is a freelance writer in Toledo, Ohio.

To start the process and keep it going, PAL looks to bring about two specific improvements: (1) to reduce by a minimum of 50 percent for each nine months of program participation the discrepancy between the grade-level equivalency a student scores on the Comprehensive Test of Basic Skills and the grade level at which he or she is expected to perform; (2) to help a student attain a minimum of 80 percent mastery of the objectives that are set for him or her on an individual basis.

Furthermore, PAL has established a goal for attitudinal improvement that requires at least 80 percent of its participants to show a more positive attitude toward themselves and their school work by the end of each year. To gauge PAL's effectiveness in this often nebulous and hard-to-measure area, the school district developed a "comprehensive attitudinal survey" which it administers at the beginning and end of the school year. The results of each testing are then compared.

So far, PAL has achieved remarkable success in meeting its objectives. In fact, each year since the program's inception in 1965, the average PAL student has gained 1.3 years in reading and comprehension for every nine months of participation. Perhaps even more telling are the day-to-day impressions one gets from working closely with the program: According to Mrs. Tennant and school superintendent George Bailey, such information barometers as the record of parent involvement, the consistently high level of student interest, and the unfailing support of the community persuasively indicate the program's overall effectiveness.

Students in Title I schools who fail to attain the 50th percentile for their grade level in reading and language arts and those who fall below grade level in reading according to specific district-wide criteria are eligible to participate in the PAL project. Students are recommended to the program by their teachers, counselors, or parents; in some cases students have referred themselves to the notice of program personnel on the basis of reading difficulties or poor attitudinal adjustment. Those with the greatest needs are served first, the emphasis in recent years shifting toward early intervention to determine and correct problems during the first few years of school.

Typically, students spend about 30-45 minutes a day in the PAL program, where there is a teacher-pupil ratio of one to five in elementary schools and one to ten in high schools. Trained parent volunteers often assist teachers with tasks that help build and develop a student's specific skills, thus providing maximum individual attention.

In many cases, the program is housed in temporary buildings or trailers on school ground. However, according to Polly Meader, parent coordinator and chairman of the District Parent Advisory Council (PAC), any trace of a stigma that might have been attached to the program in its early years because of its association with welfare funding, its focus on students with problems, or its setting away from the main building has completely evaporated. "The classrooms may be trailers on the outside," says Mrs. Meader, "but on the inside they are as appealing as any classroom you'll ever want to see. We don't have the problem of youngsters wanting to get *out* of the program, but we do have the problem of too many wanting to get *in*—even the ones who don't have reading or attitudinal difficulties."

PAL is carefully explained to parents before children enter the program. "We let them know that the program is *theirs*, not the school system's," Mrs. Meader says. "We answer all their questions and try to change their focus from 'What have I done wrong to cause my child to have these problems?' to 'What can I do now to bring about improvements?'"

Although PAL is designed to be supportive, its ultimate goal is to encourage independent learning. Cooperation and coordination between PAL teachers and classroom teachers are vital factors in phasing children in and out of the program comfortably. "Although it is a compliment to PAL teachers that children want to continue in the program even after their goals are attained, we try to build upon their successes so that they will gradually feel more competent and capable of achievement away from the PAL atmosphere," Mrs. Meader says.

What happens in a PAL classroom depends as much on the age and skill levels of the students as on the style of the individual teacher. There are certain "givens"—the requirement that teachers send home a majority of positive progress reports for each child, for example. This means that the teacher must plan activities that are sufficiently difficult to challenge a child, though not so difficult that he or she cannot solve them or enjoy a successful experience.

During inservice teacher training, a recurring theme of the PAL approach is flexibility in teaching methods and classroom management procedures. Teachers are encouraged to share with other teachers the details of what works best for them. Some teachers have found games to be effective tools for developing reading skills. Others have turned toward art or music to accomplish their ends, while still others have discovered that movement activities can lead to improvements in language skills. However, Mrs. Tennant insists that all such activities relate to sound learning principles. "Fun and games can be just that, or they can be effective teaching techniques. We never use these techniques solely to make children like us better or to make them enjoy the PAL program more. There must always be a learning objective. We believe that we can make the children feel happy to be with us through using sound educational methods and materials and without resorting to a bag of tricks."

Teachers plan activities like field trips, photography, and drama to give the students a wide range of experiences that go a long way toward encouraging self-awareness and self-expression, and helping students open up toward their teachers and toward one another. Teachers avoid using grades, comparisons, punishment, and competition as motivators, drawing instead upon individual incentives and the promise of success.

Motivation at the upper grade levels can be a more difficult proposition, owing to the fact that many students have already developed a considerable negativism about themselves, their failures, and their schools, which they often regard as hostile environments. A student whom we'll call Danny is a case in point.

Almost from the beginning, Danny had been a classic example of the turned-off, tuned-out student. His behavior patterns varied from sullen and uncommunicative to aggressive and disruptive. His absentee rate was high, and he was a potential dropout. Danny was admitted into the PAL program without a trace of enthusiasm on his part. Last fall, however, he began showing up regularly for his PAL class only, usually skipping school for the rest of the day. This conveyed a message to the PAL people. "It wasn't much, but it was something to start with," Mrs. Tennant recalls. They encouraged Danny, who became more and more involved in PAL activities and showed steady progress in reading. He made it clear, though, that he had no intention of going back to regular classrooms—ever.

The classroom teachers and the PAL staff decided that the best way to handle the situation was to meet Danny on his own terms. They never mentioned regular class attendance. Instead, every now and then, his history teacher, or his science teacher, or his math teacher would drop by the PAL room for a chat with Danny. They would mention assignments their classes were working on and offer him some of the materials which they "just happened to have with them."

In time Danny began to show up for his regular classes—sporadically at first and then on schedule. Lately his attitudes and behavior have shown remarkable improvement and his work is consistently better.

Danny's situation might have been handled differently in other schools and other approaches might have been equally effective, the PAL staff feels. But it also is convinced that the cooperation between the PAL staff and Danny's regular classroom teachers was an essential ingredient in helping him before it was too late.

Another ace in the hole of the PAL project is a special resource teacher who also acts as a community worker. This teacher counsels students individually, visits homes, and acts as a liaison with various service agencies within the community. The importance of this teacher is illustrated by a story about another boy we'll call Steven.

According to his parents, Steven did not utter his first sentence until he was five years old. "We were frantic," his mother says. "We went the whole route—hospitals, doctors, speech therapists, psychologists—nothing worked. We felt helpless." After Steven got off to a rocky start in a kindergarten class in another school district, the family moved to Adams County. When he went to first grade, it appeared that he was doomed before he even got started. He would not talk in school, and he was soon far behind in his work.

With difficulties so obvious, it was not long before Steven was recommended for the PAL project. There the resource teacher opened the lines of communication between the school and various specialists who were working with the boy. Equally important, his parents became involved in PAL's parent advisory council, his mother volunteering to work in the project classroom once a week. She says that the teacher was emphasizing self-concept and self-awareness in every reading and language experience.

Steven is now in the fourth grade. "Things didn't happen overnight," his mother says. "But the difference between then and now is like night and day. He is working up to grade level and even beyond in some areas. And talk! My goodness, he's a participator par excellence." Occasionally the need for a basic skill, which Steven missed early on, will crop up, so he is phased into the PAL reading lab until he learns the skill and catches up.

Like Steven's parents, Mrs. Meader feels that the PAL staffers' infectious enthusiasm, positive outlook, and eagerness to help are the program's power generators. "I was so intimidated by the thought of dealing with teachers and administrators before my involvement with PAL," she says. "But here school people do not see parental involvement as a threat to their professional integrity. They think that parents have a right to know what is going on in their child's education."

Each PAL class has a parent advisory council made up of anyone who is interested. There are also districtwide councils. Listed among the objectives of the councils are training parent leaders and bridging the communication gap between parents and schools. Members are informed of all aspects of the program and trained to serve as advisors in every sense of the word. "They don't ask us only to provide milk and cookies or to drive in car pools," Mrs. Meader says. "They discuss curriculum and instruction with us. They ask for our ideas about the program and for our help in making items like educational games, bulletin boards, and puppets."

One unanticipated but decidedly welcome side effect of all this effort has been a change in the councils' composition which, according to Mrs. Meader, once seemed to be about 99 percent mothers. "But times are changing," she says. "Now we have a good many dads who really participate, and there even are some grandparents." One grandfather has constructed a folding puppet theater for his grandson's PAL classroom, and another faithfully brings gourmet snacks to serve at parent meetings.

Supporters of PAL are nothing if they are not stanch in the face of adversity: At a recent county fair sponsored by the district councils, more than 400 people showed up in spite of horrendous weather conditions. The purpose of the fair was to raise money for materials for a PAL parent resource room. The room, centrally located in the district, is open regularly to parents and contains books, games, puzzles, puppets, records, and other materials which they may borrow for home use, thus keeping children's interest finely honed.

At first, parents come just to borrow materials, but sooner or later—to everyone's benefit—they wind up in informal discussion groups with other parents or teachers," says Mrs. Meader.

Besides being a catalyst for stimulating understanding, the resource room has become a symbol of the parents' contribution to the success of the program. "Just having the room shows us that the school respects our position as our children's first and most important resource," Mrs. Meader adds.

Such a broad-based program is not easy to keep under administrative rein, but the efficient Mrs. Tennant is up to the task. A self-described stickler for administrative details, she puts her personal credo to work: Leave nothing to chance. Noting that many an otherwise good program has flopped because of poor organization, she and the PAL staff have prepared comprehensive booklets on instruction, program management, staff development, and parent involvement. These booklets serve as guidelines for a systematic approach to project management and implementation. For example, the one on parent involvement explains the importance of keeping the public informed and sets forth a step-by-step procedure for spreading the news about parent programs and projects. As the booklet tersely observes, "The best activity or program in the world might be planned, but if the word does not get out . . ., no one will show up."

PAL now operates on a $160,000 grant under Title I of the Elementary and Secondary Education Act, with the school district providing some classroom space and other resources. But next year, operating as one of 16 national demonstration sites of the National Institute of Education, the PAL program will focus upon all Adams County students in grades 1, 2, and 3 who are in the lower quartile on performance evaluations in reading skills. What this means to PAL is that the program will be able to sidestep usual Title I economic criteria and test its effectiveness in all of the elementary schools in the district. Mrs. Tennant believes that this kind of flexibility and cooperation within the Federal funding structure maximizes the use of both financial and human resources and leads to the widest application of educational concepts.

In a sense it's a way of getting out the word, thus assuring that those who need PAL will at least have heard about it and having heard, will show up.

To Help Them Write, Right

It's hard enough, even with complaints in hand, to convince grammar enthusiasts that strict grammatical analysis is not only boring but dysfunctional. Here is an argument which can be used to justify your approach, which I hope will be in the direction of more time for kids to talk in class, increased writing time, both "creative" and "expository," and selective feedback on writing mistakes corrected by students—in class!

Beatrice Gross

As early as 1913 Thomas H. Briggs attempted to discover whether grammar instruction was useful in helping kids to correct language errors. Working with two matched groups at Horace Mann Elementary School (Teachers College, Columbia University) he instructed one group 1 ½ hours a week for three months in formal grammar while a coteacher instructed another group in composition and language. He then repeated the experiment with 295 children in six schools. His conclusion: ". . . no improvement that may be attributed to . . . training in formal grammar." Those trained in formal grammar couldn't recognize or correct errors any better than those not so trained.

Again in 1917 Julius Boraas found, in studying final grades of students in two city high schools in Minnesota, that no correlation could be found between grammar study and the ability to write a composition, capitalize and punctuate, or correct errors in sentences and paragraphs.

A study by William Asker in 1923 concluded that formal grammar has only a "negligible" influence upon ability to write and ability to judge the grammatical correctness of a sentence.

The studies go on and on, and are all summarized in *Four Problems in Teaching English, A Critique of Research* by J. Stephen Sherwin and published under the egis of the National Council of Teachers of English Committee on Publications. The findings regarding writing proficiency are that mere writing is not effective, grammar study is not effective, linguistic study is not effective—none of these will make a difference unless combined with motivation, selective criticism, discussion, practical exercises, and revision of the children's written work.

The pressure to mark hundreds of papers a week is one that shouldn't be added to the others you already feel. Also, it won't do much good and it might be harmful to correct everything in every paper you look at. Kids can't take it all in. What really helps is selective criticism based on frequently made errors. Pick out one or two repeated mistakes that the student needs to correct. Work with the student individually if possible. In addition spend approximately 100 minutes a week on group lessons which include practical explanations, class practice, discussion, revision, and time to rewrite.

Edward Fiske in a *New York Times* report on the work of Professor Van Nostrand supports these findings. The Brown University professor working with freshmen has "one of the most successful [programs] thus far, which depends on breaking the writing process down into 20 components; organization, selecting evidence, building the logic of an argument, etc., and teaching one component at a time." His method, described in a book available through Brown University, may give you some idea of how you can use his approach with your students. He too ignores grammar and concentrates on practice.

Welcome Back Writing

When critics complain about the relaxation of standards and suggest that we return to the clearly articulated teacher demands that are authoritarian and unbending, they forget that many children have been faced by these inflexible demands

throughout their years in school and, having no way to meet them, fail and fail again. Bety Giles considers "repairing past damages to the student's self-concept and having a student take some responsibility for his or her learning as important as practicing reading and writing skills...

"The games they are playing are for survival, not amusement... Each of the children in this remedial reading program is struggling with a fatal outlook that comes from a large collection of red marks on papers and failing grades, compounded by a full bag of defense mechanisms to hide the scars."

Gertrue E. Mitchell

They come on tough and lovable like Kotter's TV sweathogs, and the resemblance is no accident. These six ninth-graders identify with Horshack's laugh, Barberino's cool, Kotter's quips, and Epstein's and Washington's alternating hardness and muddle-headedness.

Listen as they come into the open classroom for the language lab, their final class of the day at Rockville (Maryland) Senior High. Three boys and three girls show up—the survivors of what began as a class of 12. Richard, the coolest, moans: "When I think I could be outside instead of here..."

"Aw, you and your social life," sneers his buddy Lewis.

Their teacher, Bety Giles, deposits a game at the boys' table and another at the girls' table. "I don't feel like no game," protests Freddie.

"He's afraid he'll lose," quips Richard.

The horseplay subsides as Mrs. Giles explains how to play the game spread on the table. "You pick up one of the cards," she says, "and decide if the words on it are a sentence or a fragment. If the answer card says you're correct, roll the dice and move your marker accordingly."

As she walks over to the girls, all three boys scrimmage for the answer card. Richard grabs it. Freddie goes first, reading the words on the card he's picked up: "the horse jumped over the fence" and then saying, "That ain't no sentence."

"You're wrong!" yells Richard, looking up from the answer card. The heated exchange that ensues draws Mrs. Giles back to the boys.

"Ain't I right, Mrs. Giles?" Freddie insists. He shows her the card. "See, no big letter at the beginning and no dot at the end." Two of the girls giggle.

Mrs. Giles looks at the card. "But, Freddie if those things were on the card, you'd know right away it was a sentence. They've been left out on purpose."

He is still angry. "But you didn't tell us that."

"I'm sorry," she says, "I should have." The anger drains from Freddie's face and the boys go back to the game.

This article is from *American Education*, Vol. 12, No. 8 (Oct. 1976). Reprinted by permission. Gertrue Mitchell is Associate Editor of *American Education*.

These ninth graders were assigned to the lab because they are reading and writing below sixth-grade level. Don't be misled by the surface bantering; the games they are playing are for survival, not amusement. Each of them entered public school as a somewhere-around-average pupil, but someplace along the way, each failed to learn certain language skills. In every instance the loss was critical. Even now, with a chance to catch up on the skills, they nonetheless face formidable odds. After eight years in school, these youngsters still struggle to tell a sentence from a fragment, to read and follow directions, to separate important from unimportant details, to catch the gist of a point, or to use the mechanics of spelling and punctuation. Now in the ninth grade, they have the fatal outlook that comes from a large collection of red marks on papers and failing grades, compounded by a full bag of defense mechanisms to hide the scars.

Yet, despite the poor odds, beneath the facades and banter something is happening in the remedial lab. No on-the-spot miracles, mind you, just plodding progress, both words spelled with a lower case "p." This something can be seen in Freddie's recognition that a sentence begins with a capital letter and ends with a period, though he misapplied the knowledge in the game. It is also evident in his willingness to accept Mrs. Giles' apology.

This is progress within a group of youngsters who use every defense they can muster—temper tantrums, fighting flareups, impulsive insults, brooding bouts, armored apathy—to cover up the feelings of chaos and hopelessness. "Just getting them to write a sentence," says Mrs. Giles, "is a real chore. It has taken months to bring them to a point where they don't mind working on phrasing an idea out loud, even as a class; but they'll do anything to escape writing one word on a page. Oh, they're clever and lovable about it. But they don't need love; they need skills. For that reason I have to refuse to be their crutch and instead keep them at their tasks, no matter how they resist."

The Rockville Senior High remedial lab is a forerunner of a concerted effort throughout Montgomery County, Maryland, to ensure that none of its public school graduates goes out into the world without having learned the basic skills of reading and writing. In math a similar though separate program began this September. The lab is also the high school's immediate response to the State of Maryland's pronouncement in November of 1974 that all ninth-grade students having marked deficiencies in reading, writing, and math must receive help by the end of that grade.

The State recommendation lends some official weight to attempts by Rockville's English teachers to remedy a situation they have been fighting for several years. Fortunately, the county already has a fully structured English writing curriculum, begun in 1960 and overhauled in 1968, which emphasizes the basic skills of grammar, rhetoric, and composition and which all students must take from the seventh grade through the twelfth. While the foundation is there, however, students have not always elected to use it. Like countless other school systems around the country, Montgomery County schools went through a phase in the late 1960s and early 1970s when secondary students could select many of their courses. Also, in the name of flexibility, a plethora of new titles blossomed forth in school course offerings. Although no one intended it, the liberalization enabled a student to go through high school without taking the tougher, more basic courses. The situation was particularly attractive to college-bound students who were under pressure to make high grades.

At Rockville all that began to change when Jackie Bylsma came on board to chair the English department, bringing with her a concern for the average and less able students' skills in grammar, rhetoric, and composition—a concern also shared by Bety Giles and Shirley McCann, teacher specialist in reading. Nor was the viewpoint confined to the English department. "The school community itself—teachers, parents, administrators, resource people—is coming to realize," says Bety Giles, "that reading and writing must be taught, at the very least reinforced, throughout high school. Previously both were thought of as 'elementary school subjects.'"

While the State recommendation was welcomed at Rockville, its immediate implementation posed a problem. Jackie Bylsma smiles when she looks back on the summer of 1975. "Even though the recommendation was made in November of 1974, it didn't filter down to the school level until the following June, leaving us only the summer in which to chart a beginning. The county was preparing a proficiency test for use early in 1976, but there was the problem of identifying ninth graders with marked deficiencies for the upcoming fall. And we felt that we should begin immediately."

An ad hoc committee of resource teachers attending the regular county summer curriculum and instruction workshop took up the problem. Working closely with the county board of education, the ad hoc committee drafted a checklist of 12 basic writing skills:

Alphabet (recognizing capital and small letters, alphabetizing);

Handwriting (practicing cursive letters, copying material accurately);

Numbers (using cardinal and ordinal numbers in series, translating information like time into numerals);

Abbreviations (forming and punctuating standard abbreviations);

Survival Forms (filling out forms, reading a road map, writing a check);

Fragments and Sentences (recognizing and writing a sentence, using fragments to complete forms);

Categorizing (classifying a list, distinguishing between relevant and irrelevant details, outlining);

Summarizing (taking notes, interpreting charts and graphs, paraphrasing a paragraph, summing up a point);

Mechanics and Usage (capitalizing, spelling, punctuating, using correct grammar);

Paragraphing (writing one based on a topic sentence, developing sequential sentences, using language at different levels, proofreading);

Letters and Notes (writing letters of complaint or for informational, social, and business purposes);

Daily Communication (preparing composition notes, asking clear questions, describing an incident, defining, writing down directions, explaining a process, keeping a daily record, supporting an opinion).

The ad hoc committee next designed a packet of activities for each skill. For example, under summarizing, the student must answer a newspaper want ad about a job, including a written summary of his or her background and work experience. The packets were sent to county schools having ninth-grade students.

At Rockville, Bety Giles, Shirley McCann, and Jackie Bylsma took the packets and began a task that wouldn't be finished until the middle of the 1975–76 school year: conversion of the ad hoc committee's paper-and-pencil activities into actual classroom exercises, building in components that drew upon small group work and peer tutoring. Mrs. Giles also went through every incoming ninth grader's record, noting individual strengths and weaknesses in the twelve skills.

Rockville principal Joseph B. Good decided to begin with a small pilot remedial lab for the most difficult cases, that is, students having severe deficiencies in two or more of the twelve skills. The students would receive one-half a credit for the lab; at the same time, they would also take the required ninth-grade English course.

During the first half of the 1975–76 school year, the regular ninth-grade English teachers analyzed the reading and writing skills of their students. Also at this point, the lines of communication were plugged in to parents, other English teachers, who were asked to contribute to the identification process, and—most of all—students. Those in ninth-grade English classes took diagnostic tests developed by the English department. Students who fell below a pre-established level of mastery became the nucleus for the pilot lab. Out of 300 ninth graders at Rockville High, twelve were identified as having the most need for catching up on skills. Their parents were then advised by counselors that a new course in developmental reading and writing would be offered the next half of the school year to help their children.

On the first day the twelve students reported to the lab's self-contained classroom, the staff received a shock. Pandemonium let loose in the classroom. Confusion with a capital "C." "It took us by surprise," confesses Mrs. Giles, who—even with the help of student resource teachers—couldn't handle the chaos. "We had reasoned that it was better to have a self-contained room where the students wouldn't feel threatened. We were wrong."

Once the lab moved into an area resembling an open classroom cluster, the noise level came down and tensions eased somewhat. "That seemed to be what the class wanted: to be seen like everyone else," reflects Mrs. Giles. Though they still occasionally explode or have bad moods, she says, the switch in locale has brought some order.

From the outset of the experiment, the students resisted work. By some skillful blend of patience and push, Mrs. Giles has worn down their resistance by deftly varying tasks and strategies and by using specially tailored activities which she and countless resource people—from teachers to students in other classes—have put together. She gauges about five to ten minutes for a task or exercise, no more. All the tasks, however, are tied to three basic objectives: practicing reading and writing skills, repairing past damage to the student's self-concept, and having a student take some responsibility for his or her learning. Unlike a regular English class of twenty-five to thirty students, the lab's smaller size is conducive to the kinds of small group or individualized projects necessary to treat serious problems. A student who is quiet and withdrawn, for instance, may be teamed with another who is aggressive, each taking a turn at tutoring his or her partner. The student who relies too much on merely regurgitating the material back to the teacher is firmly prodded into doing some original thinking.

Mrs. Giles' perceptions have deepened through twenty-four years of teaching. In the remedial lab she sees enough case history material to fill a psychology book. She knows, for example, that one of her students insists on being offensive so he can be hurt. By being hurt, he receives the attention he craves. Another student, beset with serious outside problems, missed a whole month of classes. Now back in the lab, the student talks about quitting. Mrs. Giles, after reassuring the student that "catching up is the path to follow, not giving up," soon has the person working on two makeup exercises. It's no exaggeration to say that the twelve students have confronted Mrs. Giles with a dozen different sets of problems, all the woes that beset troubled students from the lethargic who react to practically nothing to the hyperactive ones with short attention spans, easily distracted by surface shenanigans.

But one problem Mrs. Giles must face anew each day is how to get the group beyond the apathy that comes with being far behind in school. "No one in the lab wants to read," she says. "Instead, the students want to be fed directions and have everything neatly worked out for them. But the student resource teachers and I refuse to do this. We put it squarely on their shoulders to read directions, figure out questions, and go over incorrect answers on exercises until they understand."

In Shirley McCann's words, "Not enough responsibility has been put on the student in the past. In the lab the student can no longer hide behind a passive facade."

"They also dodge writing as though it were a plague," says Mrs. Giles. "If I insist, they'll write down one or two sentences—or what they think are sentences—and then put down the pencil, saying, 'I don't care' because they've never been any good at writing, so why try?"

But they write compositions in their regular English classes, and there's a reason behind the school's requirement that students in the remedial lab must continue with their regular ninth-grade English course. "Through the lab we are trying to catch them up on missed skills," says Jackie Bylsma, "but we think it's just as important that they not be removed from the regular curriculum."

But how does a remedial student fare in the regular English composition class if he or she is unable to put together a complete sentence, let alone turn out a full-blown composition? The process, the teachers feel, is painful but necessary. Lewis, Richard's buddy in the remedial lab, is in Mrs. Bylsma's English class. In Mrs. Giles' lab, he is one of six students; in the regular English class, he is one among twenty-five students, some of whom are ahead of him in skills. Yet, there is the distinct impression that Lewis is not lost in the numbers. Observes Mrs. Bylsma, "He is a very sensitive person who can't verbalize his feelings at all. Even if he's turned in something good and I compliment him, he can't accept the compliment in the real and sincere sense it is intended. If he's having problems, he can't explain them because everything he feels about school and classes is wrapped up tightly inside him, and the years have taught him to keep it there. With his peers, Lewis has no difficulty in expressing himself, and they clearly warm to his easygoing socialbility."

Mrs. Bylsma pulls out a sheet from Lewis' composition folder. "Here's the planning sheet for a composition Lewis wrote about the summer." In the space after "theme sentence," Lewis had scrawled: "Summer is fun because during the summer you don't have no school, any teachers and books."

"Obvious grammatical errors aside for the moment," says Mrs. Bylsma, "the theme sentence represents a breakthrough for Lewis. Writing, after all, is a tool for thinking. For Lewis, writing a composition—just a short one of three or four sentences—is difficult because he must try to think centrally. He'd much rather remain scattered and diffuse in his thinking, the very qualities that draw other youngsters to him. Basically, he's a bright person who has become a poor student. In the theme sentence about summer, however, Lewis actually achieved unity in his thinking, though not in his grammar."

For Bety Giles, it is frustrating that Lewis labors over grammar in the lab and then fails to transfer what he has learned to the regular composition class. But, given problems and even setbacks, she is not about to give up. This fall she has a new lab of ninth graders who need to catch up on basic skills. But those original six are indelibly marked in her mind, and she is still working with them. "They have reached a very critical point," Mrs. Giles says, "where they are opening up to learning." A year ago they could have been labeled "losers." But now the label might not stick. Admittedly, their road ahead is rough and only three years remain in which to travel it. But then, the six students have enough going for them that, by the time they graduate into a world where opportunity rests in part with written words, they just might make it.

All Spooko and Quiet

Now that we've decided to demand more writing from students, what shall we have them write? Peter Dixon wants us to look for life experiences that can be turned into reasons to write vividly. We don't disagree, but teachers under pressure often don't have the time that British open-classroom teachers do. How can we guarantee that we get writing from the gut?

We can push back the desks, dim the lights, and take the kids on imaginary trips. A little book by Richard De Mille, called *Put Your Mother on the Ceiling* does this (Viking Press, 1973). You may have been to encounter groups and taken similar imaginary trips: "You are walking up a mountain, there are brambles and thorns grabbing at your clothes. Suddenly you see a clearing and you move towards it, and there in the mountain clearing is a brook and an opening in the mountain. You move a large boulder away from the opening and find yourself inside. What do you see as your eyes get accustomed to the strange light in there? . . ."

A group of students under the direction of Roz Fiedel, a fine teacher and director of the Fiedel School on Long Island, uses the medium of dance and movement to take students on imaginative trips. Roz asks students to get on the floor and imagine they are in a dark, dark tunnel. "You are in that tunnel and it is hard for you to move. Try struggling out of the tunnel, try . . ." The students wiggle, their bodies pulled close, and when they come out of their mind tunnels, they write moving, frightening poem-stories of the vivid experiences they had just minutes before.

Here is Peter Dixon writing about other poetic and fictional "turn-ons."

Peter Dixon

• • •

Unfortunately, many of the "free-writing" approaches now being used in the British primary schools are scarcely better than the dull, formalized assignments I used to give. Work cards, or activity cards, are a case in point. On most work cards the level of reading ability required to comprehend the instructions does not suit the work demand of the card. In my experience this has resulted in hordes of children surrounding my desk with requests that I read the card for

---

This article was taken from **"And Now We Are Going to Write,"** *Learning,* November, 1976. Reprinted by permission.

them. Obviously this wastes my time and thereby defeats the whole purpose of having the card in the first place. But the reverse has also been true: my desk has been surrounded by children who found their cards so easy that they had whizzed through every activity suggested and were awaiting their next assignment.

Supposing, however, that the card was just right, the reading level appropriate to the content. Then what do the children find? They probably find an idea such as:

Study this picture of a cave and write about who lives in it, or an adventure which befell you when you entered it.

Look at this photograph of a horse and write all about how you were given it and the wonderful adventures you enjoyed on it. Give the horse a very special name.

At a glance these two cards might appear well considered and the kind of stimulus which will "get the children writing." I would suggest, however, that they are liable to produce the same kind of writing as the tramp descriptions.

The children will certainly write. Of that I am sure. But I am also certain that the boys will write about going into the cave fighting Batman, struggling with a few giant spiders, catching a few escaped convicts, and probably will finish up with capturing a dozen villains and getting a fat reward. The girls will likely write rehashes of girl-hero-and-horse stories, which have been done thousands of times before.

I have already mentioned the drawbacks of assigning subjects which lead children into reconstructing wearisome comic or television tales, but it is a point that needs stressing. Children are not pent-up reservoirs of creative energy waiting to emit fantastic statements in writing at a mere nod from the teacher. But youngsters do have imagination and many of the other attributes related to creative expression. If we, as teachers, learn to stimulate and effectively direct this ability, then we will be rewarded with a richness of creative statement. But we have to work for it; and working for it means a lot more than merely writing suggestions on a card for children to follow.

If I were to suggest that at this precise moment you write "An Angry Letter," your letter would probably be thoughtfully composed, carefully written, dull, and uninspired.

I suggest that your lovely piece of writing would be dull for the same reason that your children's writing is dull if you always depend upon work cards. Because you were not really involved. Creative expression means involvement at a personal level. If, for example, you discover that the chair you are sitting on to read this magazine had a huge crack in every leg, and if that same chair had just cost you $50, then I suppose you could easily write a very angry letter to the manufacturers. And if they replied that you were imagining the cracks (and anyhow they did not care), then I am certain you would write back an angry letter to end all angry letters.

My point is, I hope, obvious. We all write most effectively when we are really motivated—perhaps by anger, maybe by love, amusement, the wish to communicate with others, or one of a thousand other reasons. But there must be a motivating reason. For example, when Janet saw the headmaster's car get stuck in the freshly tarred road, and when she saw the headmaster step out of the car and slip in the tar, she certainly had plenty to write about. The teacher had only to offer Janet pencil and paper and sit back. Janet was bursting to write all about it—about the angry road crew, the headmaster shouting, the state of his new suit, the crowd gathering, and the policeman writing it all down in his little book. Unfortunately for teachers (and fortunately for head-masters), events like this do not occur daily; generally the teacher has to contrive situations which will stimulate an exciting response from the students. I do not think the answer is work cards, stimulus cards, or work packs. The answer is far more likely to lie with the child, the teacher, and the world about them. A world which is cram-full of fascinating people, places, and events.

On our school playground there was an air-raid shelter. In 1945, when the shelter had no further purpose to serve, it was sealed with a stout wooden door and padlocked. From 1945 until 1968 this wooden door kept hidden from the curious eyes of countless ten-year-olds the secrets of its inner self. One cold January Monday morning in 1968, however, my arrival at school was heralded by a chorus of children yelling, "The shelter door's been smashed in!" And so it had. Some local tear-aways had obviously been having a good time on the school premises over the weekend and the door that had prevented entry for over twenty years was a barrier no longer.

"Well, who's going in first?" I asked. I noticed that even the bigger, bolder boys shrank to the rear. As no one volunteered, I suggested we return to class and begin our normal work, but I did make it known that should anyone care to go in, all they had to do was request permission and promise to complete a piece of writing about the experience. After a quick look into the shelter myself to ascertain safety, I settled down to the day's routine. Very shortly, up they came: "Sir?" said Steve. "Me and Tim want to go." "OK!" I replied as nonchalantly as possible, and off they went. During the day, Steve's lead was followed by nearly all of the students.

To be sure, the experience was quite harrowing for them. It was pitch black inside. It was damp. It smelled stale. Every footstep echoed. But their descriptions were super, and I present but a morsel:

Drippy wet—all spooko,
Icy quiet and hollow,
Footsteps putter—or do they?
Something patters,
Something scuttles,
All spooko
And quiet.

Stephen, 9 years

Perhaps there are no old air-raid shelters on your playground—or local vandals to conveniently knock the doors down. But there are plenty of other possibilities if you condition yourself to notice.

I still take delight in the written records of our out-of-class wanderings. We looked at chimney pots:

> There they stand—dusty and
>   gloomy,
> There they smoke—quiet and clear,
> There they choke, there they
>   smoke, on a foggy night.

Robin, 8 years

We gazed at the ragged array of ducks on the park pond:

> I like Diphead even if he's always the wrong way up. He's best. I like Flap-wing and Flopfoot, but Dippy is still best—even if he never takes bread from me, and even though he can't quack properly. He's best. Yesterday he did a Ducksmile to me.

Jane, 7 years

We crowded round the local dust cart and reveled in its consumption of great piles of household refuse:

> Here is the rubbish gobbler ready to gobble up all our throw-outs. He likes old china best—just hear him crunch it! Crumple Crunch Clink Clunk Gerp. Little nails, big nails, cans and cartons—he loves them all. Show him a piece of broken china, especially blue, and he will grind his grinders with glee.

Peter, 9 years

It is my sincere wish that you will enjoy with your children the wealth of writing opportunities which surround you. For I am convinced that our children's potential for expression will be realized when they write about *their* world of motor cars, fierce dogs, strange buildings, unusual people. These are the things that really interest them—because they have been involved with them. The firce dog actually chased them, knocked them over, and might even have bitten them if it had not been for . . . The strange building which they pass every day really is strange. They have *seen* the tatty curtains, *smelled* the stale odors wafting from the front door, *heard* the peculiar wailings, laughs, shouts. They have climbed up on the front wall and *felt* the cold black iron railings which surround it. These are the things that writing is about. Experience is where the creative riches lie.

So let us summon the confidence to allow our children to write of the things they really do know. And let us begin to question the validity of the clever, commercially produced work card which so often removes the child from his world and firmly positions him in a synthetic adult-centered situation.

Hate Makes Good Copy— Conflict, Great Drama

If you intend to ask students to do more writing, and you should, you will need fresh ideas or you will get stale writing. Here are some to start you off...

Beatrice Gross

Here are two card-sets based on the story of Little Red Riding Hood:

Wolf: You are the youngest of six. You have watched your sister almost die of hunger. You don't like the family on the hill who live in the warm fancy house, and now is your chance to teach them a lesson. But you have to be charming to get the information you need. You want to know where the young girl is going so you can get her alone and eat her.
Girl: You are innocent and sweet. You have been sickly and unaware of how the rest of your family has treated the no-account folk. Above all you would never be impolite to anyone, or lie, but you find the wolf makes you uncomfortable and wish he would go away and not ask so many questions. You'd rather not have his company.

Girl: You are ten or eleven years old. You've just had a fight with your mother who told you to deliver stuff to your grandmother. But you wanted to watch a "Star-Trek" rerun, so you leave reluctantly. You have been told over and over again not to talk to strangers and know you shouldn't talk to the wolf who offers to carry your package. You think he's neat looking and would like to have him come along and carry the basket, but you are also a bit afraid.
Wolf: You see at once the girl is interested in having you carry the heavy basket, but she's not going to invite you to eat from the basket. If you help out you want something to make it worth your while. You're determined to share the loot, and maybe bring some home with you.

Another way to use folk tales for dramatic presentation (either oral or written) is to "extend" stories; writing the "real end" or the "true beginnings" of familiar stories.

Have the children act out or write the dialogue that occurred.

1. Between the wolf and his mother before he went out looking for Red Riding Hood.

2. Between the state conservation officer and the woodsman after the woodsman killed the wolf.

3. Between the miller and his daughter (in "Rumplestiltskin") after he's promised the king she could weave flax into gold.

4. Between the king and his queen twenty years later (in "Rumplestiltskin") when the kingdom is in debt because of the expenses of marrying off their first-born child. (The king thinks she should weave some more gold.)

Lively illustrations can also provoke interesting, amusing, and revealing stories. The students study a picture and write what happened before the picture was "snapped," and what happened afterwards. Students should be encouraged to let their fantasies run free and dramatize the action with dialogue. They can invent things hidden behind buildings or trees and describe them. They should be encouraged to use sufficiently descriptive language so that classmates can draw the hidden object.

When children people their dramas with stock characters from television, they should be instructed to describe the "type" assuming that the reader is from another planet (or another TV season) and will need the character pictured so well they can imagine him even without past familiarity with him.

For this exercise the covers and inside illustrations of *Psychology Today* are great, since they are heavily symbolic and open ended. Advertisements lend themselves to this kind of imaginative turn-on, as do some reproductions of old masters. You know you've chosen a good illustration if you can brainstorm at least two story lines.

By using the same techniques for an historical drama or current on-the-spot interview, social studies can come alive. Children can be helped to think of ideas for sound effects by being instructed to listen to TV dramas with the picture off, or by listening to recordings of old radio dramas which you bring in. Not only can they develop refined listening skills and be stimulated to incorporate fresh sound effects in their own recordings, but they also can gain insight into the childhoods of teachers, parents, and grandparents who grew up in a radio culture.

Obviously, there are many variations possible, the choice of which depends on your teaching goals.

Since children read with more care when the reading is preparatory to dramatic presentation, an exercise which begins with the written material and uses a tape recorder to supply the background, and ends with a "radio-drama" would be appropriate for kids who decode reasonably well but lack conviction and passion in their reading or show signs of poor comprehension.

Comprehension and analysis is practiced by children working to fit appropriate sound effects to poems or stories. Characters take on new life when acted out.

Ask your students to write a biography of the person sitting next to them in class. This works nicely, according to poet Phillip Lopate who used it the first day of class: "They were all strangers, meeting for the first time, and I explained that they would have to go on nonverbal clues: dress, posture, face. It was like staring at someone in the subway and imagining his life. They could invent any damn thing they wanted, even carry the biography to the very end (I told them I liked death scenes in biographies). They set to work . . . the best pieces were those which genuinely allowed the malice to flow."*

---

* *(Teachers and Writers Collaborative Newsletter, 4:3)*

Give your class the following instructions: "Become the person you hate the most, not necessarily a specific person but a physical or personality type that most offends you (the bully, the sniveller, or the like). You become the character to discover the forces which motivate him or her. Try walking like the person, try dancing like this person, try to discover what experiences make him joyful or despairing; get a dialogue going between several of these types."** Then write a dialogue after acting out the scene.

Ask each child to write a story that is familiar to him or her but from the point of view of one of the characters in that character's voice. You might have the children practice this as an improvisational dramatic exercise. Students, because they have different interpretations of how a character thinks and why the character behaves in certain ways, begin to see how many ways they deal with the world and why. (It is also a good handle on literary analysis.) You as the teacher will find that quiet, polite Jenny has the capacity of expressing humor and anger—when the expression is safe. Everyone has a good time being "bad." I wrote several versions of "Little Red Riding Hood" to demonstrate how this works. The first is the voice of the wolf, the second focuses on the perception of Red Riding Hood.

I was really hungry that day. Hungry and feeling cranky. You know how one gets in February when the days have all been gray and it's cold and there is nothing, but nothing, around to eat. Suddenly I saw a meal. It was that kid from down the road who had been in all year with a broken leg coming down the path with a load of muffins and some pears. I don't care much for muffins and fruit is no treat, but I'd have eaten anything that day. Well, the little bitch wouldn't share her picnic lunch with me. All them fancy folks is like that. No fellow love in them. I got tired of waiting for her to show some manners and I got me a B . . . I . . . G idea. . . .

Nothing good ever happens in February. No good holidays. Still, the foul mood of the wolf couldn't have been anticipated by the little girl setting out from her house that gray February morning. She hadn't any idea what was to happen to her in the course of that dreadful day. In fact, she was rather pleased to have company as she walked through the woods to her nanny's house. When she saw him coming she remembered her mother's warning to avoid strangers, but he seemed ever so nice and she did feel lonely . . . .

Playing further with this same theme, we can help develop two characters to be built on by the kids in an improvisational drama. It's important when setting up a "skit" that each person gets clues to the character's rationale. When they are more practiced at it, they will be able to develop the character's rationale and history on their own. This must happen before they begin to interact.

The other element of prime importance for a successful story or dramatic improvisation is conflict. In the first example, the wolf is an angry character, his anger coming out of long deprivation and exploitation, and Red Riding Hood is an "innocent" but advantaged child. The conflict is that he wants to know

---

**Ibid.

something she is reluctant to tell him. He is not above cajoling and threatening to get the information he wants and she has been taught to be polite. Who gets his way in the confrontation is left to the players. Different students in the group may play it differently, and the teacher will find that the differences are usually interesting enough to merit repeats with different children playing the parts at different times.

We can also set children to working together in pairs by offering them a conflict-card set. Each child is given the role of a character, told something about their past or present, and set to act out and write down their dialogue. When put together it can be used as a script for others.

Children beyond this level will develop even more sophisticated analytical skills when they translate stories from the passive voice to the active voice for radio dramatizations. They face the problems professional writers face: the problem of inventing dialogue to set the scene describing characters and setting up a conflict. We rarely need to describe physical things in detail since we rely on short cuts when alluding to a shared experience, so such an exercise is appropriate for the advanced child who welcomes challenge. By the way, this is an exercise in which the use of simile and metaphor would be a natural.

For students less skilled, the teacher can suggest a story that is already written in dialogue form. Some students will find it sufficiently challenging to produce a fluent recording. Striving for smoothness of presentation is particularly good for children who haven't developed reading fluency; repetitive practive under nonperformance conditions seems onerous but under rehearsal conditions is quite acceptable.

It is not always necessary or indeed advantageous to present results of play-reading to the full class. Very different lessons are learned when two or three people working together on a creative problem merely enjoy the activity and eschew the applause.

I learned this from Brian Way, an Englishman, who runs workshops for fifty adults or more in which finished products are rarely shared with the larger groups. Although natural "show-offs" (like myself) found the experience disconcerting at first, the shy participants were pleased by the anonymity and the knowledge that all of the eyes in the class would not be focused on them. For those who ache to share, you can, of course, allow time, but a certain freedom and honesty of expression emerges when children are not aiming to titillate the crowd. They can take themselves seriously without fearing they will be judged, and the sincerity is reminiscent of the dramatic play of the preschooler as compared to the "campy" productions typical in the middle years.

One exercise in imagining and sharing that delighted me in the Brian Way workshop was spare and very simple. He asked each person in the room to close his or her eyes and imagine that the sounds to follow were background sounds to a moving picture. He then beat out a steady, slow beat on a hard surface.

I "saw" a blind man with a cane walking on a deserted pier. The sky was dark with clouds, the air cold, the impact mood terror. "Now," interrupted Way, "turn to your neighbor and tell him or her about your movie and listen to his movie."

My neighbor, had "seen" a different film. He was watching cockroaches come out of the wall, one after the other, to form a grand, rather elegant, march on the sink. They were all gathered in formation, marching in formal formation as the lights went up.

This was my first experience in *selective* sharing, and it was entirely satisfactory, although I was somewhat frustrated in not hearing the scenarios of others in the large group.

You should also be looking for ways to help children master "straight" writing. I think the best way to encourage lucid, pointed prose is to lead kids into a discussion of what annoys them. They might write about some community "insanity" that needs redress or report some manufacturer for a consumer rip-off. It should be an issue that provokes kids to want to let others know how mad they are. Anger and impatience move kids and adults to seek self-expression more than does a situation of no emotional impact. After Christmas children often want to blow the whistle on toys that disintegrate. Children are annoyed when they are charged twice as much for candy at the movie theatre's candy counter than at the local drugstore; they get mad when they have to pay full price for a movie but can't sit where they like or come in after 5 P.M., or when good TV programs continue past their bedtimes, or when they are punished unfairly. Provoked, they can be encouraged to write.

But correcting, tightening, and editing are less fun. Have your class experiment as to whether editing makes a difference. (Try sending the draft out to the management or appropriate official as penned. Try sending the second typed on fancy stationery and carefully corrected for spelling and other errors.) Perhaps the class can learn from the different responses the attitude of the real world to inept, illiterate writing.

John Blessington in his book *Let My Children Work* offers some suggestions for at-home writing work that provides kids with immediate, positive feedback. To practice letter writing, he recommends that a child be asked to write to relatives who may think, because of lack of communication, that the family is deceased or dying! Everyone has an aunt or great-aunt who feels unloved because of no contact. Let the children make contact. It will be a very real experience for them—and helpful in easing the parents' consciences, too.

A Mirror for Jellyroll Jones

Most of us would consider improvisational drama as a pretty far-out classroom activity. But it can be vastly rewarding for teachers and students, and it isn't all that hard to get started and make it work. Farnum Gray and George Mager, the most gifted practitioners we have ever seen, tell you all you need to know in their book, *Liberating Education*.

Farnum Gray and George C. Mager

Teaching interns who have taken our course have called improvisational drama "pure teaching," and in a sense it is. The teacher does not have the scholarly job of providing content. He concentrates on "teaching"—or structuring—the class. The teacher provides structure by handling students in such a way that their own content is likely to emerge and they can explore it. As the course progresses and the students learn about structure, they lead some of their own classes.

In improvisational drama, the content is relevant to the students because they generate it. Instead of prescribing the content, the teacher allows it to occur.

A person's feelings and the perceptions that determine his feelings and actions often are the most important subject for his education. This was true of Jellyroll Jones, a stocky, brown-skinned twelve-year-old. For him, the most relevant content was his own hostility, and that was the content he brought forth and explored within the structure of his improvisational drama course.

The emotions and perceptions are so neglected by most schools that many people can't imagine how a student could benefit from emotional and perceptual education. Jellyroll's case should help clear up the mystery, and it should also give a concrete idea of what improvisational drama is.

Jelly had good teachers and a consistently stimulating program at the Pennsylvania Advancement School, and his experiences outside the improvisational drama class contributed to the progress he made.

When Jellyroll arrived at the Advancement School to begin his fourteen-week session, he was an extrovert—a very physical young man who did not know how to express himself physically. To get attention, he hit, bumped, and grabbed people. He seldom talked in a conversational tone, but shouted frantically as if he had to be heard quickly before everyone disappeared. Waiting his

This article is from *Liberating Education*, ed. by Farnum Gray and George C. Mager. Berkeley: McCutchan Publishing Corporation, 1973. Reprinted by permission of the publisher.

turn never occurred to him, as though he knew his turn would never come. This behavior is common among inner-city boys, and Jelly seemed largely unaware of the annoyance he caused other people. His teachers soon realized that feelings about race had something to do with Jellyroll's bumptiousness, but he had learned to avoid talking about racial matters.

For his teachers to force Jellyroll to suppress his feelings and study the conventional subject matter would have been absurd. He would not learn much if his energies were concentrated on trying to appear passive while he seethed with aggressive feelings.

Jelly took to improvisational drama from the start. In the early classes, much of the activity involved movement to music. Jelly could really move and groove, and he knew it. The dancing helped him build confidence that carried over into the dramatic improvisations, and his acting often sparkled.

Because it suspends the superiority of students who excel in literacy skills, improvisational drama is very well suited to culturally and racially mixed classes. Children from poor backgrounds are not at their usual disadvantage; in fact, their lives in the crowded slums often provide colorful and powerful dramatic material.

Jelly became so fascinated with improvisational drama (ID) that he was the first in his class to volunteer to teach. On a Friday, George assigned him to lead the warm-ups on the following Tuesday. On Tuesday morning, we sleepily dragged into the Advancement School at 7:20 to conduct an ID workshop for counselors from other schools. There was Jellyroll, an hour and forty minutes before school was to start, lying on the floor writing in a notebook. He was outlining his plan for the warm-ups. He was excited but seemed neither scared nor cocky. He was making his plans with a workmanlike attitude that seemed different from his earlier behavior at the school.

The plans were good. Jelly led the warm-ups with poise and vitality, and his classmates threw themselves into it. In discussion, the boys said Jelly's warm-ups were better than George's had ever been. George had to admit that enthusiasm had been higher than in any of the group's previous warm-ups. Jelly felt good about the boys in the class. They could have balked and made him look bad, but instead they had helped him.

Sometimes Jelly thought ID was great, but other times he was not so sure. As several other students have done, he twice went to George and said he might not come to class the next day. "That is your decision to make," George told him. "I can't make it for you." Jelly always showed up for class. In saying that he might skip class, Jelly was actually asking George to protect him from discomfort. George did not give him that guarantee, but the fascination of learning about himself consistently overcame the fear of what he might learn and kept Jelly in the class.

In the fourth week of the session Jellyroll and his classmates sat watching improvisations on cushions along two sides of a square patch of floor that served as a stage. The room was dark except for a spotlight on center stage. The class had started with warm-ups, in which vigorous physical activity alternated with deep relaxation. Then there was an improvisation in which Doug tried to convince his pal not to become a teacher. The pal was played by one of Doug's teachers, and Doug expressed a general hatred for pedagogy.

Then George introduced the second improvisation: "This is Sister Fran. Okay, Ray, you've got to convince Sister Fran not to be a nun."

"She's a nun already."

"Right. You've got to convince her not to be one. All right, get your tension up. Concentrate. Think about it. Become specific.

Sister Fran Tobin had brought a group of sisters from her school, Sacred Heart Academy of Albany, New York, for a brief visit to learn about ID and other Advancement School techniques. She had been in George's improvisational drama class for teachers at the Advancement School the previous summer, and George had asked her to take part in this class as a student. Her colleagues observed from the dark at the back of the room, along with fourteen public school educators.

As the improvisation started, Ray fidgeted in his checked sport coat and could not look Sister Fran in the eye. He had talked several times of how nuns had beaten him, preached at him, and otherwise abused him when he had attended Catholic schools, and he could hardly believe that George had put him on the stage with a hated nun.

"Hi, Ray."

"Hi. I hear you want to be a nun."

"Yeah, I do."

"Well, that's stupid."

Ray started out stiffly. He was usually rather stiff and unexpressive. As he continued heaping insults on the nun, however, he warmed up and became believable.

"Listen," Sister Fran said, "suppose I'm your sister, and you know I really want to be a nun. Are you going to tell me it's stupid?"

"I'd say, *forget it!*"

"Why would you tell me to forget it, if you know I really want to be a nun and nothing else?"

In an anguished voice, Ray cried, "Because you waste your life that way!"

From simply hating nuns, he had moved to criticizing the institution of nunnery. There was real communication and budding friendship for the rest of their improvisation. But it was the hostility Ray had showered on the nun earlier that lighted up Jelly's square face and made him bounce on his cushion. George saw Jelly's excitement, and during the next improvisation, he changed his lesson plan and devised a situation that would get Jelly on that stage to let it all out.

In the next improvisation one "actor" was assigned to convince another that he should quit school to run numbers and push drugs. Jelly and his classmates liked it. They groaned when George yelled, "Freeze," to end it. Smiling, George extended his hand to Jellyroll, who hopped up and stepped into the spotlight. George said, "Jelly is a black power leader—black militant. Okay?"

Then George gave a hand to Frank, a bright sensitive white boy who was disheartened by the hostility Jellyroll and some of his black friends were showing for whites. "You've got to convince Jelly not to be a black militant," George instructed Frank. "Get your tension up," he told the boys. "Get your concentration. Okay? Here we go."

"I've heard a lot of rumors about you," Frank said.

Bouncing jauntily, Jelly snapped, "Like what?"

"You're going to get yourself in trouble. Going to make yourself a big man."

"That's right!" Jelly grinned and smacked his chewing gum. The tension was real and electric.

"Well, what's the difference between black and white? Can you tell me that?"

"Soul brothers," Jelly said haughtily.

"Soul?"

Jelly leaned forward and crooned, "So-o-o-o-oul."

"Well, I don't care what religion or anything anybody is," Frank said, pretending not to understand what kind of soul Jelly meant. "They're still just the same inside, and I think . . ."

"That's what you think!" Jelly cut in.

"Look, did you ever see . . . uh . . . look in the news and see pictures of how the cops are beating the crap out of you guys 'cause you keep on bothering, running around, demonstrating, making trouble. Have you ever seen them? They go downtown. Break up and rob everything. You don't want to be like that, do you?"

Coolly, Jellyroll said, "Your soul do not like us."

Frank looked agitated: "Yeah. As I remember kidding you . . . going to church, you were pretty nice; but all of a sudden you've changed. You . . ."

"I still go to church."

"Yeah, but still you . . ."

" . . . once in a while." Jelly grinned arrogantly.

"Yeah! Once in a while! You're a hypocrite!"

"Ha, ha!" Jelly's laugh was half growl.

Frank said, "And look at the clothes you're wearing!"

"They're all right. Look at yours. Red socks!" Jelly shouted gleefully. He grabbed the neckband of Frank's long red underwear and jerked frenetically, crying "Yeah, yeah, yeah!"

"Freeze."

George had to enforce a structure that would keep the class physically safe. But he had to do it without making Jelly feel slapped down. To say, "You mustn't grab people, Jellyroll," might have caused a sullen withdrawal, extinguishing the spark that had been growing in Jelly since the start of warm-ups. But stopping the improvisation at that point would leave Frank feeling frustrated; he was too sensitive to be unaware of the implications of Jelly grabbing his long underwear, which to the black boy was a symbol of the white working class. Instead of passing judgment on what they had done, George simply reminded the boys of the existing structure. "All right, you're forgetting your tasks," he said evenly, as the boys held their positions. "What's your task? What do you have to accomplish up there? Get back to it. Move."

"I know I have long johns on," Frank said. "It's cold outside. But what's this black socks! What's that for?"

"The leader!" Jellyroll said proudly.

"And you're walking around every day like this." Frank imitated Jelly's strut. "And you're always starting trouble in school—and mostly with white kids."

"Ahr-r-r. So what?"

"What is it with you? What do you want to be one of them for? All you want to do is start trouble and everything. There's no particular kid's color or anything."

"There ain't?" Jelly said with a marvelous sneer.

"There ain't, as you put it. Big deal. Wow! White trash, right? You don't really mean this stuff," Frank said, grasping Jelly's shoulder and shaking him.

"Yes I do!"

"I'm not messing with you any more. If you're smart, you'll knock it off." They circled each other suspiciously and Frank said, "You know something, you're going to get yourself in a lot of trouble. Just keep it up!"

"Freeze."

George shook the boys' hands, and, with arms around their shoulders, guided them back to their seats. "Great acting," he said.

Jellyroll was not sure how much of what he had done was acting and how much was real. There was some of each in his performance, he felt, and he could think about it later. In the meantime, he basked in the appreciation of his classmates, who had been spellbound. Jelly had a good feeling about Frank, since the two of them had pulled off the success together.

Jelly was now being aggressive in a new way. He was using his aggressiveness; it was not using him. It was not frustration taking him over; he was being aggressive because he wanted to.

George had paired Jelly and Frank because he thought their interests could complement each other in the right kind of situation. He had been wrong, the boys probably would have gotten something out of the exercise anyhow. As long as the teacher does not try to tell the students what makes them tick and how they ought to change, there is no harm done if the teacher is wrong, although a teacher who usually guesses right can plan improvisations that will more effectively help students develop. It is not necessary for a teacher to decide whether a student is acting or expressing his own feelings; this ambiguity gives many students a sense of security that enables them to express feelings they might not admit even to themselves.

The class continued. "New task," George told the group. "Think of something that you're afraid of. Now become specific in your head. You must come up here and show us fear. Now concentrate specifically on what you could be afraid of. Now wait a minute, that's only half the job. Sometimes, while one person's up here being afraid of something, I will go to somebody else and tap him on the shoulder. His job is to go up and help the person who is afraid—help him not to be afraid."

George guided Cathy into the spotlight. She was a tall, blonde Antioch College student who worked at the school, and she and Jelly were good friends. Cathy crouched on the floor, trembling, face in hands. Then George tapped Jelly's shoulder. He swaggered up to the huddled girl and cracked, "Are you doing your yoger exercises?"

Jellyroll wanted very much to cheer Cathy up. But in his brusque efforts, he jerked her to her feet and banged her against the wall. When she remained frightened, he pounded his fist against the wall and shouted gutturally, "What's the matter with you?"

After the exercise, Jelly and Cathy sat on the floor in the spotlight and the boys talked about what had happened. One said, "I think Jelly must have been feeling pretty frustrated, you know."

After they had talked awhile, George said, "Tell me this somebody: Did you think he was helping Cathy? Yes or no?"

"No!" the boys chorused.

"He seemed to be scaring her more," Robby said. "When he got angry, she got even more scared."

George said, "Jelly, do you think there is an alternative way of doing this? Can you? Try it. Now this time—you may play it as you like—but this time you must try a different approach. Let's see if that's more successful."

Cathy started as before, but this time Jelly was gentle and concerned. In the discussion afterwards, the class remarked on the difference. "He helped her this time," one boy said. "This sure was better," Cathy said. "When he got angry at me, the first time, it made me more scared. When he didn't seem to get upset because I was scared, it was much easier."

Then Sister Fran was the scared one, and Ray, who minutes before had tried to convince her not to be a nun, was supposed to help her. In the discussion that followed, Jellyroll had some very definite opinions on how to help.

Late that afternoon, Jelly happily ran up to George. While talking to him, he punched his shoulder and pulled on his arm. George said, "Jelly, do I like you?"

"Yeah."

"Are you sure that I like you?"

"Yeah."

"Then you don't have to hit me any more."

Jelly got that look kids get when they've just seen the light.

Talking about drama, Jelly said he'd learned a lot that day about a different way to act in class.

"Drama isn't limited to the classroom," George said. "You can be different outside the class, too."

That look spread over Jelly's face again. Maybe he didn't have to be rough, tough Jellyroll Jones any more.

On Monday George found a typed note on his desk:

YE OLDE STORY
TO GEORGE MAGOR, (ye olde DR teach)
on the 27th day and the 11th month
we JELLY and GEORGE had a little talk about class
and over the week end I thought about
it and I really appreciate it.
YE OLDe STUDENT JELLY

In the days that followed, both adults and students praised Jelly for his striking improvement in consideration for other people. Eventually, he became everybody's buddy. In the chain reaction exercises, Jelly took many opportunities to drape an arm around someone's neck and call him friend. It was unreal. In trying to find who he was through trial and error, he went to the opposite extreme.

There was a second note, as obsequious as the first had been sincere.

Dear George
I really appreciated your kindness. Your class yesterday, I think that was the best class I ever went to. George will you please lead the class today? I was really happy yesterday when I helped you and Dan.

thanks

One day, there was an improvisation in which Herb Katz, a teacher who was visiting the class, timidly asked his boss for a raise, saying that he had not had one in years and that he really needed the money. George's instructions were that anyone who wanted to help Herb could step into the improvisation. Jelly and several others went to Herb's rescue. The others wanted to help Herb become more assertive in talking with his boss, but Jelly—acting overbearingly friendly—wanted to steal some money and give it to Herb. In the discussion, some of the boys criticized Jelly's superficial approach. They thought he was not helping Herb, but only encouraging him to delay dealing with his real problem, his timidity. Herb thought so, too. Jelly was puzzled, and he thought seriously about the criticism he received.

One day while he was acting, Jelly looked to the teacher for praise. George said, "Do it for you, not for us." It was an intimate statement, showing that George cared enough to understand Jelly beyond his expectations. Jelly learned from it, although he probably would have resisted if it had seemed like standardized advice.

The "new Jellyroll Jones" was starting to pall. Now that the magic formula of superniceness had failed, what *did* he want to be? Jelly began analyzing things. He observed and listened to people keenly. He still had a strong need for affection, but he was going after it in more mature ways. By this time he was convinced that his teachers and classmates liked him and cared about him. He became more concerned about being proud of himself than about impressing others. Once, in discussing an improvisation done by some other boys, Jelly said, "These kids are trying to please you, George. Every time they get on the stage they start looking at you." His comment showed improvements both in understanding people's actions and in honestly saying what he thought.

Like a number of other kids who have taken improvisational drama, Jelly often articulated what he had learned from his own experiences while discussing the actions of the other boys. All aspects of the class were part of the structure within which Jellyroll Jones explored himself and his potential.

One morning, George walked into the classroom and announced, "I'm not here today." Then he walked to the back of the room and sat down. Two boys volunteered to lead the class. After a while, the other boys got bored with the rather dull leadership and acclaimed Jelly as their teacher for the rest of the hour.

Jelly set up an improvisation in which two black boys were supposed to criticize each other's clothes. Chet was open in his expressions of powerful anti-white feelings, while Doug tended to butter up whites. Their argument over clothes became a bitter, personal clash over attitudes toward white people. Throughout the drama, Jelly squatted beside the stage and leaned forward, observing with rapt intensity. Was he using the situation to externalize his own internal conflict? We cannot really know, and we do not need to know.

Through his Advancement School experience, Jelly had become actively involved in a process of perceptual growth, which was changing him from a destructively aggressive person to one who could assert himself constructively. If he can continue this perceptual growth throughout his life, it will have been more important to him than anything he could have learned from a seventh-grade textbook.

Within the improvisational drama structure, students learn to practice an experiential way of thinking. The perpetual question for them is, What do I do with this experience?

An experience strikes a chord of meaning within a person. This is an internal process. The teacher structures the external situation in which the experience can occur and encourages freedom and helpfulness among the students, but he does not interpret the experience for the student or evaluate the content the student brings to the activity.

George never told Jellyroll he could not do something. As Jelly gained new perceptions, he made his own decision to stop abusing people. Had George simply told him to stop hitting people, shut up, and be still, Jelly probably would have felt threatened and clung to the perceptions he already had, and his behavior would have rigidified. Instead, when George gave Jelly his instructions for the second improvisation with Cathy, for example, the requirement that he "must try a different approach" was perceived by Jelly as a challenge rather than a threat. Rather than narrowing his vision, as he might have if he had felt threatened, he rose to meet the challenge by creating a new, more successful mode of behavior for himself.

"To be good is noble," Mark Twain wrote, "but to teach others to be good is nobler—and less trouble." It also borders on the impossible. If a student is told that he should care about other people, he might learn that concern is held in high regard, but he does not necessarily feel concern for other people.

People usually do what they perceive to be right, and the most effective way for them to make constructive changes in the way they act is to sharpen their perceptions through experience. As students learn to value their own experience, rather than merely paying lip service to what they are told, hypocrisy dimishes.

In examining one part of the development of a twelve-year-old black "underachiever" from an inner-city slum, we have tended to look through only one "psychological stencil." There are quite a few of these psychological stencils, replete with verbal labels, and teachers can benefit from knowing of them. (Knowing only one is often worse than knowing none.) But for growing children, the verbal labels seem unnecessary.

The student selects from the experience those elements that are of the most value to him. And he selects only what he is ready and able to learn. If the teacher decides what is to be learned, the student might push aside realizations that are more important and relevant to himself in order to focus on the teacher's concerns. Before a student's question can be answered, he must in some way have asked the question, he will give a cue that he is very close to the answer himself and would like another person's interpretation.

The teacher is not trying to learn something about the student and then teach it to him. He is trying to structure the classroom experience in such a way that the student learns how to learn about himself, as well as about other people and about how people interact.

Format is one important part of the structure of the class. In our courses, our usual format goes like this:

1. Warm-ups.
2. Short improvisations or simple exercises.
3. Richer, or longer, improvisations.
4. The closing.

However, format is for each teacher to decide. The most important concept in structuring is this:

The teacher provides structure by handling students in such a way that their own content is likely to emerge, and they can explore it.

Why Jessie Hates English

"What's wrong with these kids? They can't understand what they read and I can't understand what they write." Reading and writing are certainly intertwined—and research can help you know what approaches have proven helpful to some students and what simply hasn't worked. For example, texts used for grammar instruction and linguistic analysis will have little effect on the writing of students. But teachers are pressured to please parents and administrators who want to see more grammatical writing coming out of their classes. It's hard to resist this pressure, so teachers are tempted to use grammar texts that reassure those who "learned" that way and who demand their return in the name of rectifying today's reports of how badly students are now doing. What *will* our current students learn from this? They'll learn to hate English, as Sloan Wilson reports in "Why Jessie Hates English."

Sloan Wilson

Not long ago, my youngest daughter, Jessica, who is twelve years old, came home from school, dropped her book bag in the middle of our living room, and yelled, "I hate English!"

In some families this might not cause much of a stir, but I am an old English teacher, as well as a writer. My father was an English teacher and so was *his* father. As a matter of fact, my father, who enjoyed exaggeration, used to claim that all his progenitors had been English teachers, going clear back to a lone Wilson aboard the *Santa Maria*, who died horribly while attempting to give a lesson in English grammar to the Indians. They skinned him alive, Dad said, and boiled him.

When Jessie came home with her shocking announcement, my first impulse was to find the teacher who had made her hate English and give her the same treatment that the aborigines had given my ancestor. I should add here my objective, impartial view that my youngest daughter is extremely bright, especially gifted in English, and a surprisingly dedicated scholar. All right, the opinion of a father concerning his youngest daughter has to be discounted at least 50 percent. Even so, Jessie is a child who reads far more than most adults do at home, and she writes well enough to get the highest marks whenever she pens a report for a course other than English. In her English course she never has had to write much of anything. In many modern sixth-grade English courses, I had already discovered, writing does not occupy a large part of the curriculum, if any.

But what had the teacher been doing to make Jessie hate English? She was not, Jessie hastened to tell me, the kind of classroom ogre who can make a student hate anything.

"It's not the teacher, Daddy," she said with some exasperation, as though I were a very slow pupil, "it's just *English*."

"Don't you enjoy all the stories and poems you get in English?"

"We hardly ever get stories and poems. All we get, Daddy, is grammar.

This article is from *Saturday Review*, Sept. 18, 1976. Reprinted by permission. Sloan Wilson is a novelist and social critic.

That's all we're supposed to study, right through high school. I'll show you my books."

That night I spent several hours poring over my daughter's textbooks after she had finished her homework.

"What do you think?" my wife asked, poking her head into my study when it was time for bed.

"I hate English!" I replied. "These books have converted me from a life-long lover of the language to a truant."

"What's the matter with them?"

I showed her two books. They were the official kind of modern textbook that apparently is contrived to look as little like a textbook as possible. The layout looks as though it is the brainstorm of the art director of a struggling new advertising agency after a three-martini lunch. Much of the copy was apparently supplied by a deposed editor of the New York *Daily News*. Headlines scream. There are eye-catching photographs of football players and full-page reproductions of old advertisements for expensive coats, cosmetics, and automobiles. In one book, my favorite horror, there is an entire section on the grammar of Madison Avenue, which the authors obviously admire.

For a long time I have been aware that we all live in a nightmare world, but I had not realized that the schools have substituted advertising copy for the prose and poetry of the masters, which students in my antique day used to study and occasionally enjoy. Why are they doing this sort of thing?

To find out, I telephoned my *oldest* daughter, Lisa, who followed the family trade and is or, rather, was an English teacher. Unlike me, she has recent knowledge of what goes on in the public schools.

"A lot of advertising copy is used to teach English nowadays," she said. "The words are short and the sentences simple . . ."

"I'm not talking about a class for retarded children," I objected.

"Neither am I. That's the depressing part of it. Even in classes for the brightest children, the advertising copy is sometimes useful, just to keep the kids awake."

"I hate the whole system!" I exploded. "Jessie spends hours at home looking at television, and when she finally goes to school, they teach her advertisements as though they were gems of English prose! Pretty soon she's going to think and talk like a deodorant commercial!"

"Do I?" Lisa asked with a laugh. "What do you think I had to study? The lucky thing is that most kids ignore school."

I have heard it said that the students of my generation and of prior ones did not need to learn grammar because we studied so much Latin. I believe that this contradicts everything that has been learned about learning, part of which can be summed up with the astonishing news that when a boy studies Latin, he just learns Latin. My own case provides only one correction to that. For eight years I studied Latin, but I didn't acquire any lasting knowledge of Latin. I just learned to hate school, except for English, which made sense. I do not owe my knowledge of English to Latin, except for the fact that Latin made everything else appear easy.

Those who are in charge of planning English courses in the public schools do not seem to be aware of the fact that those who study grammar do not learn English—they just learn the crazy jargon of the grammarians and all their rules and regulations for English when studied as a dead language. Grammar is an attempt to codify the English language, reduce it to abstractions devoid of meaning or beauty, break it into "rules," "laws," and pseudo-mathematical "rights" and "wrongs." The fact that it is necessary to learn to speak and write grammatically does not mean that one must devote much time to the abstract study of grammar. One should, instead, study, of all things, speaking and writing.

Some youngsters can find real joy in writing a good theme and welcome a teacher's attempts to show them how to improve it, even if the corrections involve the use of a few basic rules of grammar. In a properly run English composition class, grammar has specific applications and is not taught as an abstract "science." As it should be, it is always subordinate to the basic urge to communicate, not an end in itself.

I think I know how the public schools came to rely more and more heavily on the teaching of grammar as an abstract science. As the children of parents who themselves spoke broken English flooded the public schools, something had to be done to help countless students learn whole new speech patterns. The study of grammar is not good remedial English, as the performance of so many high school graduates sadly proves, but it must have seemed a good solution at first and a much cheaper one than the complex programs necessary for helping a person change speech patterns acquired in infancy.

Although classes in grammar didn't teach children anything but how to pass examinations devised by the grammarians, they offered certain practical advantages. Tests in grammar can be graded by machines. A teacher who asks his class to write themes every day may be deluged with papers that have to be corrected line after line by a human hand. It is also true that almost any adult, after a few months of specialized instruction, can teach grammar. To be a good teacher of English composition, one has to be able to write good English oneself. As has been often remarked, English has rarely been a strong point of the teachers colleges and departments of education, which have produced most of our public school teachers. The jargon of the educators is not conducive to teaching good, clear English.

The current discovery that high school graduates on the whole read and write with more difficulty than even their recent predecessors hits educators hard. The public schools have been supported and defended as an act of faith by most Americans all during their periods of rapid growth, especially since World War II. Criticisms have been shrugged off as the work of crackpots or intellectual snobs. When the book *Why Johnny Can't Read* came out, more than twenty years ago, it sold a lot of copies, but it was never quite respectable among people who were seriously concerned with the schools. If the schools were not teaching reading well at the moment, the feeling was, the difficulties would soon be overcome.

Now decades have passed, and there is evidence that the schools are teaching reading worse than they have in the past and that writing among recent high school graduates is almost a lost art. There have been loud cries for "a return to the fundamentals." And what are the fundamentals? Reading? Writing? Of course not! In the minds of the educators, *grammar* is the real fundamental. If the proliferation of courses in grammar has resulted in the graduation of countless youngsters who can hardly read or write, the obvious answer is to give the youngsters even more grammar. If one aspirin doesn't stop your headache, take two.

Apparently no one puts himself in the position of the student who sits squirming while the teacher drills him in grammar day after day, year after year. It's easy to see why such a student doesn't want to read anything—he is taught to regard the text as a boneyard of grammar problems on which he will probably be quizzed. Writing, too, becomes a test of fitting together words and phrases in a way that is *grammatical,* not interesting, funny, or meaningful. My youngest daughter is not the only pupil in her school who hates English, and as a result, she gives it as little time as possible.

Like many other parents, I have tried to do something about this situation for my child. I wrote a long letter to my old friend David S. Siegel, the superintendent of schools in Ticonderoga, N.Y., the upstate village where we live. Dave really wanted to help. He referred the matter to the "language arts coordinator," a title that apparently means "head English teacher" in the language of contemporary public schools. He turned out to be a pleasant, intelligent young chap who is alarmingly well versed in the theories of modern public schools, but ambitious and idealistic concerning the English courses nonetheless. He organized a class for students from three grades who are especially gifted in English and invited my youngest daughter to join it. The class is known as a speed group, and now, poor Jessie reports, she is being fed about three times as much grammar as before. Her new ambition is to be a veterinarian. With animals, after all, she will be asked neither to write, to read, nor even to talk.

Perhaps in an effort to preserve some facade of respectability, Jessie's English textbooks also included some brief snippets of good books by recognizable authors. A few paragraphs by the masters, from Mark Twain to Ray Bradbury, were sandwiched between the gaudy photographs and the advertising copy, free samples of a product that many of the students may never see in its entirety.

The jazzy layout, which made a textbook look like a sales brochure, and the snippets of real writing were all sugarcoating for the main subject of Jessie's English books, which was, of course, grammar. Page after page was devoted to this dismal exercise, chapter after chapter. Many little tests in grammar were offered. Most of them I could not pass despite a lifetime of making a living by writing English.

What are "derivational suffixes"? How about a "subjective completion"? While I puzzled over "subjective completion," I thought it might be some sort of euphemism for "premature ejaculation," but the textbook tells me that it is "a word which completes the verb and refers back to the subject." Understand now?

I have here a whole bagful of nuggets of information mined from Jessie's textbook. Here is one sentence: "Just as there are determiners to signal the presence of nouns in a sentence, so too are there signal words which point to the presence of verbs—structure words called *auxiliaries.*"

That is the kind of sentence that I cannot understand and do not want to understand. People who understand sentences like that are thrown out of the Authors League and the Roma Bar, my favorite hangout.

Do you have "terminal clusters"? They are not a form of cancer, but something that adds to the descriptive power of prose, the book assures me. Are you a master of the "multilevel sentence"? Apparently it has nothing to do with the critics' favorite, the multilevel novel. Are you good at "parallel repetition" and "chain linking"? We are still talking about English prose, mind you, not wire fences. Are you a master of that new addition to marlinespike scholarship, the "comma splice"?

My twelve-year-old daughter has to be able to interpret all this nonsense. If she can't, she will fail her examinations in English, no matter how much she reads at home, no matter how well she writes for other classes.

Who invented all this hideous jargon used by grammarians? I don't know, but my quotations are from that favorite horror book of Jessie's, *Grammar Lives.* The title becomes more nonsensical the more one thinks about it. This mercifully slender volume, which presumably has been sold to many school systems, was published in 1975 by McDougal, Littell & Company. The names of the people responsible for this reverse masterpiece go on like the "crawl" preceding a pornographic movie, constituting a list of individuals eagerly seeking credit for the discreditable. The "consultant" is Karen J. Kuehner. The "authors" are Ronald T. Shephard and John MacDonald. The "editorial direction," which must have been remarkable, was supplied by Claudia Norlin. These people presumably all got together, invented or borrowed phrases like "terminal clusters," reprinted some old advertisements and snippets of legitimate prose, and then really demonstrated their talents by finding a way to make this stuff compulsory reading for hundreds of thousands, if not millions, of innocent children. They should not, however, feel alone in their guilt. Plenty of other "educators" are helping them to make children hate English and to be illiterate.

I could quote many more examples of the grammarian's art, but I have to take it easy on my blood pressure.

"Why does grammar make you so angry?" my wife asked. "Doesn't everybody have to study it?"

The answer, of course, is that for the last few thousand years nobody was asked to study grammar anywhere near as much as the pupils in most American public schools, where it often occupies most of the English curriculum. In my own youth I studied formal grammar briefly in the fifth grade. I remember it because it seemed so silly. Who but a schoolteacher would diagram sentences and make simple prose so complex? Fortunately my teacher hated grammar as much as I did. Soon she returned to assigning us themes and correcting them in detail, a much better way to teach the mechanics of the language. She also asked us to read good books—*whole books,* not snippets. When we wrote book reports, the teacher got another shot at correcting our English. I often wonder what she would have said if someone had asked her to give us advertisements for study.

VII
MODIFYING CLASSROOM BEHAVIOR

Modifying Robert's Behavior

A child who loses interest and becomes an irritating behavior problem can be your bellwether. The program itself might be causing the problem, but sometimes a child will not be attentive no matter what the activity. This kid gives you trouble by loud, abusive behavior even when you're making chocolate pudding. What's worse, he does it when the assistant principal comes in to assess you. He runs around the room and sets the others giggling. Before you know it, they're out of bounds, so the assistant principal now insists that you get *tough* as he takes the offending youngster, with stern admonitions to the class, off to his office. What do you do?

As we see it, you've got two problems. One is the kid and his behavior. The other is staying as sweet as you are without incurring the continued wrath of the assistant principal.

Here is a situation where the theory and practice of behavior modification might come to your aid. It can help you justify your continued humanity in the classroom and, you will be rewarded with a more pleasant and effective classroom atmosphere.

To justify to yourself and the administration your decision to eschew a harsher classroom atmosphere, you can point to the research indicating that any recognition of behavior, either positive or negative, frequently has a reinforcing effect.

Ponder that yourself! Being yelled at may be especially attractive to children who associate yelling with "caring." It may be the most powerful signal they get that they exist—and it's better to exist and be bad, than not to exist at all. To paraphrase Descartes, "I can make you angry, therefore I am." It can also be a most effective means of getting free of the discomfort of frustration. If the child runs around he knows he will either disrupt your lesson (and not feel anxious about not being able to do the work) or be removed for disruptive behavior (and not feel anxious about not being able to do the work).

This case study presented by Louis J. Heifetz and Barry A. Farber illustrates the steps taken to socialize and teach Robert. It is predicated on the belief that "the immediate consequences of behavior shape future behavior, behaviors that are followed by pleasant consequences are more likely to happen again, while behaviors that are followed by unpleasant consequences (or the absence of pleasant consequences) are less likely to happen again."

Louis J. Heifetz and Barry A. Farber

A CLASSROOM CASE STUDY

Robert's math class had been working on multiplication for weeks. Each class began with blackboard demonstrations by the teacher, continued with more blackboard problems in which the class as a whole contributed to the step-by-step solutions, and ended with a ten-problem written quiz just before lunch. After lunch, the graded quizzes were returned, and the students with "A" papers each went to the board and demonstrated the correct solution to one problem.

The teacher was quite concerned with Robert's disruptive behavior as well as his poor academic record. For several weeks his performance on the quizzes had deteriorated steadily. Robert was now attempting only one or two problems, usually getting neither right. During his teacher's demonstrations he often left his seat and wandered about the room; his teacher estimated that this occurred three or four times per thirty-minute math period. Robert usually ignored her requests to return, even when reprimanded angrily, until finally he would be led by the hand and seated in a chair by her desk. While the class was working on a blackboard problem, Robert usually paid no attention, except for occasionally giving an outrageously wrong answer, which elicited great glee from his peers and further scoldings from his teacher. He would be returned to his seat for the quiz, where he would typically work for a few minutes and then doodle until lunch.

Robert's teacher hypothesized that Robert's out-of-seat behavior was being maintained by her attention and the attention of his classmates, and that Robert's skill deficiencies prevented him from obtaining academically based reinforcement. In order to (a) reduce Robert's out-of-seat behavior and (b) increase his attention and performance in math, the following program, briefly outlined, was instituted; although it was designed primarily for Robert, certain aspects of the program involved the entire class.

Ten minutes were added to the beginning of math class so that the teacher could break down larger units of the math program into simpler and smaller subunits; this period was devoted to oral exercises of basic skills that are prerequisites to solving the complicated multiplication problems currently being studied (e.g., single-digit multiplication and addition problems, which Robert could solve). The teacher was careful to call on Robert only for those "mini-problems" which she knew he could answer, and she praised him enthusiastically when he did so. In addition to praise, students received one "star" for each correct oral response, which was placed beside their names on a chart in front of the room.

When Robert was out of his seat, the teacher ignored him at first (and

---

This article is from **"Modifying Classroom Behavior,"** reprinted with permission from *New York University Education Quarterly*, Vol. VII, No. 4 (Summer 1976), pp. 21–29. © New York University.

insisted that his classmates do the same); if he was still wandering after thirty seconds, she called on him for an answer to a problem which he could solve easily, and said: "Oh, I see Robert is out of his seat. That's too bad, because he misses his chance for a star. Maybe when his next turn comes, he'll be in his seat."

The format of the ten-problem written quiz was made similar to the revised oral exercise: several problems were of the easy, mini-problem variety; a few more were complete multiplication problems constructed entirely out of the previous mini-problems; the last few problems were original ones, and in these, partial credit was given for each substep done correctly. During these quizzes, Robert's teacher stood near his desk providing encouragement, occasional direct help, and pats on the back. Any negative comments made by Robert ("I can't do this stuff." "It's too hard.") were ignored, and frequent attempts were made to point out to Robert how well he was doing, how much he was improving, or how proud everyone was of his good work. Robert, of course, was now eligible for blackboard demonstrations on the basis of his correctly solved mini-problems. His teacher monitored his academic and behavioral progress by charting his quiz scores, the number of stars earned for correct oral responses, and the frequency of his out-of-seat behavior.

As he grew more confident in his skills, Robert appeared to be capable of spending more time working independently and less time needing attention. As he experienced more positive reinforcement in school and his mathematical competence increased, his behavior was becoming more intrinsically reinforcing. What aided this process was his teacher's gradual change in emphasis from praising Robert for his accurate work to praising him for his accurate, *independent* work ("See how well you can work alone!").

As the program continued and Robert's teacher began to spend less time working individually with him, moderate fluctuations in his quiz scores and his out-of-seat behavior occurred. During the initial two weeks of this program, Robert's average number of completed math problems rose from 0.8 to 3.2 to 5.8; his out-of-seat behavior increased the first week from 3.5 to 3.8 minutes, but by the end of the second week had dropped to an average of 1.5 minutes per math period. In the next several weeks, the overall trends continued in the desired directions.

Several components of this program contributed to its success: the academic demands realistically reflected Robert's current ability level; these demands were broken down into small, manageable steps; the entire class was included in the program, thereby providing for adaptive means of receiving peer attention and approval; many opportunities were provided for reinforcement; and, last, a variety of reinforcements, including teacher attention, were available to Robert as a consequence of appropriate behaviors. As a result, it was now easier, more fun, and more rewarding for Robert to perform adaptive rather than disruptive behaviors.

The approach devised by Robert's teacher was only one of many programs that could have been developed within the framework of behavior modification. An alternative procedure might have used different reinforcements (e.g., permitting Robert to be a monitor; sending home commendation cards; displaying his correct math problems on the bulletin board). She might have made math intrinsically more rewarding by appealing to other interests of his, such as a fascination with racing cars (e.g., how much distance would be covered by five cars in a ten-mile race, progressing gradually to more difficult problems). She might have arranged individual tutoring sessions, or provided homework assignments suited to his skill-level, with reinforcements to be administered by his parents. Or, she might have chosen to concentrate initially on other academic skills which she felt took a higher priority for Robert.

The success of a program does not depend upon its specific details. It really comes from precisely assessing the strengths as well as the weaknesses of a given child; from realizing how his immediate environment frustrates academic performance and encourages inappropriate behaviors; from restructuring academic tasks and using the principles of reinforcement to ensure that success predominates over failure.

Many variables—from socioeconomic status, to educational level attained by parents, to environmental "culture"—have been indicted for their role in contributing to faulty learning and disruptive behavior. But an understanding of these factors cannot substitute for knowledge of how to deal with these problems in the classroom. Recognition of such causal factors may suggest strategies of prevention, but these require broad-based programs and sweeping reforms, which are hard to sell and slow to implement. And while the hope of the future will lie in just such preventive measures, the educational needs of the present must be met by effective remedial techniques which can readily be applied by classroom teachers.

A teacher using behavior modification does not discard her ideas, her curriculum, or her personal style. She simply uses the behavioral principles as a framework for the organization of her interactions with children and adopts those techniques which are most useful for a particular child or classroom and most amenable to her teaching style. Moreover, the range of procedures available to structure a successful learning situation is limited only by the range of a teacher's ingenuity . . . .

BASIC PRINCIPLES

The frequency of a desirable behavior can be increased through positive or negative reinforcement. This reinforcement may be either primary (e.g., food) or secondary (e.g., attention, stars, toys, money, social approval, preferred activities); any reinforcement, however, should be relevant for the individual and provided immediately after the occurrence of a given behavior.

The frequency of an undesirable behavior can be reduced either through punishment, extinction, or the reinforcement of other (desirable) behaviors which are incompatible with it. This latter option, the principle of *incompatible alternatives*, is one being increasingly used by teachers (e.g., reinforcing the number of complimentary remarks made by a usually abusive student) as well as other professionals (e.g., judges sentencing youthful vandals to clean subway cars). By reinforcing a child for appropriate behaviors, this technique has the significant advantage of providing the child with more adaptive, socially acceptable means of garnering positive reinforcement.

A prerequisite for modifying the frequency of any behavior is, of course, the ability of the child to produce that behavior. When this is not the case, as in attempting to teach a new skill to a child, an original behavior must be gradually shaped by rewarding successive approximations to the final goal.

Finally, to complete this necessarily abbreviated review of the principles of operant conditioning, it should be noted that reinforcement can be applied either continuously (rewarding a given behavior each time it is performed) or intermittently (rewarding a behavior only after it has been performed several times, or rewarding the first performance of a behavior only after a certain amount of time has lapsed). Continuous reinforcement is usually applied until the desired level of performance has been reached; this is followed by the introduction of intermittent reinforcement, which tends to produce both an increased rate of responding (more frequent behavior) and an increased resistance to extinction (persistence of behavior in the absence of reinforcement).

DESIGNING CLASSROOM PROGRAMS

Programs for modifying behavior are based on the principles just outlined and proceed through the following general stages:

1. *Precisely describe the target behavior(s).* General terms like hyperactive, aggressive, stubborn, slow, or immature may be helpful for general discussion, but they do not pinpoint exactly what behaviors need to be modified or what behaviors need to be learned. A more exact description of behavior is required (e.g., the number of reading assignments completed or the number of minutes late to class).

2. *Observe, count, and chart the target behavior(s).* For example, during a two-week observation period, one might note that Richard completed an average of three reading assignments a week; or that Linda was late for class an average of twenty minutes a day. Collecting such data relating to the target behavior with an eye toward its antecedents and consequences (the A—B—C framework) provides insight into the contingencies maintaining inappropriate behavior. A knowledge of antecedents and consequences and their combined effects upon behavior allows one to manage behavior in a systematic and successful way.

3. *Set criterion goals.* For already established behaviors, these goals consist of increases or decreases in their frequencies of occurrence (e.g., increasing the completion of reading assignments from one to two per day; reducing the number of temper tantrums from four to one per week). For new skills (e.g., tying shoelaces) the final criterion goal should be broken down into easily manageable, successive steps (e.g., threading the laces, tying the first knot,

forming the loops, tying the bow). Setting many specific short-term goals is far more practical and efficient than setting vague, long-term goals. The successful completion of short-term goals is positively reinforcing for both a student and his teacher. Moreover, it enables a teacher to monitor student progress quickly and make program revisions as soon as they become necessary.

4. *Select and apply reinforcement.* The optimal type, amount, and frequency of reinforcement will vary from child to child. Often the best way of determining the appropriateness of any reinforcement is simply to consult with the person receiving it. Reinforcement should be given immediately after behavior has reached a criterion level. In addition, the reinforcement should be contingent upon the performance of a specific target behavior. If it has been agreed that Mike may watch TV only after he completes his homework, then allowing him to watch TV after he has been helpful at dinnertime has the effect of diminishing the effectiveness of the reinforcement (television watching) and therefore reduces the probability of achieving the original goal (homework completion). For similar reasons, candy may not act as a strong positive reinforcement in the classroom if it is freely available in the school cafeteria.

5. *Establish behavioral contingencies.* These may include reinforcing appropriate behavior (e.g., complimenting a child on his work habits) or terminating reinforcement for inappropriate behavior (e.g., not paying attention to abusive remarks). Particularly useful in the case of problem undesirable behavior (e.g., rewarding cooperative play in order to reduce the frequency of fighting). The designation of behaviors as "appropriate" or "desirable" is at the discretion of the individual teacher.

6. *Monitor the program and modify it according to effectiveness.* One should not be discouraged if a program is not instantly successful. Introducing new A-B-C patterns means disrupting old patterns and disconfirming well-established expectations. The frequency of undesirable behavior often increases in the initial phases of a behavior modification program as the child tests his environment to see if the old order has really changed. Out of fairness to the child and to the program, it is essential to run the new program consistently. If after a reasonable amount of time a program is still unsuccessful, one might make the criterion goal less exacting or the reinforcement more desirable or more frequent. If a program is successful, one might begin to rely more heavily on social reinforcements (e.g., verbal approval) and/or gradually change the reinforcement schedule from continuous to intermitent.

This brief overview of behavior programming is by no means intended as a prescription for action. Neither would additional detail necessarily furnish such a prescription. Good behavior modification is not characterized by a mechanical reliance on ligidly preformulated procedures; instead, one should use a behavioral paradigm as a conceptual framework for developing, monitoring, and refining strategies for effective teaching. Furthermore, certain aspects of behavior modification have been de-emphasized here (e.g., the techniques of observation and record-keeping); and many nuances of operant technology have been omitted altogether. . . .

SPECIOUS ARGUMENTS

Perhaps the most serious and most common charge leveled against behavior modification is that it is a technology of coercion. Alarmed by the specter of a psychological-scientific birch rod, critics mistakenly equate behavior modification with the use of punishment contingencies (i.e., the suppression of undesirable behaviors by means of unpleasant/painful consequences). Yet, as research has consistently demonstrated, and as behaviorists have emphasized, punishment is generally the least effective contingency for shaping behavior. In general, it is much more effective to decrease an undesirable behavior through extinction procedures, i.e., elimination of rewarding consequences. Punishment contingencies are indicated only in those rare instances when the necessity of immediately suppressing a behavior outweighs the disadvantages, like spanking a young child the first time he runs into a busy street. Regardless of whether extinction or punishment is more appropriate in a given case, either one should be combined with the positive reinforcement of alternative, desirable behaviors. In short, punishment is a small part of operant technology, with very narrow areas of application.

Other critics are concerned with the issue of "manipulation" in a larger context. They are disturbed by the potential of operant techniques to shape human behavior with a speed, flexibility, and precision heretofore inconceivable. Several reasons have been expressed for their aversion to behavior modification. Among the most common are the fear that children's behavior might be shaped in harmful directions; the belief that children's "natural impulses" should be allowed to guide their development; the idea that a child's sense of security will be undermined by parents and teachers who employ behavioral contingencies to enforce their cultural values; and the concern that children reared and schooled in such artificial learning environments will be ill-prepared to cope with the real world as adults.

It is impossible to guarantee that behavior modification will never be used in the service of corrupt intentions. It is a truism that any advance in knowledge, once translated into a technology, carries the potential for misuse. But this is a poor rationale for ignoring the techniques. The fact of the matter is that a child's behavior is constantly being shaped by his environment; and his "natural impulses" are largely the behavior patterns shaped by the haphazard consequences which the natural world provides throughout his life. An understanding of the laws of learning not only furnishes insight into the manner in which the natural environment affects a child's development; it also enables parents, teachers, and others to improve upon the natural world, to interact with a child in ways that are far more systematic, precise, and growth-promoting.

The laws of physics which govern the behavior of floods can, once we understand them, enable us to build dams and irrigation systems. Given such knowledge, a policy of laissez-faire would be folly. It would seem equally inadvisable to leave the development of children unnecessarily to chance. By not taking advantage of the available behavioral technology, a well-intentioned teacher may unknowingly limit her ability to teach. The educable retarded child who would learn to read if only the tasks were programmed in small enough steps; the child with an IQ of 115 who is banished to a "special class" simply because his teacher does not know how to rearrange the classroom environment to provide more reinforcement for adaptive behavior than for temper tantrums; the child who will never read a book as an adult because his school reading was motivated by the threat of aversive consequences; these are only three of the casualties. That the damage was done inadvertently is no consolation.

A major goal of education is to teach rules—including cultural, social, linguistic, and mathematical rules—by making them explicit and by encouraging their observance. When rules are enforced in the classroom by punitive contingencies, there is a definite threat to a child's sense of security, which is one reason why skillful behavior modifiers make minimal use of punishment. On the other hand, when more effective behavior contingencies (e.g., positive reinforcement, extinction) are used to impart rules, a child's sense of security is enhanced. In a classroom where demands are tailored to the child's current capacities, and rewards are given consistently and contingently, the result is a predictable and secure learning environment. And in preparation for adulthood in a world of capricious demands and irregular contingencies, the child is best served *not* by schooling of equal inconsistency, but by orderly and nurturant training which maximizes the skills needed in the uncertain world ahead.

TYPICAL PITFALLS IN IMPLEMENTATION

A perfect behavior modification program has rarely, if ever, been created solely on paper. As with anything a teacher does, the complexity of children and classrooms makes it necessary to revise behavioral programs while in progress. In addition to knowing the principles, a teacher can benefit by being aware of some common stumbling blocks.

Teacher attention is frequently the most powerful reinforcer available in classrooms. It can increase the number of completed math problems or the number of successful pushups. However, in addition, teacher attention can inadvertently reinforce the inappropriate behaviors of students. Gentle cajoling, yelling, even harsher reprimands are all potentially reinforcing to children who rarely obtain the more affectionate and approving forms of attention. If a student has no socially acceptable means of eliciting attention, he may choose to perform those inappropriate behaviors which have paid off with teacher's attention in the past.

The choice of suitable reinforcements and punishments is not always obvious. For example, a teacher sending a student to the principal's office assumes that this is a form of punishment; however, it may actually be reinforcing the student's undesirable behavior by releasing him from a situation in which frustration and failure are commonplace (this would certainly have been true in the case of Robert). One implication is that it is more useful to shape and reward new and appropriate behaviors than to punish inappropriate ones.

Several other common difficulties may jeopardize the success of a behavioral program. One is the problem of misplaced reinforcement. This may be illustrated by the teacher who rewards a child for scrubbing the crayon stains off his desk. The effect of this reinforcement is to increase the future likelihood of the child's making crayon stains in order to be rewarded for erasing them. By analogy, therefore, one would do better to reward a child for not fighting (e.g., for playing cooperatively) rather than for stopping fighting.

A second problem involves the premature termination of rewards. This occurs when a teacher abruptly discontinues reinforcement after a child has reached the criterion level of performance. As a result the child may revert to an earlier, less skillful performance which previously resulted in reinforcement. If, after months of being reinforced for successive approximations to the goal (successful completion of three-digit multiplication problems) Robert finally managed to get an "A" on a math quiz, and if at this point his teacher had decided that there was no longer any need for reinforcing him, then Robert's subsequent math performance and behavior might have deteriorated significantly. Behavior must not only be acquired, it must be maintained by some form of continuing reinforcement. Once criterion has been reached, the program can be phased out gradually and the target behavior can be maintained with reinforcement that more closely approximates real world conditions by being intermittent and/or less concrete and more social in nature.

One of the most difficult problems involves the escalation of disruptive behaviors. This typically occurs in the early phases of a program, when the child realizes that certain inappropriate behaviors (e.g., out-of-seat, coloring during spelling tests) are no longer being rewarded with teacher attention. In trying to regain his accustomed reinforcement, the child may resort to other behaviors which are too disruptive to be ignored for long (e.g., shouting, stealing material from nearby desks). Although it is natural at this point for the teacher to respond with a great deal of attention, the results are unfortunate: in the future the child is likely to proceed immediately to the more extreme forms of disruptive behavior in order to get attention.

When confronting an escalation problem, a teacher should consider using a "time-out strategy," which means putting the child in a situation where any possibility for reward is removed entirely for a fixed, relatively short period of time—like ten minutes—which is specified in advance. The child is simply and without undue attention removed from where the behavior problem occurred to another, non-rewarding setting (e.g., a blocked-off corner of the room, a chair just outside the door). One crucial prerequisite of an effective time-out procedure is that the classroom provide ample reinforcement contingencies which are realistically geared to the child's current skills; otherwise, time-out can become an actively sought means of escaping from an excessively demanding and insufficiently rewarding environment. Furthermore, immediately upon his return to the classroom, the child should be given a small, easily managed task (in the Robert case study, one or two rudimentary multiplication problems), whose successful performance is immediately rewarded. This combination of procedures will make it clear to him that even severely disruptive behaviors will provide only minimal "payoff" and will remind him of other, adaptive behaviors in his repertoire that are better means of gaining reinforcement.

WITHDRAWN AND AGGRESSIVE CHILDREN

A fact of life for many teachers is the apparently "unworkable" child who seems impervious to even the most intense and prolonged intervention. Often this child is extremely withdrawn or extremely aggressive, and as attempts to change his behavior repeatedly fail, his "passivity" or his "aggressive" nature come to be seen as the underlying cause of his intractability. However, it is crucial to realize that these labels are not explanations of behaviors, but merely convenient shorthand for describing behaviors.

Being shy or teasing others or refusing to comply with adult requests are all behaviors that most children occasionally display; extremely passive or aggressive children simply display such behaviors with greater frequency and/or greater severity. Therefore, the working assumption is that the environmental contingencies encountered by these children have—in comparison with those encountered by other children—more consistently and more strongly reinforced passive or aggressive behaviors. The passive child, for example, may have learned that by not participating in class he avoids being criticized; the aggressive child may have been reinforced with teacher attention for his fighting, or learned that aggression is most effective in suppressing other students' teasing. Regardless, then, of the entrenched appearance of such behaviors, the same basic rules of learning have governed their acquisition and can effectively be applied to their modification.

The use of behavioral principles with passive or aggressive children proceeds according to the same six-stage program outlined earlier. It is, however, imperative that a teacher working with these children expect progress to be both more erratic and more gradual. Initial resistance can be expected, and initial progress may well be discouraging.

Often a teacher may need to begin by monitoring just one specific undesirable behavior and providing reinforcement for an adaptive, incompatible alternative. A teacher could do this by giving the passive child a check (or star) for every instance within a given period in which he interacted in any way with someone else in the classroom; similarly, a teacher could reward the aggressive child for every two-minute period in which he was sitting at a desk, performing task-relevant behavior.

An alternative method might be the negotiation of a "contract," with the teacher suggesting more appropriate classroom behaviors and the student offering suggestions of specific rewards—so many points for sitting at a desk, working at a task. The contract may be written up and a copy kept by each party. In the initial stages of the contract the teacher might need to assign points after every five-minute period and provide immediate back-up reinforcement (a star for one point, candy for five points); eventually, the frequency of these counting periods could be reduced, the interval between points and reinforcements extended, and the expected behaviors and types of rewards changed.

In summary then, the teacher must reinforce even minor approximations to the final goal, attempt to ignore inappropriate behavior, and tolerate occasional setbacks or even escalations. The systematic application of these principles can, however, significantly improve the classroom behavior of even extremely passive or aggressive children.

Compliments Provoke John

What do you do when Robert's "reinforcement" is John's "punishment"? Madeline Hunter knew the class she was subbing in was tough, so she was pleased when "even John came to join the others on the rug. Wanting to strengthen his 'good' behavior, I used the positive reinforcer, 'Good for you, John. You really knew how to act.'

"It was as if I had thrown a firecracker into a volcano. . . ."

Madeline Hunter

"Boys and girls, Mrs. Hunter is going to be your teacher."

"Oh, no!" was the wail of unanimous rejection from the first grade class who did not want anyone to replace their teacher.

What an ego-impaling experience! I am not a new teacher or a substitute teacher. I'm a teacher educator who has had lots of experience in the classroom, but I barely survived this encounter with these first graders.

It all began in an inner-city school when a first grade teacher needed to be "sprung" from her classroom for a conference. A substitute was on the way but had not arrived. If I had known she would never arrive, I might not have been so generous with my offer "Let me take the class. I haven't worked with a first

This article was originally published as **"Much I Had Forgotten,"** in *Today's Education*, Vol. 63, No. 4 (Nov.–Dec. 1974). Reprinted by permission. Madeline Hunter is Principal of University Elementary School and Lecturer, Graduate School of Education, University of California, Los Angeles.

grade in some time, so the experience will be fun for me." Fun? Little did I know.

I was not even alerted when the first grade teacher said, "Oh, no, Mrs. Hunter, you'd better not. This class has a—uh—real personality." I was to find out later she was a master at understatement to describe them so nicely.

When I first entered the room, children were milling around; no one seemed involved in much of anything; and John, whose name I learned in the first thirty seconds, was buzzing around pestering everyone. The teacher, somewhat embarrassed, explained that she had been waiting for the substitute so she had not started a lesson in case the substitute preferred to do her own thing.

As I took in the situation, the cold realization dawned on me that I would not be enjoying a group of industrious six-year-olds intently involved in fascinating tasks. Instead, I would have the chore of putting together a disintegrating class by creating something to occupy them when I did not have the slightest idea of what they could do, where they sat, what materials or books they had, or even their names.

Except, of course, for John's.

In the first few minutes in the room, I had four opportunities to learn his name as the teacher pulled him out of the paper cupboard, told him to stop hitting Stacy, made him return the stapler to the drawer from which he should not have taken it, and told him he must stop interrupting.

"Give me a book; I'll read to them," I said grimly. "Then go ahead to the conference or you'll be late."

Generous and thoughtful? Not at all. By then I knew that no sweet smile and cheery greeting was going to pull that group together. I surely did not want the teacher or any other adult to be in the room to see my floundering. There I was, a supposedly competent educator, with a feeling in my stomach that reaffirmed my belief that it is a lot easier to talk about successful teaching than to accomplish it in the real world of the classroom.

It was at that moment that the teacher introduced me to the class, and I was welcomed by their "Oh, no!" Then, rolling her eyes to heaven, the teacher left.

I tried not to take the children's rejection personally. After all, they had never seen me before so they could not possibly know how rusty my first grade teaching skills were. Even though the professional me could acknowledge this fact, the personal me had a hard time accepting their rejection.

How must regular substitutes feel when children daily demonstrate a negative reaction to their entrance into a classroom? Or unsuccessful teachers or student teachers when pupils' negative responses confirm their suspicion that they are not really as competent, or even as likeable, as they would desire to be?

I began trying to gather the group on the rug, praying that the book had some spellbinding potential. John, I found, was not the only innovator when it came to following directions. Trying to get the group together was like trying to handle popcorn. I would get two or three children settled, then while I was gathering some others, I would lose the first few. (Any experienced teacher will recognize my situation and my feelings. I found myself grimly wishing that some legislators, business people, or parents who are critical of teachers could be in my spot.)

Slowly, as I used the educational theory I knew, the group began to cooperate, and even John came to join the others on the rug. Wanting to strengthen his "good" behavior, I used the positive reinforcer, "Good for you, John. You really know how to act."

It was as if I had thrown a firecracker into a volcano. Pleasing the teacher was the last thing John desired. I had barely uttered my words of praise when he jumped up from the group shouting, "I don't wanna listen to the dumb book" and proceeded to dance on top of the tables.

Fortunately, I understood reinforcement theory. If I had not, I would have taken the bait and reacted to John's antics—which was exactly what he wanted me to do. Instead, I gritted my teeth and pretended not to see him, which took some doing.

When he bopped another boy on the head with a book, I was lavish with my attention to the victim. "Why, I'll bet there isn't anyone else who is so grown up he can keep right on listening after being hit like that. You're acting just like a *sixth* grader." Whereupon the boy sucked in his breath, sat tall, and withstood John's onslaught.

Clearly, I could not turn this class loose to work by themselves. My only hope for survival was to weave a spell and keep them on the rug for the remainder of the hour until lunch.

The writer of the story I was reading never would have recognized his tale, for I began to spin it out as long as possible. The story, called "The Uncatchable Mouse," as I recall, had a refrain that went something like this: "The trap went snap. It caught the . . . but it didn't catch Henry."

I had the children clap each time I said *snap* and added "No, sir" at the appropriate places in the refrain. "It didn't catch Henry" became "No, sir, it didn't catch Henry. No, sir, no sir, it didn't catch Henry. No, sir, no, sir, no, sir, it didn't catch Henry." The more No, sir's I added to the refrain, the more intense the children's attention and anticipation.

When I got this survival skill really launched, the child I pointed to indicated with his or her fingers the number of times all of us chanted the No, sir. (More time burned up, for they all selected four or five times, and lunchtime and salvation got closer and closer.)

Through this ordeal, three me's were involved, the *classroom teacher me*, the *personal me* (with my ego bleeding), and the *teacher educator me*. Each watched the others perform, feel, and think.

The *classroom teacher me* knew a lot of psychological theory and, as a result of years of training and experience, had encountered similar problems and had a repertoire of professional skills to use.

As for the *personal me*, realizing how it reacted was a real shock. For the first twenty minutes, smarting with humiliation, I found myself praying that no one would come in and see me in the mess. Teachers had often wondered if I were an ivory-towered theorist, and I found myself facing evidence that seemed to indicate that I could not really bring it off in the real world of the classroom.

When I first tried to get the children to the rug, the personal me thought, "What if I were being videotaped?" (I had videotaped teachers countless times.) I would have died of mortification.

Later, when the group was responding positively to the story, I wished someone had been videotaping the lesson. I wish parents and legislators could see the agony behind difficult teaching and the seeming eternity of chaos out of which the professional is responsible for drawing educational order. I wish they could see the slow, minute steps, not all of them forward, which lead a reluctant (even recalcitrant) learner toward becoming an eager, involved learner.

How useful it would be for new teachers to see a pro getting children ready to learn. How important for those beginners to see the abrasion of the ego that occurs to all of us. How essential for them to perceive that what turns chaos into productive learning is professional competence which builds desirable self-concepts and feelings of worth and achievement for the learners—not wishful thinking or divine revelation.

A frightening aspect of the personal me emerged—the revengeful me. I found myself thinking, "Just you wait until I get rid of the rest of these kids, Master John. Then, you and I will have a session at lunchtime, and you'll learn how to listen and how to follow directions." I was appalled by the retaliatory reactions my damaged ego was generating.

I did not like John one bit. There I was, a supposedly successful educator, and he was making a monkey of me. I thought about all the university courses that stress understanding the child. Phooey. How can teachers withstand the emotional and nervous stress that unmanageable pupils present unless they also have the professional skills necessary to deal productively with such pupils? These courses must present those skills, as well as a case for understanding the child.

The *teacher educator me* was experiencing the moment of truth. If this situation was difficult for me after years of experience, what must it be like for new teachers who do not have the theoretical know-how plus experience to guide them through such potentially destructive educational arenas? The teacher educator me found an even more profound respect for the Herculean task of the classroom teacher than I had had before. All of us who are telling teachers how it ought to be done should try doing it ourselves to keep us humble as well as realistic. And we had better make sure that our teacher preparation translates theory into the practical skills and understandings critical to success.

As the story proceeded, John, unable to elicit a negative response from me, was finally "educationally seduced" into joining the group, who were having fun, clapping and chanting their way through the story. Time, story, clapping, chanting, and professional skills merged to produce a participating, enjoying, behaving group.

But I was not deluded. Had I changed the educational prescription and expected anything more than participatory entertainment activities, I would have had an atom bomb on my hands.

Finally, the teacher returned to find her replacement chanting and clapping with an enthralled, involved class that included John! And what happened to *her* ego and *her* professional self-concept? She worked daily with kids who were difficult to manage and now saw another adult working with them in a manner that made everything look easy. I saw the despair in her eyes.

I told the class that I had enjoyed being their teacher and I hoped I could teach them again. The group responded with a warm "Yes, come back," and John, the child for whom I had been planning a thumbscrew at noon, added, "Come back tomorrow!"

"What a darling little boy!" I now thought.

Afterwards, I tried to explain to the teacher what a problem I had had on my hands with her class, how I had prayed for the first twenty minutes that no one would come in the room and see the chaos there, how hard I had worked to pull the group together, and how John had defied me. But she did not believe me. She thought I was only attempting to protect her wounded ego.

My short first grade teaching stint taught me or reminded me of some important principles that are easily forgotten by those of us who are no longer in the classroom. We forget

How much easier it is to enthrall a group for an hour than to teach them day after day.

How teachers feel when they are not performing as well as they wish they were—especially when it's possible that someone will come in the room and observe them.

How teachers feel about a child who shows the world that they are not as competent at coping with difficult pupils as they would like to be and how their feelings about a problem youngster change when his or her behavior changes for the better.

How teachers feel when they see someone else who appears successful with a child or a class that has given them trouble.

How essential valid programs of teacher education and continuing in-service are in helping teachers learn necessary professional skills so that they can cope with the daily problems they will face or are facing in the classroom.

How excruciatingly difficult and emotionally exhausting teaching is.

I am going to take a class again and again so I will never forget.

M & M Motivation

A token reward, the material symbol of teacher pleasure, is the most conscious and concrete symbol of behavior modification techniques, and very controversial. I myself enthusiastically defend *and* reject its use—depending on the circumstance.

Beatrice Gross

Among the advantages of material reward, claim its adherents, is that the teacher is reminded to look at and for good behavior. The rate of positive comments from the teacher increases dramatically. Also each child gets increased attention because the teacher keeps her eyes open for opportunities to reward the child. And if the teacher should forget, the child feels it is permissible to remind her. The amount of work done increases as behavior improves, they say, and the system works especially well with "disadvantaged" children.

There is some concern that teachers will manipulate children for doubtful ends: material reward has been used to maintain "law and order" in the classroom. Worse, it's been used to eliminate behavior which many think of as natural for children: moving, skipping, talking to and looking at other children.

Ten years ago, when I first heard of behavior modification used in a school, it wasn't so labeled. Harold L. Cohen, artist-designer turned educator, used the technique at the National Training School for Boys, a youth house for youngsters who had turned off and tuned out and *been* turned out by the schools and their families. Some were charged as delinquents, others were kids who truanted or had been found "incorrigible" or were school failures. Most figured they wouldn't make it in the "straight" world. They had found ways to get immediate gratification and didn't have a strong future orientation.

Cohen invited each boy for an informal chat in his office where he offered to supply them with soda, girlie magazines, time at the pool table—whatever they liked that was legal—in return for reading a bit and answering some simple questions or working on math problems. The boys weren't pressured to learn or put into classroom seats which they found oppressive, rather, they were offered an opportunity to earn pleasures in a frankly quid pro quo arrangement. It was clear payment for performance—up-front, frankly explicit, and minus the rhetoric and subtleties which usually mask it.

"Normal," achieving kids know they must work hard at homework to get high scores on SAT's so they can choose the best colleges and graduate into good-money, high-prestige jobs. These boys lacked the background or social training that encouraged them to plan ahead for the "bottom line," so Cohen moved the incentive up to a priority position which they could appreciate. Gradually, according to Cohen, he exacted more work for each privilege, and eventually the boys found sufficient satisfaction in their work to function without rewards.

In this instance the token method seemed appropriate and reasonable.

But when one learns of first- and second-graders who once loved to draw and paint but turned away from favored activities when the "token" was removed, one is shaken and fears the hidden curriculum of the token system.

And then there is the problem of the token itself. Many parents and teachers strenuously object to their children being given candy as a reward for work, realizing the problems and pain such a reward causes later in life.

We also know that teachers often reward behavior that may not be in the best interest of the child as a learning, questioning person, such as not raising pressing but unanswerable questions or never contradicting the teacher. As a rule, I think the "target" should be given a choice as to whether he or she wishes to be involved in such an experiment. We should be alert lest we turn activities that are pleasurable into duties, and we should constantly monitor our goals.

Those who work with children can anticipate other problems endemic to the method: What will happen when unobserved behavior goes unrewarded? Will the child learn to behave appropriately only when the teacher is around to notice it and reward it? Could this problem be solved by having peers dole out recognition and rewards? Could the children themselves handle their own rewards? Self-monitoring and peer recognition are both employed by adults practicing behavior modification on themselves, and it is believed that these methods are more effective in maintaining modified behavior than are token rewards.

If you feel that despite the drawbacks you want to try token rewards with your group, be selective and remember it is no panacea. "A common educational research hypothesis is that lower-class children will be more motivated by material rewards than will middle-class children. . . . The hypothesis is often taken as a 'given' by researchers, who cite a number of studies for support."* But this hypothesis is unproved according to Charles B. Schultz and Roger H. Sherman in an issue of *Review of Educational Research*. "Of about sixty studies, most of them conducted within the past decade, some did support the hypothesis, *but most did not*" (Winter 1976).

Unfortunately for those who need an easy answer, the conclusion of the study was that "the type of reward (material, social, or feedback) that will best motivate a student depends on the individual student."

And of all the criticisms the most poignant for me is this: By giving tokens or withholding them, one can remove the joy and excitement from activities that once were engaged in for fun.

---

*John Hollifield, **"Research Clues,"** *Today's Education*, September–October 1976; David Green and Mark R. Lepper, **"How to Turn Play Into Work,"** *Psychology Today*, September 1974.

Trying to Get Workable Ethics in the Classroom

One approach to changing behavior—the behaviorist approach —has already been presented by Heifetz and Farber. On the other hand, you might find Cam Smith Solari's method more compatible with your goals.

She describes her method of working with junior high school children by making the children more aware of their actions and the consequences of these actions. As she says, "One gets very tired of being reasonable with students causing problems and its nice to have them handle it themselves."

Cam Smith Solari

When one asks what acceptable behavior is, in any group, it comes down to a question of the kind of behavior which does not do damage to others and is to the benefit of oneself and others. When any individual or group wants to survive, ethics comes into being. Ron Hubbard defined ethics as: "Rationality towards the highest level of survival for the individual, the future race, the group, and mankind."

I use this definition and consider learning a survival activity whether it is practical or aesthetic learning. In the learning group of a class, I consider an individual has his ethics pretty well "in" if he takes responsibility for himself, does his part and his own work, and is considerate of the working needs of his classmates. Ethics are "out" if he is insensitive to others and causes problems. Out-ethics are a problem if the classroom experience isn't very interesting, or in a class where students have been suddenly put on their own responsibility and don't quite know what to make of it yet. The instructor in the second case has to try to handle problems as quickly and as quietly as possible, while the group learns to be responsible for their own behavior.

With students who have been compelled to sit in quiet rows for years, there doesn't seem to be a way of "lifting the lid" just part way. If you really want to teach responsibility to students who are used to imposed control I think you have to breathe deeply and stand back and let people see that *obviously* a few agreements are needed.

For minor or major disturbances that occur in class, I ask the students involved for a written report about what happened. This isn't a letter of apology or anything else; just a report. The important thing is not to take time to argue with the student or give verbal reproof, because this is rewarding some-

This article is from **"What It Is, What It Ain't,"** *A Teacher's Report.* Reprinted by permission of the author. © 1972 Cam Smith Solari.

one who is causing a problem with your attention. I hand someone with out-ethics a report to do and immediately get the "facts" in writing, like: "He tripped me when I came in the room so I called him a name," or "You're not being fair and I wasn't doing anything," or "He had it coming so I hit him," or "I was just playing and she got her arm hurt." It doesn't matter *what* is written and whether the "facts" the student gives are true or not. What it does is to get him to put some attention on himself and his own actions. I've found that after a student has had to do a few reports and I keep asking for exactly what happened, the "facts" get more accurate and he will say what *he* has done.

For even something minor like having to use the restroom during class, a student signs a statement with date, class, time, and a note to the effect that he needed to be excused from class that day. Nothing is said, and the note is filed. Students stop needing to use the restroom.

For more major things like hot arguments between two students in the middle of class, both are required to write out the full story . . . or draw it if they are too angry to write. If one is "innocent" but involved in any way they still have to do it. (It is often the "innocent" ones who never do anything who really create trouble.) Drawing is often much better for ethics reports since it is a quicker way of communication. The important thing is to get the emotional charge off immediately and not to have to talk or argue about it.

For the most part, good indicators like smiles and readiness to go back to work are seen in students who write or draw a "mad" report. Reports are never censored or disagreed with. If they were they wouldn't work again. It has to be pretty safe and with no one "getting after him" before a person can look at his own actions and evaluate himself. Then it has to be safe to improve, and improvement is all that is wanted.

Another variation of an ethics report is more involved than slapping a paper down in front of an angry student and saying "start drawing!" This one I made up as a detention assignment one day for two boys who had just had (another) fist fight in class:

1. Have the students tape paper together to make a strip about 20 or 30 feet long. (The taping is part of it since they have to do it together.)
2. Have them divide it into frames like a strip of movie film.
3. Have each student take a crayon and both start in the first frame drawing a scene between two people. Each student draws a character. (The first frames are likely to have the characters killing each other.) This is continued frame by frame together, until they are drawing their two characters in good communication with each other and both students look happy and are acting like they like each other.
4. Then the instructor who has been reading a magazine or something and watching out of the corner of one eye, notices what has happened and says, "That's it! Both of you go home."

One gets very tired of being reasonable with students causing problems, and it is nice to have them handle it themselves. In a few minutes enemies have turned into friends using this communication report. The two fighting boys I first had do it asked to stay after school again the next day to draw another giant comic strip.

Following the same basic ethics principle of having *students* handle whatever is wrong, if any damage ever happens nothing is said except that the person who caused it must make it right again. Students in my classes have had to make other students stop crying, wash desks and floors and walls, communicate, sew up rips in clothes, and do whatever they must to correct something they have done to the environment or another person. They feel wonderful after that instead of feeling sorry or "punished."

For having out-ethics one is no longer part of the group until he has handled whatever it was, and wants to continue. It is considered handled when the student says it is handled and looks cheerful, and his group or coach wants him back. The separation can be either an understood separation from the group because he has had to drop what he was doing and write the report, or it can be actual physical separation to another part of the room or out of the room, depending on how far his ethics went out. I found in the social studies class that merely "firing" someone from his group was amazingly effective in helping him get his ethics fast. The whole group begins to notice ethics. The more a class really is a good place to be and the learning experience is happening, of course the more rare an out-ethics problem is.

What Could Be Wrong With Praise

Beatrice Gross

Unlike rewards of candy, praise doesn't rot the teeth or encourage materialism. So what could be bad? Praise well placed would seem to have nothing but good effects. Its use is encouraged for infants who can, with lavish praise, be toilet-trained in one day: it helps "weight watchers" and "smoke-enders." In fact, most self-improvement programs build in time for applause and praise. Observers of Chinese schools report that children applaud each other for correct answers while they attach no blame to wrong answers, which seems to result in an extraordinarily healthy climate for learning and cooperation.[1]

Of course some encouragement can be unconsciously destructive. Barbara Sher, designer and director of the Women's Success Teams, blames the tender loving concern parents show in times of a child's "failure" with the child's unconscious desire, in later life, to fail. She asks her audience, "Can you

---

[1] Elizabeth Kellogg, **"Education in China Today,"** *Outlook*, Summer, 1975.

recall unmitigated joy at the success you had when a child, or are your most vivid memories of moments of reassurance when you failed? Wouldn't you be more successful as adults if you'd been cheered on more for victories and commiserated with less?"

Shouldn't you want to be known, then, as a teacher who praises and encourages her students?

Well, there is a problem with praise, according to some research studies. Jane Stallings, in a Stanford Research Institute study, examined seven Head Start programs and focused on teacher behaviors that produced desirable child behaviors, such as independence, task persistence, cooperation, and question asking.[2] Her finding is most disturbing, regarding the effect of praise on independence. She reports that the child who becomes dependent on praise becomes a teacher watcher rather than one who behaves and thinks independently. This of course, confirms what John Holt described in *How Children Fail.*

If teachers want to help children become more independent, praise should be used sparingly and above all specifically, says Stallings. And if you want to further encourage children to work without constant adult direction and intervention, you should base your program on materials other than textbooks and workbooks. You should ask more open-ended questions and avoid direct questions with right or wrong answers. (Unfortunately, the very things she says you should avoid have been found to be effective if one is looking for techniques that lead to good results in achievement tests.)

Children accustomed to high amounts of praise will not get involved in innovative or complex reasoning because they have been conditioned to go for the quick payoff, according to Mary Rowe of the University of Florida.[3] They will tend also to guard results until the teacher asks for them, acting alone rather than in cooperation with others. They will check more often with the teacher, waiting to get her attention, perhaps because they don't want to do a task wrong or because they know they can't expect help from "competitors."

Must you make a choice between having independent children or high achievers? A number of investigators demonstrate the effectiveness of praise on achievement in elementary school children,[4] but Taffel, O'Leary and Armel

---

[2]Presented by Jane Stallings, Ph.D., at the Early Childhood Conference on Evaluation, Aug. 6, 1974, Anaheim, California. Contact Stanford Research Institute, Menlo Park, Ca. 94025.

[3]Mary Budd Rowe, *Teaching Science As Continuous Inquiry* (New York: McGraw Hill, 1973).

[4]Wesley C. Becker, Charles H. Madsen, Carole R. Arnold, and D.R. Thomas, **"The contingent use of teacher attention and praise in reducing classroom behavior problems,"** *Journal of Special Education,* 1 (3) 1967, 287–305; Ace Cossairt, R. Hall and B.L. Hopkins, **"The Effects of Experimenter's Instructions, Feedback and Praise and Student Attending Behavior,"** *Journal of Applied Behavior Analysis* 6 (Spring 1973), 89–100.

offer an alternative route.[5] They studied the reactions of second-graders to either praise or reasoning and found that "verbalizing reasons to a child for engaging in an academic task is as effective or more effective than giving him praise for doing so and is certainly more effective than giving him no reasons or praise statements at all."

Maryann Gatheral found that in junior high school abundant praise may make kids so overconfident they don't concentrate as well on tests.[6] Of course, for some adolescents being praised in front of their peers is an embarrassment leading to social segregation.

Often teachers praise low-achieving students in hopes they will take heart, but such praise may deceive them into thinking they are working sufficiently hard, only to have them face real competition later and be crushed by the experience. Yet we also know from experience that many of these children are systematically criticized or ignored at home and need encouragement. What should we do?

It is certainly a dilemma for teachers of children who would like to encourage high achievement, independence, cooperation, persistence and a good self-image. Must one choose one good over another? Isn't there a conflict between behavior modification programs which guarantee success by the use of praise and this advice to hold back praise?

Mary Rowe, at the University of Florida, suggests that praise be used for simpler tasks, for drills or encouraging acceptable social behavior, and that the praise should be pertinent. The more in-depth the learning, the more you should encourage the students by showing an interest in their work or ideas.

Check whom you praise and what you praise them for. You must be careful that you don't give generalized praise to low achievers or girls while you reserve specific admiration for high achievers and boys. Such comments as "You're doing very well," "Good job," and "Just fine" are not as valuable as "You set up a great experiment," "I'd like to follow up that point," "That's a connection I hadn't thought of." You must learn to convey admiration that's not mere flattery.

Don't substitute general criticism for praise. A critical remark must also be specific and followed immediately with an indication of how to do the task right. Even better than that, give the students the time (uninterrupted) to talk and explain why they think what they do. Encourage them by asking a follow-up question showing your interest in what has been said or done. And be patient so they can answer thoughtfully.

---

[5]Susanne Johnson Taffel, K. Daniel O'Leary, and Sandra Armel, **"Reasoning and Praise, Their Effects on Academic Behavior,"** *Journal of Educational Psychology* 66 (3) 1974, 291–295.

[6]Maryann Gatheral, University of California at Davis, as quoted in **"Your Praise Can Smother Learning,"** by David I. Martin, *Learning*, Feb. 1977.

"Stifle Yourself" First

With all the new materials available we still don't get children to think. Why? Mary Budd Rowe found that it's because we can't stand silence. Teachers talk too much and too soon.

Rowe taped numerous class sessions and found that most teachers gave students just one second to answer. If the teacher didn't get the answer in that one second, she repeated the question or directed it to another student. When the teacher did get an answer she waited even less than a second after the student stopped talking and shot out another question or comment, or changed the subject. Rowe studied three hundred tapes of classroom interaction, so her concern is well documented.

On occasion my own children accuse me of "asking questions like a teacher." It must be this kind of behavior they are thinking of.

In classrooms where teachers gave a total of three seconds before they jumped in, the kids began to really develop their ideas, advance new theories, talk for longer periods, answer with more complexity, and volunteer comments more frequently without being called upon. While the "pushy" teacher got an average of three voluntary comments per period, the more patient teacher could count on an average of seven.

Pausing longer reduced the number of "don't know," "we..ll I think..." answers to more secure statements, and the quiet ones in class began to speak up. Teachers who waited began to find they had classes of much smarter kids than they had imagined.

Did the slower-paced method of running a class change the test scores? Not necessarily—and when it did, it wasn't always in the direction of higher grades.[1] But when you consider that more children felt better about themselves and probably retained more for longer periods because the material was better integrated, perhaps you could be willing to sacrifice the higher test scores. This is a problem, since classrooms which use a high rate of drill, practice, and praise do produce children who achieve higher test scores. Compared to classrooms that are more exploratory, they also produce children who accept more responsibility for their failures, take more

---

[1]Mary Budd Rowe, "Wait-Time and Rewards as Instructional Variables: Their Influence on Language, Logic, and Fate Control," *Journal of Research in Science Teaching*, 11 (2), 1974.

responsibility for their successes, and who have lower absence rates.[2]

Unfortunately, achievement tests still have not been standardized to measure the thinking capacity of children or their ability to use information. Most achievement tests ask for a quick and superficial recall of facts. For those teachers who are secure and want their children to be more secure and intellectually stimulated, counting from one thousand and one to one thousand and four before asking the next question can help. For untenured teachers under pressure, I leave you with the data. Look to your conscience to select your method of testing.

Sondra M. Napell

INTRODUCTION

Many instructors unwittingly behave in ways which not only frustrate their own goals, but also actively discourage significant (as opposed to rote) student-learning. . . .

At issue is the relationship between intent and actions: what teachers do and how they do it delivers more of an impact than what they say. . . .

SIX NONFACILITATING BEHAVIORS

Insufficient "Wait-Time"

"Wait-time" is the amount of time after an initial question has been posed before the teacher answers it himself; repeats, rephrases, or adds further information to the question; or accepts an answer from a student.

More than just a few seconds are a necessary prerequisite for mental information-processing (Moriber, 1971; Rowe, 1974). When the teacher becomes a nonstop talker, filling every possible silence with his voice, what chance do students have either to think over what is being said, formulate intelligent responses, or ask for clarification? . . .

Students who note that the instructor answers a preponderance of his own questions without waiting for a response soon grow dependent upon the

---

[2]David D. Franks, Susan L. Wismer, and Stephen V. Dillon, **"Peer Labeling in Open and Traditional Schools,"** published by the University of Denver, July 1974.

This article was originally published as **"Six Common Nonfacilitating Teaching Behaviors,"** in *Contemporary Education*, Vol. 47, No. 2 (Winter 1976). Copyright © 1976 by Sondra Napell and *Contemporary Education*. Reprinted with permission of the author and Indiana State University. Sondra Napell is the Coordinator, Graduate Assistants Teaching Programs, University of California, Berkeley.

teacher to do their thinking for them. In like manner, an answer too rapidly accepted has the effect of cutting off further information-processing and analysis by the rest of the class. We may attest verbally to our aim of encouraging independent thinkers, but unless we consciously work to expand our wait-time, we will have rhetoric with little resultant change in behavior.

Rowe (1974) reported that when teachers were trained to increase their wait-time from one second to 3-5 seconds several changes occurred in students' behaviors: length and number of unsolicited but appropriate responses increased; failures to respond decreased; and the incidence of student-to-student comparisons of data increased. Instructors who are interested in repeating this experiment in their own classrooms can measure their wait-times ("one, one-thousand, two, one-thousand," etc., sufficing for timing purposes) and then deliberately expand these periods of silence-for-thinking both after a question is posed and after an answer has been given. Sharing the concept of wait-time for thinking with the students often enables the teacher to maximize his efforts and gives the class an insight into learning skills.

The Rapid-Reward

What is the effect on students' processing of information and analysis of data when an instructor says to the first respondent to his question: "Right, good"? As if to assure that further thinking will be terminated, the teacher either proceeds to reword, repeat, and exemplify the answer, or goes on to the next topic. Learning being a highly individualistic process, people learn at different rates and in varying ways. Rapid acceptance of a correct answer favors the faster thinker/speaker who has completed his thought processes; those in midthought are terminated prematurely.

A variation on this theme is the softly voiced, hesitant answer of the student seated nearest the instructor. Because many students commonly respond softly to the teacher if he is within close proximity, an awareness of the consequences of this behavior is crucial. Many a student seated out of earshot has become frustrated, bewildered, or lost interest when a softly voiced, difficult-to-hear answer is rapidly rewarded. To ameliorate this situation, encourage student-to-student dialogue, discussion, and peer critiquing of each other's ideas. The following are suggested: extended silent time after an answer is proffered; a questioning glance around at other students tacitly requesting comment; a question to those in the rear, "What is your analysis of what was just said?" and, most important, physical movement of the teacher from place to place about the room in order that as many students as possible enjoy close proximity to the instructor, "front row seats," at one time or another during the class duration.

The Programmed Answer

The following are examples taken verbatim from classroom dialogues and best exemplify this third pattern.

1. "What are some of the enemies of the praying mantis? Cats kill them, don't they? How about other animals? Or insects?"
2. "What thoughts have you about impeachment? Do you think the proceedings are too lengthy? That partisan politics play too great a role? Is there enough evidence?"
3. "What reasons do you have to use that formula? Was it suggested in the homework chapter? Had you ever used it before? Or seen it used in this context?"
4. "What happens when we add the sums of the rows? Do we get skewed results?"
5. "Look at this shrub and tell me, what observations can you make? Do you see the dead stems? Are they damaged from insect teeding?"

The programmed answer not only deprives the respondent of expressing his own thoughts by steering him toward the answers that the questioner expects, but also conveys the message that there is really little interest in what he thinks or says. While the reasons offered by those who make a practice of this pattern are usually altruistic (i.e., "Silence after the posing of a question is embarrassing to the student"; "I feel impelled to help out by suggesting clues"), one needs to ask himself honestly: "Is it I or the student who is uncomfortable after a second or two of silence?"; "Do I have confidence in the students' ability to think about the question and formulate a response?" and, more important, "Am I interested in what the student has to say or in determining which of my answers he prefers?" While programming can be an effective tool when one desires to guide students' thinking, suggest possibilities, or model logical thought processes, it is important to be aware of its limiting effect in opening up a wide variety of possible ideas. It is via the latter route that an instructor can demonstrate his interest in the students' ideas and himself model inquisitive learning behavior. A willingness to listen helps to create in the classroom a community of learners in place of an authoritative, superordinate-subordinate relationship between teacher and class.

Nonspecific Feedback Questions

Many instructors feel justified in assuming that their students have no questions if no one responds when they ask, "Are there any questions? Do you all understand?" Purportedly designed to give the instructor information as to the clarity and comprehensibility of his presentation, these questions usually fail to solicit feedback. Why? We can isolate several possibilities, two of which are the nature of students and the nature of the questions.

What type of student will (bravely) call attention to his own ignorance when the question is posed to a class: "Does everyone understand?" Interestingly enough, it was a student who suggested that those who do respond comprehend most of the concept, lesson, problem, etc., and need only a minor point made clear. Others, whose lack of understanding is more comprehensive, whose confusion is more widespread, may be too intimidated to call attention in such a public way to their situations. Often the latter are so confused that they cannot think of questions to ask. Yet these are the ones who most need our assistance. How can we determine what it is they do and do not understand?

Contrast the following pairs of questions:
1. "Who doesn't understand this?"
2. "Marx's concept, 'the withering away of the state' can be a difficult one to grasp. Let's try to summarize together some definitions of what this means."
1. "Does anybody have any questions?"
2. "Let's think of some other examples now of situations in which this principle is applicable."
1. "Does everybody see how I got this answer?"
2. "Why did I substitute the value of θ (theta) in this equation?"
1. "Who wants me to go over this explanation again?"
2. "What conclusions can we generalize from this specific graph?"

The teacher needs to ask himself, "What is it important for the students to say or do in order that I be able to determine the extent of their understanding?" He can then formulate and pose one or more questions which will give a more comprehensive sounding of the class's problems and questions.

The Teacher's Ego-Stroking and Classroom Climate

Think of the effects on students' willingness to respond to teacher-posed questions when statements such as the following are made:

1. "Since I have explained this several times already, you all should know what is the effect of an increased demand upon this supply curve."
2. "Obviously, when you use this formula you'll get_____?"
3. (After having listened to several students' answers) "The real answer is this:_____."
4. "Does everybody understand the explanation I just gave? It should be clear by now."
5. "O.K. Now rephrase your answer the way you think I would say it."

Students need to feel that it is psychologically "safe" to participate, to try out ideas, to be wrong as well as right. The teacher's behavior is a most important determinant in the establishment of a safe or comfortable climate. Learning, an active process, requires that the learner interact with ideas and materials. Constant teacher-talk, feeling compelled to comment on each student idea, deciding to be the final arbiter in decision-making processes, interrupting, controlling, intimidating either through expertise, or the threat of grades—these are but some of the behaviors which prevent students from engaging in the active process needed for significant (as distinguished from "rote") learning to take place. It is interesting to note the increased levels of student participation when instructors do not conceal the fact of their ignorance, when they sometimes hesitate about certain questions or information, when their responses are dictated more by an honest desire to assist the student than to demonstrate the extent of their own knowledge.

A few of the possible behaviors which can encourage the establishment of an environment conducive to participation are the teacher's remembering and referring to students' ideas, yielding to class members during a discussion, acknowledging his own fallibility, framing open-ended questions which provide for expression of opinion and personal interpretations of data, accepting the students' right to be wrong as well as right, encouraging joint determinations of goals and procedures when feasible (i.e., "How can I help you best to learn this material?"), sharing the responsibility for learning with the learners (i.e., permitting students to answer their peers' questions; freeing oneself from the burden of thinking that what isn't covered in class, the students cannot learn elsewhere; encouraging group presentations of the material to be covered, etc.), and soliciting student participation in their own learning evaluation such as feed-in of test questions and joint correction of examinations.

Fixation at a Low-Level of Questioning

Bloom (1956) has postulated that cognition operates on ascending levels of complexity. One begins with knowledge, or informational details, and moves upward through comprehension, analysis, and synthesis to evaluation. Questioning can be a central feature in promoting the development of conceptual abilities, analytical techniques, and the synthesis of ideas. Skillful teachers use questions to guide thinking as well as test for comprehension. Too often, however, as illustrated by this sixth recurring pattern, teachers' questions become fixated at the informational level, requiring of students only that they recall bits and pieces of rote-memorized data: information-level questions. For example:

1. What is the formula for finding the force between two charges?
2. What are the years usually ascribable to the writing of the Bible?
3. What is the definition of "quality demanded"?

One-word or short-phrase answers, those capable of being sung out in unison, constitute the preponderance of question-and-answer dialogues in many classrooms and necessitate little interrelating of material, sequencing of thoughts, analyzing of data. While a solid base of factual information in learning is clearly important, fixating students' thinking at this level discourages the development of the more complex intellectual skills. Questions such as those listed below encourage the students to use informational knowledge in order to analyze concepts, synthesize complex relationships, and evaluate the new data:

1. Describe some possible effects on the demand curve of a rent-control law.
2. What would happen if we inserted a metal conductor in between the moving charge and the current?
3. Why must the information in Table One change when we consider these new data?

Being conscious of the levels of questions one is asking and attempting to structure the questions toward analysis, synthesis, and evaluation can do much to combat a fixation at the information-level of thinking.

Conclusion

If asked to formulate the goals of the educational process, would not most teachers include the nourishment of intellectual curiosity, encouragement of independent learners, development of people able to engage in the more complex thinking process? Yet instructors' behaviors such as the six described in this paper militate against the achievement of these goals. . . .

Giving Children Experience In Power

The schools, thought for years to have been the agency most responsible for upward mobility, were reanalyzed in the sixties by social and educational revisionist historians such as Colin Greer, who found most educational gains followed in the wake of economic success.

The reason immigrant groups succeeded, posited Greer, was that as the parents became more powerful and able to take control of their lives, their children were motivated and better able to take advantage of what schools offered.

Now, as always, the children of the very poor, who feel stuck in the lowest class, feel powerless and unable to cope. The despair felt by these children permeates their learning style: a style characterized by either too much passivity or haphazard, unproductive aggression. It is displayed frequently and dramatically on graffitied walls, and by broken windows and trashed classrooms.

What can you do? You might work for social change. You might help the parents of your children to get political clout by organizing for jobs, and for available social services. In the classroom you can find ways to give children an experience in power which might aid them to overcome debilitating inertia and anger and focus their energies constructively.

Dan Cheifetz

POWER GAMES FOR THE CLASSROOM

Setting up learning situations in power can establish important psychological precedents for children. Teachers can validate and extend this learning by bringing "power games" into the classroom—such as "Simon Says." In this game, each child has a chance to be Simon. Each has a turn at affecting the course of action, as well as becoming the object of all eyes. Some tension accompanies this opportunity—"Will I do well? or goof it up?" But almost anything the child does is accepted by the others because he is "playing the game." The game, with its set procedures, rules, and implied contract for social behavior, gives the child a secure structure within which he can confidently step up to experience his moment of strength and importance, and accept with more or less equanimity, his success or failure.

Another game children in my classes play is "I Am Your Master." Each child takes a turn as "master" (some prefer to be called "magician" or "wizard") with the power to turn the others into any creature or thing he wishes. The game begins with the children seated. They rise only when the master proclaims, "I am your master." The master turns them into snakes, robots, or whatever. But the master doesn't wield his power in a vacuum. After the children have obeyed his commands, they have a chance to express how they feel about the way he used his power. Older children may comment verbally. Younger children may feel more comfortable responding with gestures or sounds. In either case, however, touching the master is forbidden.

Children learn that while it may be exhilarating to possess power, there's no guarantee that everyone will like the way they used it. And by listening to what turns people on or off, they get a hint of how to use power effectively.

Power issues abound in just about every area of the curriculum. In studying Napoleon, or the American presidency, or powerful literary characters such as Fagin or Captain Hook, for example, the question "How does it feel to be powerful?" is central if students are to have a personal grasp of the subject. Playing "Simon Says" or "I Am Your Master" is one way to give children that grasp.

GAMES FOR PAIRS

"Power Pairs" is an improvisation game that connects directly with some of the power issues of modern society. Work with the class to develop a list of relationships in society in which one person is powerful and the other,

This article is reprinted by special permission of *Learning*, The Magazine for Creative Teaching, (March 1976) © 1976 by Education Today Company, Inc.

subordinate or weaker, e.g., *coach-player, parent-child, big sister-little sister, cat-mouse.*

Then divide the class into pairs and have each team improvise a dialogue for one of the power-subordinate relationships. ("You may not watch TV until you clean your room." "Aw, Mom, my favorite show is on. Can't my room wait?") After a time, have team members switch roles. Then ask for volunteers to present their improvisation to the whole class, and follow with a general discussion. Rich class discussions have emerged from such subjects as how power can be used benevolently, or abused; how different it feels to be in a powerful position than in a weak one; how a person with power in one situation can be less powerful in another (for instance, big sister has mother to contend with; the cat has the dog).

With my group in Harlem, I tried another activity called "Sculptor." Pairs are formed in which one child is the "sculptor," the other is the material the sculptor works with—clay or stone or wire. The sculptor shapes his material into a tree, robot, kung fu fighter, etc. He can do this with whispered instructions or he can physically place his partner's body in the position he desires. When the sculptor is finished, other members of the group try to guess what the sculptor has produced. (A child might also create a group sculpture using several people as his medium.)

Obviously, certain rules are necessary. The person being molded is not to resist the sculptor in any way, regardless of what he may think of the idea. There should be no guessing before the sculptor has finished, and no personal criticism of the sculptor.

You can easily tie this activity into a unit you are teaching. If the class is studying prehistoric creatures, for example, or transportation, or structures, you can instruct sculptors to create something within that particular category.

CREATIVE POWER

As the children in my group developed more cohesion and a spirit of cooperation, I gave them opportunities to exercise more sophisticated, creative power. On one occasion, for example, I gave each child the chance to lead a group improvisation. Everyone was to think up an idea that involved many people or animals or objects, and some central activity—a bus ride, a circus, or a panful of popcorn. Members of the "cast" were to take the positions the leader indicated and were to follow the leader's instructions, though everyone had some freedom within the activity (for example, each corn in the popper could jump in its own special way as it got hot; the bus riders could each pick a character to play). I led them in one of these improvised sequences, and then I threw the floor open to the students.

The first to volunteer was the class bully, Bella. She was a tall, strong-looking black girl who usually wore an insidious smile. She did not mistreat anyone physically but used threats and sarcasm to dominate some of the girls in the group. Girls not in her clique she regarded as strays, no-accounts (as indeed they regarded themselves). Whenever I asked for opinions from the group, the girls usually waited for Bella to respond, then agreed with her.

Bella often used her power destructively. During one session, for instance, while one of the "strays" was telling a story as others acted it out, Bella, who was in the audience, began giggling with one of her friends. I stopped the skit immediately and asked her to pay attention. She retorted that the story was "corny" and the people in it looked "dumb." I upbraided her rudeness and defended the story and its players, but she had given it the kiss of death. When the story resumed, all energy and interest had drained away.

Now Bella was leading a group improvisation. First she put some kids in a subway car, demonstrating how they were to sway to the motion. Then she said, "The subway wrecks! Everybody fall down!"

The children spilled down all over the place. Bella went among the fallen asking, "Anyone hurt bad? Is there a doctor in the house?"

Someone came forward looking official and began examining the injured. At Bella's direction, a nurse offered assistance. The uninjured helped the injured. The police came . . . the ambulance. Bella supplied the sounds.

In the middle of the disaster, Bella decided she wanted more action, so she pulled some of her friends from the subway wreck and led a protest march with imaginary picket signs. Then she directed some boys to make fun of the demonstrators. She turned her best friend into a crazy woman of the streets who yelled at everybody. She told the two children left in the audience to put on roller skates and interfere with everybody. It was all a little like a Robert Altman film, a kaleidoscope of hassled, disaster-a-minute urban life—colorful, fast moving, quite sophisticated and, despite the incipient chaos, amazingly well staged.

Bella was in everyday touch with her power self. Unfortunately, the only way she knew to be a leader was to be a bully. Now, however, the bully seemed to retreat. Her natural magnetism and energy—the qualities that made others *want* to follow her—emerged. The satisfaction she felt at making her fantasies come alive infected everyone in her cast, and a two-way flow of excitement took place. She didn't need threats here because everybody was having a good time obeying her commands. And maybe in the process she glimpsed a new way to feel important and to get others to follow her lead. It was certainly fertile ground for Bella's natural gifts of creative leadership to flower.

The next master improvisor was Ted, a good-looking black boy who laughed a lot and seemed willing to try anything zany. He turned the group into a Sunday morning congregation. He gave no instructions but began by clapping his hands as he improvised a gospel song. Then he became the minister, shouting the fear of God into his congregation and inspiring their fervent responses:

"You all sinners?"

"Yes, Lord!"

"Whatcha gonna do about it?"

"Sin no more!"

"Hallaluyah!"

But Ted was not one to play the straight role for long:

"You got the Devil in you?"

"Yes, Lord!"

"I got the Devil in *me!*"

"Oh, my!"

"And I *love* the Devil, I do!"

"Uh, huh!"

"And you got to love the Devil, too. Hallaluyah!"

Then he pulled a friend from the congregation to lead, and one girl did a spontaneous "Afro-Indian" dance. It was rousing and funny, an affectionate parody of a kind of power many of these children knew intimately.

PLAYING TEACHER FOR TEN MINUTES

Near the end of the term, I offered each child a chance to be teacher and plan a ten-minute period for the group. "You can plan any activity you wish," I said, "though I would prefer you do the kind of thing we've been doing in the group. However, the final decision about what you do with your ten minutes is up to you."

Only two of the thirteen in the group refused to take a turn at leading. Several children copied what others did as the safe way to handle the unfamiliar situation. One child resorted to "Everybody just play." Another child led the group in her favorite game, "Ducks and Drakes." Two children led "Simon Says": one of them let other children play Simon; the other stayed Simon for the whole ten minutes. One boy led the game "Sculptor," specifying that all the statues had to be about sports.

A few assumed leadership with natural ease, but for most, it was clearly a risk. For them, I believe, it was an especially valuable experience—their very first chance to lead a group, to see how *their* ideas, *their* plans, worked out, and to find out how the group responded. For them, the world was turned upside down for ten minutes. They were actually *doing* something a parent or teacher does: making decisions about how they wanted others in their charge to spend their time and energy; explaining an activity, leading it and taking responsibility for their actions.

Children (and many adults, too) often think of power in superhuman terms—the physical power of a Six Million Dollar Man or a Wonder Woman—or in terms of armies, kings, and presidents, or parents, teachers, and principals. Power, to them, is something someone else has. But in the ten minutes that each child led our group, he or she was learning that power need not be the exclusive possession of adults, forbidden to children. These children were having a taste of what power and responsibility actually feel like in their lives.

I'm aware this is not an easy issue for an educator—or any adult for that matter—to come to grips with. The idea of giving children power runs head-on into our own insecurities. I myself have felt uneasiness about trying some of the activities described here. "Watch out—those kids will run all over you," warn the inner voices. "You'll lose control!"

But there are no real reasons for such fears. Give children guidelines and firm limits in a situation, and they're glad to stay within them. I've noticed that whenever I've given children some power—or observed others doing so— they seem to respect the teacher more, not less. They're pleased that the teacher has shown confidence in them. Children don't want or need (nor can they handle) complete power. But they do need to know how power feels. They can gain experience in self-assertion and leadership and creative mastery only if we adults are willing to share some of our power with them, if we can create safe but challenging situations in which they can test their abilities to wield power.

Some Thrive on Stress

Beatrice Gross

Some school terms it seems that nature has conspired to give you a group of children matched in personality, either all so passive you think you might age from sheer boredom, or, more likely, all so off-the-wall you fear you will never survive the constant outpouring of energy needed to keep in step with the intensity of the kids. Most often your class is mixed.

A recent study by William Revelle, a professor at Northwestern University, and two students, Phyllis Amaral and Susan Turriff, suggests you would do well to match the pressure of your demands regarding assignments and tests to the type of kids you are teaching. Variations in pressure can make for really dramatic improvement in the way individuals in your class will perform.

According to their work, introverts do better on certain intellectual tasks when they are relaxed than when under a tight deadline or time pressure or when keyed up by caffeine.

On the other hand, extroverts do better with the stimulation of some caffeine and under time pressure, but don't function as well if they have no time pressure.

A mixed group will score equally well under either condition (a time limit or no time limit), but that's because part of the group goes up as the other part goes down.

This kind of insight may help with your pacing for continuing education as well as helping you plan different experiences for different types in your class. By varying demands and building-in relaxing exercises (such as practiced as part of meditation or for natural childbirth), you will be helping all the children to marshall their energy for painting or sums.

"Learning" to Give Up

Sometimes we teach negative attitudes without realizing what we are doing. Here is an example of how we teach futility and helplessness.

Albert Rosenfeld

We all have an intuitive knowledge—supported by personal experience and common sense, reinforced by religious beliefs and folk wisdom—that our attitudes toward life are of critical importance to our enjoyment of it. Whether we overcome our problems or not (or in some crisis situations, whether we even survive or not) may depend on whether or not we have hope, whether we give up or keep on trying.

Over the past few decades, biologists and psychologists have been carrying out some fascinating research that reconfirms how powerfully our mental outlook can affect the outcome of our life situations.

You can, for example, do a simple experiment (as Dr. Curt Richter of Johns Hopkins has done repeatedly) with two rats: hold one rat in your hand firmly so that no matter how valiantly he struggles he cannot escape. He will finally give up. Now throw that quiescent rat into a tank of warm water. He will sink, not swim. He has "learned" that there is nothing he can do, that there is no point in struggling. Now throw another rat into the water—one that doesn't "know" that his situation is hopeless and that he is therefore helpless. This rat will swim to safety.

Another experiment (done by Dr. Martin E.P. Seligman of the University of Pennsylvania), this time with dogs: suspend a dog in a hammock into which he fits so snugly that he cannot get loose. Give him electric shocks. He will struggle for a while, then just lie there and submit. Later, take the same dog and put him down on one side of a grid that is only half electrified. Though he is perfectly free to get up and move to the unelectrified side, he will sit where he is, enduring the shock, resigned to his fate. Put another dog down in the same spot—a dog that hasn't been taught to be helpless—and he'll move around until he finds an area that doesn't shock him.

Okay. Fine for rats and dogs. But what about people?

Seligman has been one of the pioneering investigators of the ways in which people's perceptions of themselves as being helpless can in fact render them helpless. His seminal book, *Helplessness: On Depression, Development and Death*, has influenced many other psychologists to pursue this fruitful area of research. Here is a sample Seligman experiment:

This article is from *Saturday Review*, Sept. 9, 1977. Reprinted by permission.

Take two groups of college students and put them in rooms where they are blasted with noise turned up to almost intolerable levels. In one room there is a button that turns off the noise. The students quickly notice it, push it, and are rewarded with blissful silence. In the other room, however, there is no turn-off button. The students look for one, find nothing, and finally give up. There is no other way to escape the noise (except to leave the room before a previously agreed-upon time period has elapsed), so they simply endure.

Later, the same two groups are put in two other rooms. This time, *both* rooms contain a switch-off mechanism—though not a simple button this time and not as easy to find. Nevertheless, the group that found the button the first time succeeds in finding the "off" switch the second time, too. But the second group, already schooled in the hopelessness of their circumstances, doesn't even search. Its members just sit it out again.

There is an obvious parallel here. In each of the three cases—rats, dogs, and students—the situation had changed decisively, but because their efforts for alleviation didn't work in the first instance, the "helpless" subjects didn't even try the second time.

Yes, you may say, but the students knew that at a given point the experiment would be over and the noise would stop. Otherwise they would have been more highly motivated to keep on looking. Besides, in the first instance, no matter how motivated they may have been, no matter how hard they may have tried, there simply *was* no way to turn off the noise. Their efforts would have been futile. Aren't many life situations like that—no matter how hard you try, you're doomed to lose?

True enough. In at least one of Richter's rat experiments, for example, he wanted to know how long a rat would keep swimming to try to save itself. The rat swam for sixty hours before it drowned. Were some other rat intelligent and articulate, it might observe this and say: See, what was the point? All that effort for nothing. Wasn't that a foolish rat, to try so hard?

No one suggests there is a guarantee that you'll win if you try. But most of the rats in these experiments did, after all, swim to safety. And even in this one instance, the experimenter might have changed his mind in the interim or been influenced by some outside event to stop the experiment. In most human life situations, the outcome is not rigidly preordained. Many studies in clinical medicine, psychology, and anthropology indicate that seriously ill patients who have hope are more likely to survive than those who don't, that those who are highly motivated tend to last longer—and are happier in the knowledge that they are putting up a fight.

Some population groups are more susceptible to feelings of helplessness than are others: the elderly, for instance; and as one might suspect, blacks; and women of any color.

In a series of classroom experiments, Dr. Carol Dweck of the University of Illinois found that when girls fail in school, they tend to blame the failure on their inability to master the subject matter. But boys ascribe failure to not trying hard enough. Because girls are considered to be neater, better-behaved, and harder-working, teachers assume that they are already doing the best they can. Because boys are considered to be sloppier and less diligent by nature, teachers tend to tell them, "You can do better. You're just not trying hard enough." The boys believe it. They do try harder, and do better. Thus, for paradoxical reasons, girls are inadvertently programmed to feel more helpless about improving their situations.

Consider another series of classroom experiments being carried out by Dr. Rita Smith, a former student of Seligman's who is now in the African studies program at Temple University in Philadelphia. She has been comparing the helplessness quotients of black and white children. Though the research is incomplete and the results not yet published, it is already quite apparent to Smith that black children, especially those from poor families, give up much more easily than do white children of similar economic status. If you give the two groups a problem that has no solution (as in the case of Seligman's college students in the room with no turn-off button), the black pupils not only quit trying sooner but when given a solvable problem next, they are more likely to be convinced a priori that it can't be done—at least not by them. The white kids tend to stay with the problem longer, and they don't assume they can't solve one problem because they failed to solve the other.

Smith attributes these results to the *experience* of black children in a world that does not respond very reliably to their attempts to exercise more control over their lives. The giving-up attitude becomes even more pronounced in the tenth grade than it was in the second grade (the two age groups Smith has been working with). By then, the kids have had eight more years of experience to reconfirm the apparent uselessness of trying.

Whether you look at rats, dogs, or people, it's now abundantly clear that those who try harder do better. Intelligent organisms, says Seligman, automatically know how to help themselves: they keep trying; they have hope. Nor does this healthy tendency have to be learned. In fact, it is so built-in, says Seligman, that even special training doesn't enhance it. Most of us, to one extent or another, are guilty of teaching others helplessness and of permitting ourselves to learn it.

Science has many uses. Experiments such as those described may not provide us with any technological breakthroughs. They do not "conquer"any diseases. But they do give us scientific validation of, and therefore greater confidence in, the value of traditional virtues such as perseverance and hope—which, in these times, is no small service.

Thus through research are our homely.truisms doubly confirmed: hope is healthier than despair, perseverance is more sensible than giving up, and helplessness can be self-imposed and therefore self-defeating. The same can be true even in the affairs of nations. One wonders how guilty of defeatism we all, including our statesmen, may be, when we keep saying, There always have been wars, and there always will be wars; people are no damned good, and you can't change human nature; and so on. Whatever the case in point, the fact that "it didn't work last time" has nothing to do with next time. Next time we may swim to safety. Next time we may find a spot on the grid that doesn't give us a shock. Next time the room may have a turn-off switch.

Damn the T.V.

Beatrice Gross

I've spoken to teachers who say that kids simply aren't as creative as they used to be. It's not just that the teachers are teaching more and enjoying it less (as the ad campaign has it), but that they find their messages to kids about what constitutes thinking or how to come up with one's own solution to a problem, aren't being heard, let alone acted upon.

For example, I approached a geometry teacher I know who teaches tenth grade. I had learned he was promoting a new way to teach geometry, which depended on the kids memorizing each and every step in the Regents' review book.

"Don't leave out even one equivalency mark or you'll be marked off," the kids reported him saying.

This seemed like a crime against Euclid, so I pursued the teacher in an effort to either straighten out my misconception or straighten out *his*.

This besieged man was at his wits' end. As he told it, the kids were not only encouraged by him to come up with their own proofs—they were courted, charmed, provoked, forced, and all but beaten, to no avail. He would bring in several proofs of the same theorem; he would ask kids to come up with solutions to problems they had not seen before, problems he had not seen before, but nothing worked. Finally in desperation he said, "If—and only if—you cannot understand how such problems are solved, how one gets from the questions posed to a solution, and it's late and you are discouraged, depressed, and hopelessly confused—you might have to simply memorize the book solution."

Unfortunately, that's all the kids heard. So they reported home that he was making them memorize the solutions.

Why did they wish to hear that? Why do they look for uncreative tasks to do?

Stanley Stern studied the effects of TV viewing on creativity for his doctoral dissertation at the University of Southern California School of Education.

Dividing 250 intellectually gifted fourth- through sixth-graders into groups, he set them to watching TV programs. Stern gave the children a battery of creativity tests before and after the prescribed watching, and found that all the children programmed to watch TV (even those watching educational TV) declined in all areas of creativity except verbal ability. Those who watched cartoons, exclusively, declined substantially more than the others.

Why? We don't know all the reasons. But we know that TV eliminates the need to use the imagination; it absorbs active playtime energies; it is used by viewers to avoid dealing with problems (which then don't get resolved); it takes the place of friends and family, and the joys and pain of interaction. And it does these things by consuming an enormous amount of the child's waking time.

The average child living in the United States will spend more time in front of the TV screen *before entering* school than he or she will *in* school from grades one through six. By the time the typical student is eighteen, two years of his or her life will have been spent in front of the tube.

Given the amount of time kids spend watching, I think teachers ought to seriously consider using less audio-visual and more moving and making and doing activities.

But make no mistake—it's not easy to wean kids away from the tube, even when the children and parents are aware of the dangers. Withdrawal seems almost as much of a struggle as it is for the drug freak or confirmed smoker.

Although our son Peter enjoyed the intellectual discipline of school, he was addicted to the tube at home. While he watched, phones went unanswered, food dropped onto his lap, and afternoons turned into nights.

But he fought his addiction, and when he was eleven years old he wrote two poems which show his use of and his struggle to overcome TV dependence.

Blank Screen,
You stand there on the stage
So Empty,
So like me.
Waiting for something to happen to it.
But I don't want to be like it.
I'll get up and do something for myself.
Thank you, screen.

To some extent the lure of the tube is a result of the difficulty children have in coming to terms with a world which is often fear-provoking and unmanageable. Peter's poem about the shark seems to speak to that feeling.

Shark

You swim through the water.
You streamline in and out.
Your fin cuts the water like a knife through cream cheese.
But oh my God.
He sees me.
He's coming toward me.
Can't swim . . . he's too fast.

I'll have to do it.
I rushed towards him quickly and turned the channel.

Perhaps you should share with children and parents your concern, and bits of research you may come across, which will strengthen their resolve to move towards healthier solutions to life's problems. You will be seen as a sympathetic, all-around caring professional who is open to hearing from them about all problems their children are having.

Second Thoughts

Arthur Berger feels that the emotionless Dr. Spock of "Star Trek" fame is a negative "model" of sorts. He is not pleased by what this says about Spock's audience. I feel, on the other hand, that David Banner, the mild-mannered, sweet-tempered doctor who when angry turns into the raging uncontrollable Hulk can also be identified with, because we all fear our anger. Do the same people find these two opposite characters fascinating? Are they popular because they both speak to a part of us—albeit each to a different part?

Or is T.V. merely a narcotic upon which the audience grows increasingly dependent?

I wonder if this question can be answered for the whole audience or if we don't need to discriminate more in our generalizations.

Arthur Asa Berger

. . . The average television set is on something like five hours a day in a typical family; preschoolers watch an average of three hours of television a day; by the age of eighteen, the average young person will have watched 15,000 hours of TV and been exposed to between 400,000 and 650,000 commercials.

Yet, despite these figures, there has been relatively little attention paid to the influence of television on the socialization of children, on their food preferences, personality development, general social attitudes and values, and a host of other phenomena. Work done on TV violence indicates that its level

This article is from *Human Behavior* Magazine. Copyright © 1977. Reprinted by permission. Arthur Asa Berger, Ph.D., teaches at California State University, San Francisco.

tends to be harmful, but what about other effects of TV viewing? We underestimate the impact of television upon ourselves, our children and society. . . . and because of myths about the government protecting us or the morality of the broadcasting industry.

I would like to propose a "model" of sorts that explains why television tends to have such a grip on people. In my research, I noticed that an important television theme, represented by Mr. Spock of "Star Trek," is the emotionless man. As I wrote in my book, *The TV-Guided American:*

> As a symbolic hero, he is most significant—he represents the emotional cripple, the mechanical man, the man who has such control of himself and his feelings that he seems to be a robot. As such, he represents millions of people who find themselves in the same situation: we are afraid to have emotions; we suppress our feelings because we fear that if we do have feelings we must, inevitably, act on them, and these actions could be destructive.

This notion that Americans are in flight from emotions was supported by Herbert Hendin, the distinguished psychiatrist, in *The Age of Sensation.* Abram Kardiner, in a review of this book, discusses Hendin's findings that young people try to live "emotionfree" lives and strive to replace *affect* (emotions) by accumulating "fragmented sensory experiences" and through drugs. This, in turn, has had a devastating impact upon family life, which is now in danger of being destroyed. As Kardiner writes, "In the end it is the family that is being destroyed by the egocentricity of each member." Egocentricity here meaning both emotional self-centeredness and selfishness.

So far so bad. But where does television enter into the picture? That link was provided by yet another psychiatrist, Julius E. Heuscher, M.D., in his book *A Psychiatric Study of Myths and Fairy Tales.* Folklore, he notes, emphasizes the importance of a harmonious, gradual human development. "The child who is being presented with an overabundance of adult-life conflicts and desires," he says, "and who thereby is being pushed toward grownup ideas, tends to become afraid of growing up and is therefore stunted in his maturation process."

Is it possible that television has played a major role in this fear of growing up that Heuscher talks about? He mentions the problem himself, although cautioning that research has not demonstrated that television is the culprit, stating:

> The changes in values and behavior, the increased passivity and the lack of wholehearted and lasting commitments among the young (and not so young), are undoubtedly due to numerous factors among which television has not been established as the essential one. However, we cannot remain complacent and let things drift along until demonstrable, permanent, serious side effects are undermining the health of the population.

Here's how I believe the vicious cycle in television works:

1. Childhood (and other) television viewing leads to a fear of becoming an adult (and being involved in all the inherent conflicts).

2. This fear of becoming an adult leads to an incapacity to have sustained and wholehearted emotional ties and commitments. (The existence of this has been suggested by Hendin.)

3. This incapacity leads to fear of marriage, nonrelational sex, fear of feeling (and of flying) and so on.

4. These phenomena are not satisfying to those involved, leading to anxiety, pain and escapism (through drugs and other means, such as television viewing) to obtain "relief."

5. Television watching becomes a narcotic upon which we are dependent—to escape from imprisonment within ourselves, to have vicarious experiences and so forth. But at the same time that it provides "relief," it also reinforces our childhood fears, by presenting us with characters who do not feel (such as Mr. Spock) or conflicting adults (whom we do not wish to emulate). It may even be that fear of being an adult is connected with our notions, given us to a great degree by television, that adults are "violent."

What this all suggests is that television, in some way, creates the very dependencies that viewers use it to try to overcome; we become, then, prisoners of our television sets, which leads to our becoming prisoners of ourselves.

Obviously, this is an enormous subject and one I cannot do justice to in a brief article. I do not want to suggest that television alone is responsible for the various problems we find ourselves afflicted with. But I do think it is more involved than we imagine. Whether we are prisoners of the television set is something we may all think about—next time we reach for the knob.

Student Know Thyself

Beatrice Gross

The more learning is researched, the more we realize how people differ in their needs. Some people work best under pressure, others must be relaxed; some focus on one fascinating area of study, while their neighbors are naturally gifted dilettantes; some like noise, others hate it.

I think one of the most valuable tasks to set children to is to help them analyze some of their own peculiar needs so they can find out how they learn best.

About a year ago I came upon an analysis of body time and its effect on creatures large and small. I learned that a laboratory mouse could be killed by a loud sound when at the low ebb of its energy (determined by its personal time clock), yet be totally unaffected by the same sound if exposed to it at a high energy peak. The first laboratory animals used to test thalidomide were evidently given the drug only during their peak times and so did not evidence any ill effects. After humans were found to produce deformed children as a result of ingesting the drug, the tests were repeated, but this time test animals were given the drug *throughout* the day and it was found that animals who got it when they were in a weakened state also had deformed offspring.

People, like animals, have peak efficiency times. Being able to identify these peak times and low times could mean the difference between successful and unproductive study. You might help students by having them chart times when they feel positive well being and tolerate pain easily, are creative and efficient, and also those hours when they are overwhelmed by minor pains, can't see straight, have accidents, and lose emotional control.

Not only is time an issue, but conditions too can make a difference. My daughter Elizabeth, at fifteen, undertook a study of how background music affects concentration, the results of which changed her study habits.

She hypothesized that teenagers studied better with the radio on, since she and her friends felt more relaxed when they listened to music. All her friends were convinced that this was true, asserting that they would be able to work longer if relaxed, and therefore listening to music would be beneficial.

Elizabeth used a randomly mixed number chart with a distracting background as a gauge for testing this hypothesis. The subject had to find in sequence numbers from 10 to 99 on the chart, with music and without.

She found to her surprise that every one of the students she tested took two to three times as long to find the numbers in sequence on the grid when they were listening to music as when they were without distraction.

She has not worked with a radio on since her experiment.

Other obvious study tricks should also be examined. I saw one young man writing each word on a spelling list ten times. "How many times must you write them to learn them?," I asked. "I don't know," he answered.

"Have you pretested yourself to find out how many you really need to practice that way?" He hadn't. Yet this is a question his teacher should ask if she intends to make competent learners of her students rather than mere busy-work experts.

VIII
OTHER PEOPLE ARE ALIVE AND DIFFERENT

Other People Are Alive and Different

Ronald Gross and Beatrice Gross

In his posthumously published autobiographical novel, *Maurice*, E.M. Forster says of his hero at one point in his life: "He had learned that other people are alive—but he had yet to learn that they are different."

Maurice is no fool—when Forster says that he had learned that other people are alive, he meant something beyond a simple awareness of their existence. He meant a gut sense of their inner reality, the disturbing insight that they are the center, each one, of a whole world; that their existence has the same inherent value as one's own. And when Forster says that Maurice has yet to learn that other people are different, he means something more than the surface differences we all take for granted in one another. He means the deeply different realities of our individual lives, the fact that we live in quite autonomous worlds which miraculously, somehow and sometimes touch tenderly at the edges and even sometimes overlap.

Your awareness of the uniqueness of each child is critical to creative teaching. To hold it steadily in view can change everything: your perception of the child, your way of teaching, and your understanding of how to reach each child.

So much emphasis is put on being "fair" that we often forget that fairness means being respectful of individual differences rather than merely even-handed in doling out favors or punishments.

In our four-year-old daughter's nursery class was a rough, charming boy named Robby who almost always had problems "lining up." Elizabeth came home one day and explained with satisfaction how she had helped Robby out.

She, who was fourth in line, pushed into Sandy who was third, who pushed into Robby, who pushed Michael clear out of line. Michael had to go to the end of the line and Robby could be first. "You see," explained Elizabeth, "Robby really needs to be first." "And you Elizabeth? Don't you need to be first? Ever?" "Well," explained my four-year-old daughter, "sometimes I want to be first, but Robby, he *needs* to be first."

Teachers and children should be able to understand and give more to the child with special needs. They should also ask of him some favor easily awarded by him to others: the boy who needs drawing out, the new girl who needs a partner. By our actions and consideration, we can show that we accept differences in others and confirm our singular "aliveness" by allowing our differences to show as well.

A fine teacher we know uses a "show and tell" format to help children share the secrets of their hearts. "I have here a beautifully wrapped box, a lovely thing, covered with fancy silver paper, and I give it to you, Charlotte, and you open it and find your very favorite thing is in the box. It's anything you want it to be... What is in your box?" As Charlotte goes through the motions of unwrapping this imaginary box, the teacher wonders aloud, "I wonder what it will be? A visit with your grandmother from Detroit? A quiet evening on your dad's lap? An alligator? A puppy? A cozy quilt that doesn't have any stuffing coming out?... What's in your box?"

Do You Know What Retarded Means?

Sandy Gart moved children, not only across the invisible age-segregating line, but into a group that is one of the most feared and reviled in our society.

Her class trip to the world of the retarded provided more than a glimpse of people who are different. She actually helped and encouraged her children to try befriending exceptional people—a step that teachers must encourage if our society's heartless disregard of the handicapped is to be counteracted.

Sandy Gart

The visitor to our classroom stepped forward, "I'm Wendy Forgash, a teacher of special education at the Rosemary Kennedy School for retarded children. Do you know what retarded means? Her eyes scanned each face as she awaited the response. Reluctant hands began to appear.

"I think retarded means that a person can't walk too good and may need a wheelchair or something."

"I think retarded means that a person forgets things all over the place."

"I think retarded means you're just very slow at doing things."

On and on they went, trying to explain their impressions of a retarded person. Each contribution was an opinion, never a certainty.

"You get the message," said Wendy suddenly. "No one seems to know for sure, and although you describe one or two retarded people that you have known or met, your understanding of the word is pretty vague."

The next hour passed quickly. She spoke earnestly, placing each word upon their young ears with great care. She told them about the Kennedy School, the type of children she worked with, the facilities available, and what

This article is reprinted from *Instructor*, copyright © November 1976 by the Instructor Publications, Inc., used by permission.

she did. The unknown—the different—was described with enthusiasm and compassion. Absorbed in every word she said, the veil of uncertainty began to lift. Perhaps the veil could be lifted completely, I thought as an idea forged ahead in my mind. At the end of the session, I asked Wendy about the possibility of taking some of my students to visit the Rosemary Kennedy School. She asked me to make a preliminary visit to discuss the idea.

Several days later I arrived at the Kennedy School. I walked silently through the corridors, becoming absorbed in everything I saw. What a happy place! There was so much warmth and togetherness. The children were eager and friendly.

"You're nice," said one little guy as I stopped to talk to him in the hall. "You have a pretty face," and he reached up and cupped my face in his small hands.

If my kids could see this, it would be a first step toward understanding. I went back to our classroom and told them, "We're going to visit the Kennedy School. The children are great."

We spent the next week getting ready. We had meetings and discussions. We role-played possible situations. Sometimes we just talked, sharing ideas, feelings, and anxieties. There were lots of the last. Some were afraid they might laugh; some were afraid of crying. They were afraid they wouldn't understand or be understood. We talked a lot about similarities.

"Of course they sometimes cry and feel sad, the same as you. They get angry, too. But, most of all, they just want to be accepted, understood, and loved—like you."

The children were given opportunities to search out each other's feelings and attitudes. There was a growth in self-assurance and self-awareness as the children became bound together in a common goal.

It was a beautiful day, as we took our seats on the bus to start our trip. Each child wore a boldly printed name tag and a very pensive expression. The kids were still apprehensive, unsure of what was going to happen; but most of all they wanted to be accepted and liked by the children at the Kennedy School.

As we pulled into the parking lot, there were waves and smiles. We approached the classrooms we were to visit and there was a large sign: WELCOME BIRCH SCHOOL.

"You see, they're happy to have us," said one of my girls.

What followed was more like a homecoming party than a first visit. The children hugged and kissed and laughed, and started to play with each other immediately. As the day progressed, they read to each other, sang together, had a puppet show, played records, sewed, and painted. They were all children, spontaneously responding to each other.

Everyone was absorbed with one particular child. "That's Joanne—a twelve-year-old Mongoloid who weighs 183 pounds. She comes to school, but does absolutely nothing. She just sits and waits for her lunch, then eats and waits to go home. Look at her now! She's laughing and playing with one of your girls. She usually never laughs, never smiles, never talks. But, look what one child can do. I can't believe it!"

The day continued and the children went into the gym where shrieks and cheers echoed from the walls. Even Joanne shuffled shyly into the gym and was greeted warmly. Stimulated by other children, she participated in some of the activities.

As the day neared an end, they sang a song, "Friendship," for us and gave us the decorated rocks they had made. We packed up our gifts and left many games and work sheets we had brought for them.

Joanne was seated at the window ledge, her head resting on her folded arms. She sobbed pathetically and called out a few times.

"We're your friends, Joanne. We'll be back," they cried.

The bus was unusually silent—everyone deep in his own thoughts, retracing the events of the day.

"Well, what are you thinking. . .?" Before I finished the sentence, they pleaded with me to let them go back again—the decision was unanimous.

Back at school the kids kept diaries, wrote reports, and summaries. They shared their newly found knowledge, but more important they shared their feelings. They talked about how they felt before, during, and after the trip. Their enthusiasm spread to other students. Everyone who heard them wanted to go. Follow-up visits were scheduled for other groups.

Parents, too, were pleased with the results. I had just finished describing our visit at a round-table meeting of parents. A father paused briefly, and said, "I have a sequel to your story, Sandy. We have an eleven-year-old son. He goes to school, comes home, and plays—*alone*. This has been going on for most of his young life. He has no friends—he is a retarded child."

Those seated motionlessly around the large table waited as I searched his eyes, waiting for him to continue.

"Within the last couple of weeks my wife told me that other children have appeared asking him to play. Now he's bombarded with friends. We couldn't understand it, but now we know—something good is going on in Merrick."

Is Something Wrong
With Their Brains?

Beatrice Gross

There are many studies focusing on children not "ready for learning." The problem is discouraging and we all want to find a solution.

TV may be responsible, as may food additives, the lack of zinc in children's hair, the fluorescent lights in the classroom, radio frequencies, or an increased incidence of brain damage due to induced births. All of these have been seriously proposed as reasons for learning disabilities.

It also may be that "learning disabilities" is merely a new growth industry and one which many parties seek to exploit. As Diane Divoky and Peter Schrag point out in *The Myth of the Hyperactive Child*, this new "well-intentioned movement" had already put between 500,000 and 1,000,000 American children on amphetamine-type drugs by 1975 and the numbers of children so treated doubled every few years.

What actually is a learning disability? Leslie Hart, author of *How the Brain Works*, thinks we misuse the diagnosis both because we don't understand how the brain works and because it is easier to blame the child than to accept our responsibility.

> If, then, a child whose physical visual apparatus is not impaired confuses letters, the first assumption must be that the patterns involved have not been well learned, which is a much simpler and more probable explanation than that there is something wrong with the brain. To say, "But the other children have learned" is to suggest that all children are alike and have had fairly identical experiences. That, of course, is obvious nonsense—but we must marvel that the remark is made so frequently.
>
> Often, in talking to a group of parents, teachers, or others, I show color slides of a number of common flowers, or birds, or trees, and ask the viewers to identify them. Some people score well, but most of them score poorly. Then I point out that since they have been exposed to these subjects with great frequency over many years, and since a few people can name them, the others must be brain damaged! If not, we should not identify young students as having brain damage if they are confused by letters or numbers that take many forms.
>
> If learning disabilities did involve something wrong neurologically, we would expect no relief short of medical or surgical action. Indeed, it might be well to insist that only those with a medical degree and full qualifications should attempt to "treat" the child in any way. Teachers have no more authority to try to correct a neurological condition than they have to help a student with a twisted spine or defective heart. Only when we see the problem as one of *learning* has even the specialist the right to attempt a remedy. And, of course, where improvement does occur, individual instruction of better than classroom quality is the most likely means. A diagnosis of "visual dysfunction" rather than "hasn't yet learned" can cause misunderstanding, obscure the true problem, and, in all probability, send us off in the wrong direction.*

Hart maintains that there *is* considerable evidence that the brain (actually the neocortex) "downshifts" in times of threat or danger. "Most of the subtle learning ability of this newest brain gets shut down. For example, we see this shutdown demonstrated in an automobile crash; minutes later we cannot recall the color of the car or how many people were in it."

---

*Leslie A. Hart, **"Misconceptions About Learning Disabilities,"** *The National Elementary Principal* Vol. 56, No. 1, (Sept.–Oct. 1976). Copyright 1976, National Association of Elementary School Principals. All rights reserved.

The most conmon cause of learning disability symptoms that stand out in the case histories is threat to the children in the form of demands made far too early or marital battles that keep them in fear and unsure of their security. Again, from Leslie Hart:

> . . . . To obtain good results, present understanding of the brain suggests that we need to create a setting as free as possible from threat, and that we need to use methods as divorced as possible from those of usual teaching. We also need to recognize that the learning problem arises not from "something wrong" in the child's brain, but from the inhibiting effect of threat to the child by adults who may or may not mean well. The child is the victim who is in need of help of the right kind, but not "treatment."

Beneficial approaches include one-to-one assistance in learning by people who are seen by the child as nonthreatening (an older child or elderly volunteer may fill the bill); considerable use of materials and machines (typewriter, tape recorder) rather than verbal instruction; discontinuance of constant "failure" evaluations; and removal of the crippling "LD" label.

Hyperactive?

I see a child labeled hyperactive and learning-disabled in a Long Island classroom. His mother is being called in that afternoon by the school nurse to be told he must be medicated. He is, I'm told by his student teacher, always out of order; he hits kids in the hallway, doesn't focus in class, can't sit still.

This morning the boy is sitting quietly and working at his desk. As I enter the room looking for him our eyes meet. I smile and wink at him. He winks back. When I sit to work with several children using small blocks to clarify "take-away," he is quick to grasp the concept.

Later he comes to the teacher with his spelling work. She looks at the sentence he has devised to show the meaning of *class* and says, "Marco, this is absolutely wrong. I don't know what you can be thinking, but as usual you are wrong and must have been dreaming when I explained."

"See," she shows me his work, "this is what I mean. He has written 'I am in the due class.' "

My Italian is weak but I point out that due means two. She harrumphs.

"He's been left back once, you know, and should be again."

I shake hands with Marco as I leave and tell him how much I enjoyed my visit. He has not once hit a child, jumped out of his seat, talked too loud, or messed up the equipment I brought with me. My student tells me that this was an unusual day.

"Mostly, as anyone can tell you, he acts wild."

But I know that the teacher, who doesn't have any manipulative equipment (homemade or bought) in her first-grade classroom, may be making a terrible mistake. I think she has in some way caused this child to act up in rebellion and frustration.

You might say, "It's not that way with the kid I'm to get next year. Let me tell you about the reports I've gotten." Or, "Let me tell you what I've just been through."

It may be that those who, like reading specialist Sharon Stern Schanzer, value chemically induced behavior modification, have a point, but as you read this, remember that Marco was described to me in the same way.

Sharon Stern Schanzer

David* was nine years old when he came to our school for an evaluation. He was an alert youngster who, for some reason, was failing every subject in school and was acting out both at home and at school. The family history indicated that David's mother had had a difficult pregnancy, which included toxemia, making it necessary for her to remain in bed for most of the nine months. The boy's developmental milestones were appropriate for his age. His parents, however, recalled that he never walked; he just ran everywhere. Although David's parents spent much time with him, they were never able to persuade him to sit down to play a game or to concentrate for more than a few minutes. This pattern had continued throughout his nine years.

In both nursery school and kindergarten, David ran around the room for most of the day and was not able to spend much time in either individual or group activities. Yet, his teachers reported, he had a good background of general information, and he appeared to be bright. At this same time, the parents observed that their second son (four years younger) appeared to be much calmer than David.

David continued to have difficulties in school, both behaviorally and academically. He was given individual tutoring in reading three times a week and speech therapy twice a week, and he was allowed to move at his own pace in the classroom. His parents consulted both a psychologist and a psychiatrist to help them cope with David's excessive activity and volatile behavior at home.

---

*David is a fictitious name.

This article was originally published as **"The Reality of the Learning Disabled Child,"** in *The National Elementary Principal*, Sept.–Oct. 1976. Copyright 1976, National Association of Elementary School Principals. All rights reserved. Reprinted by permission. Sharon Stern Schanzer is learning disabilities itinerant teacher at the Cornman Diagnostic Center in Philadelphia.

During the course of these interviews, the suspicion arose that this youngster might have a learning disability problem.

A complete psychological and educational evaluation revealed that the boy had a full-scale IQ of 115 on the Wechsler Intelligence Scale for Children (Verbal 119, Performance 106), was approximately three years behind in all aspects of academic work, and was unable to concentrate for more than a few minutes on most activities. Perceptual tests showed some difficulties in the areas of visual-motor integration, visual discrimination, and auditory discrimination. This nine-year-old boy stated that he thought he was dumb because he couldn't read and write well. He also said that he didn't like to play with other kids because he couldn't run or play ball very well.

A neurological examination revealed that there were no hard signs of neurological impairment. In these tests, he evidenced the same hyperactivity, coordination, and perceptual problems that had appeared in the other testing. His medical history, however, showed that David had experienced two convulsions tht were accompanied by high fevers. The neurologist recommended that David be placed in a special class for learning disabled youngsters and suggested a trial period of medication (Ritalin). The doctor cautioned in the report that the youngster's medication should be reviewed frequently in order to see if it was still warranted.

At the age of nine, David entered a class for learning disabled children in a Philadelphia center. He was in a group of eight children who were all about his age, and, like his classmates, he was given an individualized program in almost every subject. He spent at least one hour a day in individual instruction with either his teacher or an aide; he participated in a specialized gross motor class with the perceptual therapist three days a week; and he received speech therapy three times a week. Conscientious efforts were made to teach him on his true "instructional" levels rather than on "frustration" levels. Evaluations were made regularly in order to be sure that he was really improving, or if he wasn't improving, to find out why.

For example, it was determined that, because of David's poor auditory discrimination, he learned phonics and spelling better when a linguistic or pattern approach was used rather than a phonetic one. The use of science materials and projects was emphasized because he showed so much interest in them. The use of concrete objects and a number line helped him to learn the number facts that he had never mastered, and graph paper helped him to line up a row of numbers without losing his place.

An individual schedule was made up for David (as well as for the other students) each day, from which he learned to tell time and follow a schedule. His independent work periods gradually lengthened and his skills and controls also improved as he met with more and more success.

At first, David had temper tantrums when he didn't understand a direction or when he made a mistake. Because the number of children in the classroom was small, however, the teacher or aide was able to speak to him quietly and find out the reason for the problem. A separate "office" area was available to him when he wanted to be alone. David was also asked to evaluate his behavior at the end of the day so that he would be aware of the difficult moments and be able to discuss the situations that had upset him. He was rewarded with free time when no temper tantrums occurred. The tantrums decreased dramatically, and after about four months, they became almost nonexistent. But David had difficulty getting along with the other youngsters. He could not play with all seven of the children at the same time, and so he was encouraged to play with just one or two children at a time. In order to further reduce his frustrations, he was also encouraged to use play materials and games that were on his correct perceptual-motor level.

During David's two-year stay in the program, his medication was reevaluated three or four times. The amounts of medication were gradually decreased, and attempts were made to remove it completely. At first, when David did not receive the medication, marked deterioration in his controls and concentration were noted. By the time he graduated from elementary school, however, he no longer required medication.

David returned to a Philadelphia public school sixth-grade class after two full years in the learning disabilities program. He was on grade level in reading and spelling and about a year behind in math skills. Although he was somewhat frightened about returning to school, he was confident about his skills. He had good controls; he was able to express himself when he was confused or didn't understand a problem; he could also work independently for long periods of time; and he got along well with both teachers and students.

This youngster graduated from elementary school with good marks in all subjects but math. He was able to move ahead in his classes, and he maintained good grades in junior high school.

According to Peter Schrag and Diane Divoky, in their book *The Myth of the Hyperactive Child*, the school district committed many wrongs against this child and his parents. Among the components that were used to help David (and that would be considered wrong by Schrag and Divoky) were psychoactive drugs, the label "learning disabled," a small special class, and behavior modification techniques.

Before deciding, however, whether these techniques were correct or justifiable, let us consider two questions:

Were these methods of treatment successful with this particular youngster? Why didn't this youngster succed in the mainstream of education even when he was provided with special tutoring, speech therapy, and a teacher who allowed him to go at his own pace?

In response to the first question, it cannot be denied that David made significant gains when the four components were used at different times. It is also a fact that several hundred other children who had been failing in the school district are now succeeding in the mainstream of education after spending two to three years in the special learning disabilities program. All of these children were placed in special classes on the basis of psychological, educational, and neurological examinations. A small percentage of them were also involved in behavior modification and medication during part of their stay in the program. Moreover, it does appear that the methods of treatment were successful for these particular children.

In response to the second question, many factors should be considered. First, we should keep in mind the large number of children in our public schools. A child in a classroom of thirty-two students cannot get the same attention as a child in a classroom of eight. In fact, is it realistic to ask a teacher with thirty-two students to provide the special perceptual and academic remediation for those students who may need individual instruction and attention throughout the entire day? Even if children with special needs go to specialists throughout the day, they may still need individual help when they return to their classroom.

Furthermore, children with severe learning problems need a consistent, integrated program in which everyone involved is aware of and working to meet needs and goals that are specifically determined. This type of integration is easier to manage in a full-time special program than when the child is bounced back and forth between specialists and the mainstream throughout the day. It should be emphasized, however, that the majority of children with learning problems can benefit by remaining in the mainstream and receiving special services. Full-time special placement should be used only when severe problems exist and when other alternatives have not been successful.

It appears, then, that there does exist a small percentage of children who, despite good intelligence, good sensory acuity, and no severe emotional problems, do not seem to be able to learn adequately. These children continue to have learning difficulties even after their parents have received counseling and after supportive services have been tried in the school. Difficulties in the gross motor, fine motor, language, and social areas persist, and the child falls more and more behind.

Should there be programs to help these children who are several years behind perceptually, academically, and socially?

The answer seems clear: a learning disabilities class is the correct placement for a small percentage of students. For the majority of children with learning problems, other alternatives—such as transitional classes, resource rooms, itinerant service, and individual tutoring—work best. If these other alternatives are tried and are not successful, however, should these children be denied a special classroom in which they may thrive? Is it ethical to allow children—even one child—to fail rather than to achieve at their potential level? Is it not "dehumanizing" to allow someone to fail?

This same answer seems applicable to the specific components of the program. For some children, the individualized instruction and small group environment are sufficient to help the child behaviorally and academically. But what about the perceptually impaired child who continues to be hyperactive, distractible, and unable to concentrate even within the special class? If behavior modification and medication do help children to acquire controls and help them to learn, should they be withheld from children who need such help? Is it not the prerogative as well as the responsibility of the system to provide children with opportunities that will enable them to succeed? If that is not the school system's prerogative and responsibility, whose is it? Or, if it is no one's, do we just sit by hoping for the best?

Schrag and Divoky have clearly pointed out the abuses that can occur in labeling, medicating, and using behavior modification with masses of children. Certainly, such abuses are not to be condoned. There *are* programs for the learning disabled, however, that do work and that do not abuse children—programs in which children who have failed begin to progress and experience success. It is unreasonable and illogical to abolish all programs for the learning disabled because of specific misuses that have occurred.

The key to successful programs of this type is the word "caution." Decisions concerning the learning disabled child's education, as well as all children's education, should be made with extreme caution. Listed below are some specific caveats that must be taken into consideration concerning these children:

1. Thorough physical, psychological, neurological, and educational evaluations should be made by qualified specialists to help clarify the nature of the problem.
2. It must be determined whether it really is a perceptual disability that is causing the child's learning problem, rather than physical, emotional, or intellectual factors.
3. Other alternatives within the mainstream of education should be tried for a reasonable length of time to determine whether they would be sufficient. These alternatives might include individualized instruction within the regular class, tutoring, itinerant service, resource rooms, upgraded classes, and smaller classes.
4. Recommendations concerning the child should be made jointly by a team of experts who know the child well.
5. The child who is placed in a learning disabilities class must be severely behind in perceptual and academic skills. Special education is not for children with mild problems.
6. People who teach learning disabled children should be thoroughly trained in child development, classroom management, and the diagnosis and remediation of perceptual and academic problems.
7. Behavior modification techniques should be used by a trained person with the ultimate goal of having the child internalize the positive behaviors without the need of external reward.
8. Medication should be recommended only by a qualified physician after administering a complete physical and neurological examination. It must be monitored cautiously and be reevaluated often to see if it is necessary.

9. Children's progress in the special class must be evaluated frequently. Educational programs must constantly be altered in light of the child's changing needs.

10. The goal of the learning disabilities class is to return the youngster to the mainstream of education within the shortest period of time.

It is with this cautious yet flexible perspective that educators can begin to face the reality of the learning disabled child. With these caveats in mind, the team of specialists can proceed to help youngsters achieve at their potential levels.

Divergent Thinkers Use Blankets Differently

Beatrice Gross

Everyone in education these days seems to be discussing the effect of left-right dominance on differing patterns of thinking and behaving. When we were growing up our parents didn't know about left-right dominance. They sorted kids by calling one "a dreamer," another a "professor," a third a "practical boy." Less scientific, but what did our parents know of cognitive styles?

Psychologist Liam Hudson talks of "convergent" and "divergent" thinkers. This urbane Englishman is interested in what differences exist between equally bright boys with different thinking patterns. He explains why some kids perform so much better (or worse) than their tests predict, and why they do so in certain kinds of classrooms under certain conditions.

He begins with the child with "standard" intelligence, the kind most understood by schools, whom he calls the *converger*. The converger likes to take action, and his answers reflect a practical approach. As a rough rule, the converger is substantially better at the intelligence test or any test requiring a single "most correct answer" than he is at open-ended tests. The *diverger* is the reverse.

What is an open-ended test? One that asks, "How many meanings can you think of for each of the following words?" Or, "How many uses can you think of for each of the following objects?" Or, "Given the title _____, draw the picture."

You might like to try to answer such a question before reading on to determine which kind of thinker you are—or at least which tendency you have: "How many uses can you find for a barrel? A paper clip? A blanket?"

Two examples of how bright but different students answer these questions may give you some idea of the variations in thinking. One youth, who listed his interests as playing the clarinet, singing in the choir, and reading books (mainly foreign), answered: Uses for a barrel? "Storing beer; sitting on; using as a raft; gnawing; loud-speaker holder; as a musical instrument." Uses for a paper clip? "Holding paper together; wire; pin; toothpick; to undo and waste time; making darts; as a button; cleaning nails." Uses for a blanket? "Sleeping in; using to stifle burning; to keep warm; lag pipes; round a camp fire; suffocating people; muffler and insulator for sound; for clothes."

Contrast these answers with those of an equally bright student of the same age and from the same school whose interests are model building, hand-built railways, and sports: Uses for a barrel? "Container for liquids, sitting on." Uses for a paper clip? "Clipping paper on; when straightened as a bit of wire." Uses for a blanket? "Sleeping in."

Clearly the questions interested one boy much more than the other. And if you found that some of your answers were even stranger than you'd like to admit publicly, Hudson tells us that convergers are less likely to produce a "violent" response than divergers, but when they do produce one, it is more likely to be really ghoulish.

Again, using the three questions mentioned above, some of the stranger responses were

1. To put spikes round the inside and put someone in and roll the barrel along the ground. (Barrel)
2. Wrapping up dead wife so as blood doesn't stain car seats. (Blanket)
3. Smother my sister. (Blanket)
4. Suicide. (Paper clip)
5. As a thumbscrew. (Paper clip)

You may think that this kind of question cannot and should not be taken seriously and might sympathize with a student who walked away from such a test altogether, but if a student responded this way to a standard IQ test, he would be committing academic suicide. Yet judging someone on a test they despise handicaps them.

Besides playing with questions like the above and perhaps using them to resort and reshuffle the kids in your class, of what relevance is this to you as a practicing teacher?

Most teachers find convergers (or conventional) thinkers easy to work with. They like to follow rules, they are more likely to accept expert advice, and are good team members. They are neat, tidy, and well mannered.

A teacher beset with divergers who can't settle down might try providing the kind of work they are most suited for. You may be especially eager to find problems that challenge these children, for, if Hudson's characterizations are correct, they are often more emotional than convergers. Typically, they are "blurters."

Like them or not, you must take personality differences into account when planning experiences for the whole class, for the teacher who plans only for one group is going to get flak or failure from the other.

Cheating on Miss Mortenson

We all know in our hearts that our influence on certain children may be lasting and profound. Few of us will receive a thank you as articulate, albeit belated, as this one.

Eda LeShan is one of today's leading child psychologists. Remembering her teacher's respect and forbearance, she believes that if every child could have teachers like Miss Mortenson it could change the world.

Eda LeShan

Helga R. Mortenson, 1895-1975. "I am an artist, for I am a teacher of children. . ." were the opening lines of a poem written by Helga Mortenson at the start of her career. She was a teacher from 1914 to 1958. . .Miss Mortenson taught fifth, sixth, and seventh grades. . .

Excerpts from a school newsletter, 1975

I was startled to see the name—and then felt a sharp wave of pain; a deep sense of loss that surprised and shocked me—and then such remorse that I had never let her know how much she had meant to me; I had never asked her if she'd known about my cheating.

When I knew her, Miss Mortenson was a sixth-grade teacher. I recall her as very tall—lanky—with black hair pulled back severely in a bun. Of course she seemed very old to me; she must have been all of thirty-eight. She was never my classroom teacher. But in the dim recesses of my child mind, I have loved her all my life. How I wish I had told her the story—tried to find her—let her know that I think she changed my life.

In my elementary school we had after-school clubs every Friday afternoon. Most of my memories of those early years are filled with feelings of being dumb and ugly. As far as I was concerned, all the other girls were prettier and smarter than I was and none of the boys on whom I had crushes ever paid the slightest bit of attention to me.

I remember only one place where I *always* felt completely happy—and that was in Miss Mortenson's Friday Literary Club. I remember Miss Mortenson's classroom; she specialized in ferns—all over the place; and colorful posters of foreign places. During our club meetings, she sat in the back of the room, sprawled, her long legs stretched out on a couple of chairs or along the floor, her posture most un teacherlike, it seemed to me. It was perfectly clear that she was enjoying herself.

This article was originally published as **"Empty Notebooks."** Reprinted by special permission of *Learning*, The Magazine for Creative Teaching, March, 1978. ©1978 by Education Today Company, Inc.

There must have been ten or fifteen of us in the club. Miss Mortenson treated us with great dignity. I can feel the warm glow of her approval right now as I think about her. We were *writers*; that's why we were there, and Miss Mortenson had a passionate devotion to writing. Nothing was required of us; we were there because we wanted to be. Each of us was given a lined notebook at the beginning of the year, and we could do as we pleased with it; write stories and poems in it, make notes on stories Miss Mortenson read to us—or scribble in it if we felt so inclined.

There were never any assignments, but we knew Miss Mortenson would be delighted if we felt like reading whatever we might write to the class. I was never afraid of disapproval in that classroom—never too shy to express myself. Miss Mortenson seemed so delighted with us and treated us with the respect of colleagues. So much so that we were, for that brief hour or two, a lot kinder to each other.

During the first year and a half of belonging to the club, I wrote a great many stories and poems—even a one-act play—in my notebook and read them out loud each week. The group would then discuss my work, making suggestions, commenting on which parts they liked best, what they thought might be improved. Because Miss Mortenson treated us like writers worthy of attention and respect, we never made fun of each other or were cruel in our comments. We were, to say the least, a different group than we were anywhere else the rest of the week. We took turns as authors and audience. It was a blissful oasis for me—sometimes calm and quiet, sometimes full of laughter and joking. Miss Mortenson never told us to sit up straight, and we lounged across the desks and chairs in imitation of her postures, I suppose. Some of the club members wrote very funny stories; others wrote jokes—we had a couple of very funny stand-up comedians in the group, and no one laughed harder or enjoyed them more than Miss Mortenson. Sometimes, if a story was sad, she would blow her nose very loud and wipe the tears from her eyes. "That was a *Wow*," she'd say. She had a deep, rich voice as I remember it. I was soothed; all the worries and shyness and feelings of inadequacy faded in her presence. She *liked* me!

The middle of the second year I got sick and was out of school a great deal. I also had a sixth-grade teacher who scared me half to death. I never seemed to catch up on my work and sixth-grade arithmetic terrified me. It seemed to me that there was no torture in the world equal to tests on fractions and long division. There was also a workbook on grammar. That was my classroom teacher's favorite subject. She gave long lectures on the importance of correct forms of speech in writing. I simply could not memorize the different names for various parts of speech. I failed one test after the other. She had steely gray eyes that stared at me accusingly, mournfully, every time she returned a test to me. The teacher assured me that my failures would lead to a disastrous life. "I understand that you think you want to become a writer," she said. "Well, I am very sorry to tell you that unless you make a greater effort, Eda, that is an impossible ambition." She lectured me regularly, personally, and at length on the necessity for developing "sound mental tools," if I wanted to accomplish anything in life. I felt tired, harassed, discouraged, and frightened, all the time.

Except on Friday afternoons. But now I never seemed to have time to write any stories or poems. I would come to the club meetings with nothing written in my notebook, week after week. Miss Mortenson just looked disappointed. After several weeks she said, quietly, "We miss your interesting stories, Eda."

The following week when she asked if I had anything I wanted to read, I said, "Yes." I went up to her desk, sat down, and opened my notebook. The pages were totally blank. I began "reading" out loud—making up a story as I went along, my eyes moving along each line on the paper, turning the pages at what seemed to me the appropriate places. Apparently the story I told was one of my best. Miss Mortenson was very enthusiastic and thanked me for taking the time to write a new story. "Isn't it a pleasure to hear such a good story," she said to the group.

Week after week I reappeared with my empty notebook. Week after week I "read" my stories. Each was discussed seriously and enthusiastically. I took notes in my empty notebook of criticisms and suggestions. Sometimes I thought I saw a puzzled, thoughtful look on Miss Mortenson's face, but I was never sure if she knew what I was doing. She seemed kinder than ever, and when I graduated from sixth grade, she said, "I wouldn't be at all surprised if you became a famous writer some day, Eda."

I came back to visit a few times during high school, but after awhile other preoccupations, other loyalties, other pleasures took over and for forty years Miss Mortenson faded into a distant, vague memory. I began to think about her again about five years ago. I had become a writer, all right; there were about ten books and several hundred articles to prove it. I was a writer and in some ways even a storyteller—but not the kinds of stories I had written for Miss Mortenson. What I had been writing was nonfiction. Along the road of growing up, the writer in me had been deflected into other areas—nursery school teacher and director, college instructor, child therapist, parent and family life educator. I wrote as an "authority" on special subjects.

Then, about five years ago, I began to wonder if I might ever get back to writing fiction. I remembered the Literary Club and Miss Mortenson. It suddenly occurred to me that Miss Mortenson *must* have known about that empty notebook, and that I had always known that a time would come when I would want to set aside all the other demands of my life and begin to fill the pages of that notebook, at long last.

Looking back it now seems to me that Miss Mortenson seemed concerned about me, that she questioned me gently, lovingly. She had kind, soft eyes and she would look at me thoughtfully and say, "It must be hard, catching up with all your work," or "I guess you have so much to do these days." Once I think she even whispered to me, "Don't be scared of Miss P. Her bark is worse than her bite."

She surely must have known I was cheating; telling her I'd written a story when I hadn't at all—stories which immediately faded into oblivion because not a line of them ever appeared in my notebook. What a gift that teacher was to me! I can still feel that heightened sense of awareness as I began each story. I *felt* like a writer—without writing a word, without passing grammar tests; I felt like a writer because Miss Mortenson sat there smiling, attentive, really listening—and *enjoying me*. Never demanding more than I was able to give; respecting talent without asking for proof. That quality of teaching has been a beacon all through my life. I know that if every child could have teachers like Miss Mortenson, it might change the world.

And now she is dead and I never asked her if she knew. I guess I know the answer. I have been a teacher too, and I have long since been thirty-eight years old, and if that happened in a class of mine, I surely would have known. It is too late to say "Thank you." I wish I had. But I think I may now be ready to fill those empty notebooks with stories.

What Are Little Girls Made Of?

One half of your class may be damaged, in need of special attention. When we examine the material we teachers provide for girls to read we can begin to understand why it might be so. I think you will find that this piece and the editorial guidelines that follow open your eyes to the damaging image girls must overcome to grow straight and tall.

Lenore J. Weitzman
and Diane Rizzo

Textbooks have always been a cornerstone of our education system. Although the main function of textbooks is to convey specific information, textbooks also provide the child with ethical and moral values. Thus, at the same time that a child is learning history or math, he or she is also learning what is good, desirable, just.

This second type of information—which sociologists refer to as the "latent content" of textbooks—provides standards for how men, women, boys, and girls should act. This latent content was the focus of research we carried on for the last three years. During that time, we have analyzed the latent content of the most widely used textbook series in the United States in each of five subject areas: science, arithmetic, reading, spelling, and social studies. (A grant from the Rockefeller Family Fund supported the research.) Through computer

This article was originally published as **"Sex Bias in Textbooks,"** in *Today's Education*, Vol. 64, No.1 (Jan.–Feb. 1975) Reprinted by permission.

analysis, we obtained data on the sex, age, racial distribution, and activities of the textbook characters by grade level and subject area.

This article will summarize the ways in which the two sexes are portrayed and the type of behavior encouraged for each.

SEX DISTRIBUTION

Since women comprise 51 percent of the U.S. population, one might expect half of the people in textbook illustrations to be females. However, males overwhelmingly predominate in all series: Females are only 31 percent of the total, while males are 69 percent. Of over 8,000 pictures analyzed, more than 5,500 are of males. Girl students using these books are likely to feel excluded.

SEX DIFFERENCES BY GRADE LEVEL

The percentage of females varies by grade level. In all series combined, females comprise a third of the illustrations at the second-grade level, but only a fifth of the total on the sixth-grade level. In other words, by the sixth grade, there are four pictures of males for every picture of a female.... Thus, as the textbooks increase in sophistication, women become less numerous and, by implication, less significant as role models.

This decline in female role models makes it harder for a girl student to identify with the textbook characters and thus may make it harder for her to assimilate the lesson. Covertly, she is being told that she, a female, is less important as the textbook world shifts to the world of adults—to the world of men.

This declining representation of females is particularly striking in some of the series. For example, in the second-grade spelling series, 43 percent of the illustrations are of females, but in the sixth-grade series, the percentage has declined to a mere 15 percent.

SEX DIFFERENCES IN ACTIVITIES

The pictures of children show three striking differences between boys and girls. First, boys are portrayed as active, skillful, and adventuresome; girls are typically shown as passive—as watching and waiting for boys.

Second, the boys are depicted as intelligent and as mastering work-related skills, girls are shown engaging in domestic activities or in grooming themselves, trying on clothes, and shopping. Third, girls are depicted as affectionate, nurturing, and emotional, but boys almost never embrace or cry. Thus, the young boy is taught that to be manly he must control his emotions. In the same way that girls are constrained by images which stereotype them as pretty and passive, boys are constrained by images which stereotype them as strong and unemotional. The textbooks thereby encourage both sexes to limit their development.

Adult men and women in textbooks are even more sex-stereotyped. While only a few women are shown outside the home, men are portrayed in over 150 occupational roles. A young boy is told he can be anything from a laborer to a doctor. He is encouraged to imagine himself in a wide variety of roles and both to dream about and plan his occupational future.

In contrast, the future for young girls seems preordained: Almost all adult women in textbooks are housewives. In reality, however, nine out of ten women in our society will work at some point in their lives. By ignoring women workers, the textbooks fail to provide the necessary occupational role models for girls and thus unnecessarily restrict future horizons.

SEX DIFFERENCES IN SUBJECT AREAS

There are systematic differences in the treatment that girls and women receive in different subject areas. The percentage of females in illustrations varies from a high of 33 percent in social studies to a low of 26 percent in science. These subject differences are important in understanding why children like certain subjects and want to major in them—or why, in contrast, they feel unwelcome because of the covert messages they receive.

In science, the most male-oriented series, 74 percent of the pictures are of males. The science texts seem to imply that the world of science is a masculine domain. When boys are shown, they are actively involved in experiments—looking through microscopes and pouring chemicals. In contrast, when girls are shown, they observe the boys' experiments. The epitome of the male prototype in science is the astronaut. But only boys are pictured as astronauts and, in the text, only boys are told to imagine that they can explore the moon.

In mathematics textbooks, many problems are based on sex-stereotyped roles, with men earning money and women dividing pies. Further, despite the Equal Pay Act of 1963; we found math problems in which girls were paid less than boys for the same work. (It would be hard to imagine a textbook publisher allowing an example in which a black child is paid less than a white child.)

In the reading series, story titles provide a good indicator of the relative importance of males and females. Boys predominate in every grade. The series examined had 102 stories about boys and only 35 about girls.

Even the female heroines reinforce traditional female roles. For example, Kirsten, the heroine of a third-grade story, wins over the girls who have rejected her by making Danish cookies and having the most popular booth at the school fair. The moral in this story is that girls can succeed by cooking and serving. But Kirsten slights herself and the very skill that had earned her favor when she says, "It's easy; even I can do it, and you know how stupid I am." Thus, even when girls succeed, they tend to deprecate themselves. In contrast, boys show a great deal of confidence and pride.

Both the reading and spelling series demonstrate a surprising amount of antagonism and hostility toward females. In the spelling series, female characters are yelled at and pushed around. In the reading series, they are shown as stupid and clumsy three times as frequently as males.

In social studies, the best series studied, women were often skillful and important. Here, mothers play a crucial role in passing on their cultural tradition to their daughters. Although we applaud these positive pictures of women, it should be noted that mothers in the series teach only their daughters, not their sons. Similarly, fathers teach only sons. Thus, traditional sex roles are perpetuated. Today, boys need to learn to manage in the home and to be parents, and girls need to learn about vocations and the outdoors. Textbooks could expand rather than contract children's potential.

Although this series has the largest percentage of females in pictures, still 2 out of 3 are pictures of males. Women are in the section on the home but are absent from the sections on history, government, and society.

After studying these textbooks for three years, one cannot help but conclude that children are being warped by the latent messages in them. We urge teachers to examine the textbooks they use and to check the ways in which sex roles are stereotyped. Only teachers can change the impact that these books will have on our young people and on the next generation of adults. Teachers can tell their girl students about the world and the real options they have in it. Teachers can encourage them to dream and can help them plan.

What is sorely lacking in textbooks and thus desperately needed in the classroom is a new image of adult women and a wide range of adult role models for young girls. Girls—and boys too—should learn about the history of women in this country, about suffrage and the current women's liberation movement, and about female heroines of our country and the world. What a difference it would make if young girls could point to adult women with pride and feel that they themselves have an exciting life ahead.

While we must all create pressure to change the textbooks, in the meantime, it is up to teachers to counteract the latent messages in them and to create positive images of adult women in the minds of students.

Guidelines for Equal Editorial Treatment of the Sexes

In an effort to avoid sexist assumptions in their publications, the McGraw-Hill Book Company and other publishers have drawn up guidelines for equal treatment of the sexes. The following adaptation from the McGraw-Hill guidelines may prove helpful to teachers as writers and as speakers and in discussions of sexism with their students.

In discussion, treat men and women primarily as people and not primarily as members of opposite sexes. Stress their shared humanity and common attributes—not their gender differences. Do not stereotype either sex or arbitrarily assign one sex to a leading or a secondary role.

1. Though many women will continue to choose traditional occupations such as homemaker and secretary, do not typecast women in these roles but present them as individuals interested in a wide variety of professions and trades. Similarly, do not present men as constantly subject to the "masculine mystique" in their interests, attitudes, or careers.

View girls as having, and exercising, the same options as boys in their play and career choices. Encourage girls to show an interest in mathematics, mechanical skills, and active sports, for example, and do not make boys feel ashamed of an interest in poetry, art, or music or an aptitude for cooking, sewing, or child care.

2. Represent members of both sexes as whole human beings with *human* strengths and weaknesses, not masculine or feminine ones.

3. Refer to women and men with the same respect, dignity, and seriousness. Avoid references to a man's or a woman's appearance, charm, or intuition when irrelevant. Say, "The Harrises are an interesting couple. Henry is a shrewd lawyer, and Ann is very active in community affairs" and not, "Henry Harris is a shrewd lawyer, and his wife Ann is a striking brunette."

In describing women, avoid a patronizing or girl-watching tone, as well as sexual innuendoes, jokes, and puns. The following are examples of practices to be avoided: focusing on physical appearance (a buxom blonde), using special female-gender word forms (poetess, aviatrix, usherette).

Avoid stereotypes such as the following: scatterbrained female or fragile flower. Also avoid jokes at women's expense—such as the woman driver or nagging mother-in-law clichés.

In referring to females—

Say *women*, not *the fair sex*.
Say *the women*, not *the girls* or *the ladies*, when speaking of adult females.
Say *wife*, not *the little woman*.
Say *feminist*, not *libber*.

In describing males, especially men in the home, avoid references to general ineptness. Do not characterize men as dependent on women for meals or clumsy in household maintenance or as foolish in self-care.

Treat women as part of the rule, not as the exception. Assume that generic terms, such as doctor and nurse, include both men and women, and avoid modified titles such as woman doctor and male nurse.

Speak of women as participants in the action, not as possessions of the men. Do not use terms such as *pioneer*, *farmer*, and *settler* as though they applied only to adult males. For example, instead of saying, "Pioneers moved West, taking their wives and children with them," say, "Pioneer men and women moved West, taking their children with them."

4. Recognize women for their own achievements. Introduce intelligent, daring, and innovative women, both in history and in fiction, in class discussions as possible role models for girls.

5. When referring to humanity at large, use language that includes women and girls. Whenever possible, avoid terms that tend to exclude females.

The word *man* has long been used to denote humanity at large. To many people today, however, the word *man* is no longer broad enough to be applied to any person or to human beings as a whole.

Here are some possible substitutions for *man*-words:

humanity, human beings, and *people* for *mankind.*
artificial, synthetic, and *manufactured* for *manmade.*
human power and *human energy* for *manpower.*

The English language lacks a generic singular pronoun signifying *he* or *she*, and therefore it has been customary and grammatically sanctioned to use masculine pronouns in expressions such as "one...*he*" and "anyone...*he*." Nevertheless, avoid when possible, the pronouns *he, him,* and *his* in reference to the hypothetical person or humanity in general.

Replace occupational terms ending in *man* whenever possible by terms that can include members of either sex unless they refer to a particular person. For example, say *mail carrier* or *letter carrier*, not *mailman; fire fighter* not *fireman; supervisor*, not *foreman; business executive*, not *businessman; sales clerk*, not *salesman;* and *member of Congress*, not *Congressman.*

The Dumbest Kid

We all know him: the dumbest kid. T.M. Walsh traces his rise to momentary success in school and his predetermined descent into the failure he was "destined" for.

T.M. Walsh

I should have told the kid to use another name. Still there's no wisdom in setting a young man on a deceitful path. He'd be lying enough out of sheer necessity as he made his way up and down the nasty slopes of life.

Perhaps what gave everything away was that stupid snapshot. If they'd have just kept his picture out of it, everything might have rolled along, real nice. Albert Johnson is a common enough name and they might not have

---

This article appeared in *The Teacher Paper*, Portland, Oregon, Copyright Fred and Robin Staab.

wised up on the name alone. Albert was such a handsome-looking pirate, I suppose Conway figured that the snapshot would add a touch. Conway was a competent neighborhood editor first, last, and always.

Still it wasn't really Conway's fault or Albert's or mine. The fault lay with the stupid educational system which was every bit as dumb as Albert himself.

Albert was a seventeen-year-old blond Casanova with whom my lively dark-eyed fifteen-year-old daughter was temporarily enamored. He was a lanky, lean-muscled, blue-eyed, free swinging Norseman kid, practically inarticulate, up to his neck in trouble at school, and exactly the last young man I would want for a son-in-law.

I recall my wife's saying to me one night as we got ready for bed: "I don't like the idea of Diana going around with Albert. He's just not her type."

This was true, Diana was one of those unfortunate people who is a natural student. She was always at the top of her classes and always receiving silly awards for her scholarly abilities. I advised her not to take these honors too seriously, because I believed the educators who went in for this nonsense were sadly deficient in good sense. I don't think it's a good idea to divide mere children from one another by such awards.

"It doesn't mean a thing," I said. "Diana is very pleased that the handsomest kid in school is interested in her. She'll soon grow tired of him."

"But he's so dumb!" my wife exclaimed.

"Don't say that about him," I admonished. "There's no such thing as a dumb human being. If Albert were the only person on earth, he'd be the pride of the universe."

"As long as there's anyone else on earth, he won't make much of a stir. He's so dumb!" My wife was positively fascinated by Albert's dumbness.

In a worldly nonphilosophical sense, she was right. I once asked Albert what two squared was. He didn't know, although the following year he would be a senior in high school. He had no conception of grammar, history, civics, politics, or anything that young people are supposed to know in school.

He had lots to report on the fight he had with other students. One day he said to me, "There's a couple of guys in my biology class figuring to gang up on me. I'll whip the both of them."

My interest aroused, I asked him to demonstrate his fighting stance. It was a stance neither I nor anyone else had ever seen before. He stood up and clenched his fists, looking for all the world like a baker simultaneously kneading two lumps of dough on a low table, or a farmer gripping a low-handled plow. His clenched fists were at the level of his hips.

I tried to teach him the importance of a left jab, a right cross, and how to block a punch. But it taxed his brain to the point of nervousness, and he finally balked at my instruction, saying, "No, I just better fight them my own way."

It really didn't worry me, because Albert was such a strong, strapping lad. I felt sorry for his two opponents whoever they might be. I learned later that the fight hadn't come off after all.

One day I asked Albert what he would like to be.

"I'd like to be a sports writer," he said with fervor. The poor kid loved sports, but he was not allowed on any of the teams because his grades were so bad. And there was something else. His heart had a bit of a murmur. It couldn't have meant much because you never saw a stronger seventeen-year-old boy. He believed he could never be a sports writer, but he thought such a life would be the nearest thing to paradise that the world could offer.

"I could teach you to be a sports writer in fifteen minutes," I said in the way I have. "There's nothing to it." My wife frowned when she heard I said this, and later she protested, "You shouldn't tell that poor ox things like that. He'll just be hurt. Now you have him and Diana all excited."

I don't know what my wife was worrying about because I did teach him to be a sports writer in fifteen minutes. It wasn't me who broke his heart.

I remember the day very well I taught Albert to be a sports writer. Albert, Diana, and my wife and I were seated in the room we used as the den. It was practically bare except for a leather couch and overstuffed chair and the desk on which my typewriter rested.

Maybe it took me twenty minutes to teach Albert sports writing. Anyhow not much more than that. I remember I picked up the newspaper, sat down at the typewriter, and put down forty different verbs from the sports stories. I handed him the list and said, "Next Friday go to the football game and write it up. Remember now the secret is the verbs. Remember that the halfback doesn't run over the tackle for five yards. He slams or bangs over the tackle for five yards. He doesn't run around left end. He skids or sweeps around left end for five yards. If one team beats another by a big score, you use 'clobbered' or 'swamped.' If it's a close score, you use 'edged by' or 'squeaked by' or some suitable verb. Get the idea?" He said he did.

"Now then," I suggested, "write up next week's football game, bring it to me, and I'll type it up for you. Then you can take it over to Conway, the editor of the *Pickyune Times* newspaper, and see what he thinks of it."

My irrepressible daughter, Diana, grew enthusiastic about the idea. She decided that she would write an article about club activities in the school.

The following Friday night Albert brought me the story he had written. Although every third word was misspelled, he had plainly mastered the principle. I typed up the story of the football game and the next day, which was Saturday, he and Diana went over to see the editor. Conway was quite pleased with Albert's report on the football game. It was arranged that the young fellow should cover the school sports once each week for $7.50 per story.

Diana was disappointed because the editor wasn't interested in school club activities.

Every Friday night for three weeks Albert brought me his story in longhand, and I typed it up.

So he had achieved his fondest dream in life. He was a sports writer. After the third week he didn't bring me his story, but somehow took care of all the details himself. Possibly he had one of his cute girl friends helping him with the spelling and typing.

But there it was on the sports page every Monday:

SPORTS FLASHES FROM EAGLETON HIGH
by
ALBERT JOHNSON

I devoured his weekly reports. And, on the seventh Monday, I noted with pleasure that a picture of Albert's handsome mug stood at the top of the story.

On the eighth week I opened the newspaper to the sports page, and my heart sank. I read:

SPORTS FLASHES FROM EAGLETON HIGH
by
DICK TURNEY

Dick Turney's bespectacled, scholarly face beamed out from the top of the article.

"What happened?" I asked Diana when she came home from school. "Did Albert get tired of writing sports?"

"No, she said, "the principal made him stop. He thought since his grades were so bad, it wasn't right for Albert to do it. So they fixed it up with the editor to have Dick Turney do it. He's a scholarship student."

So the dream of a lifetime was snatched from my protégé, and his task as arbitrarily turned over to a kid who was meant for better and more serious things.

Diana didn't care too much because she had already wearied of poor Albert's childish outlook on life. She was now fascinated by a skinny droopy-eyed young fellow who played the guitar and could recite numerous stanzas from Omar Khayyam.

But I burned with resentment. Since the goddamned school was incapable of educating the kid, they should have been pleased that he was showing something on his own.

Could it be that each of us has a line of destiny to follow from which there is no escaping? I saw Albert getting out of a rattle-trap truck one day about five years later. I hurried over to ask him how he was doing. His hat, clothes, and face were covered with cement dust. He had difficulty remembering me. He told me he was helping a man put in driveways. Albert's wife and three unkempt infants, crowding the cab of the truck, seemed hard-pressed and weary. Then I looked more closely at Albert. His face had thinned and he had the aspect of a lean, overworked man. I felt that Albert was destined to be overworked and tired all his life.

The Discarded Set

Many special children have been segregated into separate classes. It is not politic to question this approach these days, yet we would be remiss if we didn't share the disturbing possibility that some of these children have their own secret reasons for seeking school failure, and that they are being closed off from the mainstream by tracking.

The tests can be faked, and have been, even by institutionalized mental retardates who could control their IQ test performance when they thought it in their interest.*

Annette Covino, a "special ed" teacher, struggles to find a way to help each child in her class. Her search for appropriate materials and patience is not unique to her role, only heightened. Most teachers aren't subject to this unremitting pressure, and few have the honesty to admit: "Linda was the only child that I ever physically hurt and it made me hate her and me. . . ."

Annette Covino

Adam was my boy. If ever a teacher and a kid had a thing going it was me and Adam. Two people—one young, one old; one male, one female; one black, one white; one labeled retarded, the other overeducated—but we had a real thing going. Rapport, communication, soul, transference, call it what you will, we understood each other. It was like a beautiful chess game. In all of the subtle interplays, neither one of us ever made a mistake. To the brink but never over. Small, lithe, and expressive, Adam was never just plain. He was moody or serious or mocking or sympathetic or defiant. And I gave him lots of play.

"You old white witch," he'd start, "you say you want to help me but you don't want to help me. You never come to help me. You're ugly and white."

"Say it out, boy," I'd say to myself, "say it strong and say it clear. I can take it. I've got it made. But you've got to stand up and fight now."

I remembered reading Adam's record folder. The teacher he had last year had written that Adam could not keep up with the class, but when she tried to give him easier work he would not do it but kept on with the too difficult work and had no success.

---

*Benjamin M. Braginsky and Dorothea D. Braginsky, "**The Mentally Retarded: Society's Hänsels and Gretels**," *Psychology Today*, March 1974.

What can that do to a kid that needs to prove himself and is compulsive? He is caught in a trap. He cannot admit that he needs to do easier work, and he cannot satisfy his need to finish the job perfectly. I thought of the three loose-leaf books he had filled by the end of the term. They were overflowing with work. Never had he failed to finish an assignment perfectly. He drove me wild.

"Help me, Mrs. Covino," he was forever crying out, "see, you never want to help me when I need you."

"Damn you," I thought sometimes, "leave me be, boy. Don't do the goddamn work, but leave me be." But there was no stopping him. He knew he could count on me and he drained me until the paper had a big, red 100 on top. And of all the children in the group Adam was the only one that grew academically before your eyes. All of a sudden Adam could read. All of a sudden he could do multiplication. I'd watch him sometimes when he was quiet, working so strained and hard, and I'd think that it just wasn't fair for him to work and try so hard and not be able to make it. He was my ongoing private project, and I stood near his desk most of the day and gave him every spare minute I had and ounces of energy I couldn't spare. And he was worth it, but when I didn't have it I had to give it anyway.

"I always come in meaning to be good but you make me mad, you white witch," he'd say. But when I was reading the story in the afternoon, he'd move his chair up to the front of the room next to mine and rest his chin on my arm as he tried to follow the words. But when the day was over he'd look over theneat row of work with the red 100's on top and he'd say, "Gee, I did pretty much work today." Or he would pick up a book and start to read to me and say, "Gee that's a real hard book I can read." So I didn't really care or maybe I didn't really care most of the time.

Adam ended the year much straighter inside than he had come in. And he had learned an awful lot pretty fast for a boy who had been labeled retarded. But I knew that it wasn't nearly enough.

• • •

"What's the name of that handsome boy in your class?," the regular teachers would ask. "My, I do like him, he's so polite." And I guess he was. Handsome and polite. If that's what you care about. But somehow James and I never had enough overlapping area to understand each other. We had a kind of respect for each other but almost no real understanding. Handsome and well built and polite as he was, James was always coming out garbled. His speech was al mixed up and he never could tell the difference between puppy and puppet. His belongings spilled over his own desk and an extra large table that was his. His handwriting spilled over the paper as though his letters were nothing more than random marks. James didn't want liking or loving or help-ing. He only wanted you to be fair. In his own groups he had always been the scapegoat, the spark of trouble. Not the cause. The cause was in the dynamics of the groups and fires would have flared up even without James. James was too anxious to be the match in one way, but yet he still craved recognition of his real role. Maybe that was why being fair was so important to him.

"It's not fair, Mrs. Covino," he would say, "I was first." And somehow it meant much more to him than to any other child.

"All right, James," I would say, "I guess I made another mistake. You were really first." The bitterness and anger would fade and he would smile. And this fairness filled him with pleasure and it was as if it were a live thing that we shared. After a while we added another line to the repartee.

"It's all right, Mrs. Covino," he would say with great pleasure in his giving role, "I can wait, you can go to her first." I accepted his gift with all the pomp and ceremony it warranted.

Peggy was the only middle-class child who spent the year with us. As far as I know, her mother was the only parent to ever complain about the group. At one point Peggy was the only white child in the group and her mother reported that her child was upset and cried at home about this. At the end of the year I overheard the following conversation between Peggy, Shelley, and Julia.

"Did you tell her yet?" Shelly asked.

"No," Peggy replied.

"Go on," Julia urged, "tell her you want to be black like us. Tell her tonight."

Peggy was tall and thin and fair. Of all the children she looked the most different from the "normal child." She had heavy braces and heavy glasses and was most unattractive. Maybe it was not really her looks but the reflection of her mother's feelings about her that made her seem so unattractive. The worst thing was her speech. It was poor speech and almost unintelligible without listening experience, but even that was not crucial. Of all the many difficult aspects of the group the most difficult thing for me to take was Peggy's whining. It grated on raw nerve endings like the constant screeching of chalk across the blackboard. It was high pitched, singsong, and constant. At the end of the year when Peggy was able to give me a loud and clear "I won't," I was pleased and when she added, "You can't make me," I was almost happy.

Somewhere along the way Peggy had truly been robbed of hope and any learning was meaningless to her. She did what she had to do with constant prodding and supervision but she never cared how it was done. And in a while I didn't care either. The records indicated that there had been very little academic improvement in the last few years. But Peggy had a friend in our group. She and Shelley sat together and worked together and walked to lunch swinging clasped hands, and that was my only gift to Peggy. The atmosphere of the classroom had made it possible for her to have a friend. They worked together. Shelley opened her friend's book to the right page each morning and handed her her coat when it was time to go home. She got her a tissue when her nose was running, which it always was. That was on the good days when Shelley wasn't upset about something at home or mixing it up with James. And Peggy and Shelley had lots of good days. They were the only children in the class who came to the school picnic and they came together. And I think the best time for Peggy was when the girls were dancing. It was about the only thing that made Peggy come alive.

Her mother was a lovely looking, mink-stoled lady who had been born in Germany. Her father was a large man who sold insurance. Peggy had two socially acceptable younger brothers.

"If only I could find one thing that she could excel at," her mother said. And that was really it because she would never find that one thing and there wasn't anything about Peggy the way she was, that her mother could like. Truthfully I didn't like her much either, but it probably would have been different if she had been younger. So Peggy took endless lessons of assorted kinds.

"I am going to be a ballerina," she said. "I been taking dancing a long time." Only the sad reality of the situation barred laughter.

"You may dance very well," I said, "but to be a ballerina and dance on the stage is very hard work and very few girls can be ballerinas."

"I will dance on the stage," she whined. "I have a ballet suit." It was neither retardation nor immaturity that prompted those remarks. It was her mother's need.

"My mommie and daddy say that you have to give me harder math and stuff. You just keep on giving me the same old baby stuff and my mommie and daddy don't like that." I could only guess at the conversations that went on in her home.

Peggy had a rare experience the year we were together. She became a member of the elite inner circle of our group. Her friendship with Shelley was the opening wedge. From her first days as a victim to her later days as a tormentor of Karen, she traveled a long way. In the end she whined in a lower pitch and complained in a louder, stronger voice. She also found a true black friend. I doubt if her mother would wish to thank me for the changes.

If Adam was my special boy, then Julia was my special girl. I knew from the beginning that she wasn't retarded. Her eyes had a kind of sparkle and she just knew too many things. Not about reading or arithmetic but about the world. And we had special feelings for each other. Once, when I had been out the day before observing Mrs. S.'s class, she came in the next morning and put her arms around my neck and gave me a kiss. I have had my fair share of different kinds of kisses. I don't think I have ever had a kiss more honestly given. I had told the psychologist in the beginning that I was worried about Julia. There was not much that I could do with her academically. She could not admit to herself that she had to work on the level that she did. And I felt that to push was to help destroy the child. It said on the record that she needed psychological help. I asked the psychologist how I could help her to get it. "Make out a pink slip," he said. "She's not really our problem because she comes from M." I am not a pink-slip-making-out person and I thought of the effects of the pink slip on the mother and I made out no pink slips. And I had a strong urge to scream out, "Are we not all God's children even if we come from M?" This is strange because I do not really believe in God. But I smiled and was quiet and Julia and I managed.

When the class had first started, Julia's position was based on having the loudest voice and yelling the vilest words the most often. She was always tensed up, alert, and raring to find something to go at. When the whole tone of the class became less aggressive, I worried about Julia. She had lost her tool and I had no substitute for her. She looked real forlorn for a while and that upset me more than the yelling. And I guess that what finally made up for her loss was me. We liked each other and she knew it. She was the only child who ever said, "I ain't never coming to school with no other teacher but you." Most of her days were spent hopping and jumping around as though she was a fighter waiting for the action to start.

"Sit down," I'd say, "and do your work."

"No," she'd say, "you gonna make me?"

"No," I'd say, "I'm just asking."

"O.K., Mrs. Covino," she'd say and sit down for as long as she could bear it.

It's funny about the routines. Some lines got to be so popular you'd think they came from Joe Miller's *Joke Book*. Once when James needed help it took me a moment to get there and by then he had found the answer himself.

"See, James," I said, "it took me so long that you found the answer by yourself. I was too late." He was real pleased with that and it got to be a regular thing.

"Hurry and help me," he'd say," hurry or it'll be too late and I'll get it by myself." I'd pretend to put the speed on and run over.

"Did I make it?," I would ask anxiously.

I had told the school psychologist and anyone else who would listen that Julia was brain damaged and emotionally disturbed and couldn't cope and needed help. At the end of the year the psychologist found out that he was responsible for what he thought he hadn't been responsible for all year, and a lot of testing was done in a great hurry. Julia was the first to go. And surprise of surprises, was he ever excited to find out that she wasn't retarded after all.

So pretty much Julia and I compromised on the work. I let her do the work she thought she should do and hoped that she would get some incidental, if not sequential, learning out of it. She kept busy and didn't learn as much as she should have, but we were friends and we both were the better for it and who can say that a year with a friend doesn't mean as much as a year's growth in reading?

Allison was the reason, I think, that the class had started in October. Her family had moved here from Brooklyn over the summer and there was no room in the special classes for Allison and her twin sister. And their mother was not the person to see her daughters not getting what she had in mind for them to get. There were seven children in the family and, for relief purposes, no husband. When Allison was unhappy on the school bus and her mother decided that the bus was too crowded for her daughter she went straight to the principal, and I'll be damned if he wasn't out there the next day counting bus children. She is a remarkable woman. She is a black, lower-class replica of the middle-class Jewish mother. I wonder if she knew how to make chicken soup.

When this lady came to the community and found a house and got wel-fare to pay for it she wasn't about to let her girls sit home more than a few days. And it seemed to be pretty much policy in special education to shift the bodies around in such a way as to eliminate the strongest complaints. Like the naughty boys in school, you only got noticed if there was trouble. And the special education department was very vulnerable because of a question that they didn't even want whispered. How come the retarded classes were made up almost entirely of blacks and the brain-damaged classes were almost all white?

So when our class started in October it was Allison's first day in the school system. What can I say about Allison? On the record that she brought from a city class for the retarded, it stated that my twelve-year-old Allison was unsatisfactory in preprimer reading and first grade math. The first day she came in and straight off headed for the coat closet and hid under the coats. When I finally coaxed her out and got her settled it was time for music. Music was in a room down the hall. She screamed and clutched her chair as though the most horrible kind of unknown torture awaited her. "Think fast," I said to myself. I had to get that class to music and Allison was part of the class. I gave her the kitten puppet. "He can be your friend,'" I said. "You can keep him with you. I will hold one hand and he will hold the other." I didn't even know if she understood me. But she did and she clutched me and the puppet and she sat in music. At the very end of the term she still went under the desk when strangers came in.

It was Allison who set me thinking about how variable functions can be. She read at preprimer level but there were many things she could do as well as I could. She could visualize a dress, an arts and crafts project, or a puzzle. She was the only child to figure out that if you do a puzzle on the floor and you put a heavy paper under it before you start, then you can pick it up and put it on your desk to finish tomorrow. She had a nice shop teacher going for her and I bet she made more things in shop that year than any other kid in the school. I don't know what she learned and it took me a while to learn how to work with her but she became a very busy girl. She wrote endless letters and sent them with endless wrapped presents to an endless string of people. She copied stories and made word cards and looked up words in the little dictionary. She liked to have piles of math papers around. She was always asking for things to take home. Sometimes she reminded me of the little old ladies who live in the subways and have large shopping bags filled with the odds and ends of their belongings. The bus driver complained about the large bags. There was some talk of stealing but she never stole from me because she never had to. Allison needed these things around her and she was welcome to what she needed.

When I tried to push the academics too far she would sit and cry. "I have nothing to do," she would say. And the tears would stream down her face. I knew what she meant. She had nothing to do that she could feel good at. So we would start some project and I would say that when she finished her reading she could work on the project. She would smile and try to wheedle a little less work and we would bargain awhile and finally settle the problem. I was silently glad that she did not come to school every day but was kept home to babysit at times. Even though I enjoyed her she was a terrible energy drain. Allison and Julia and Adam, I could never really get angry at them. You took so much from them that you didn't mind putting it in. But they were always needing you and the days when you just didn't have it were too bad.

Allison could be real mean when I wasn't there and lash out rough and hard. I do not understand the why and how of Allison and I stand humble in my ignorance.

Karen came in the middle of the school year. All of her school years she had been in a school for the trainable retarded. She was one of the few children to make it from one category to another because our class was labeled educable retarded. Karen was twelve years old but she was small and physically imma- ture and could pass for a second-grader. Her almost unintelligible speech was the catalyst that won Peggy her inner circle status. In the beginning it had been Peggy who had been the butt of the retarded bit. "Peggy makes us all look retarded the way she looks and talks," my black children would complain. When Karen came they switched from Peggy to Karen.

If you think that suffering creates understanding and empathy, you'd better forget it because Peggy joined happily in giving what she had been get- ting. What other variables do we need to add to suffering and experiencing to lead to empathy and understanding?

Karen sat near my desk almost until the end of the term when Linda took over that position so that we could all survive. Karen was not entirely isolated. Allison and Mary often worked with her. But Allison could shift into reverse real fast and I had to keep alert to protect Karen. The happiest times for her were the days when Allison was absent and she and Mary worked alone. But Karen seemed happy all of the time and worked hard and took great pride in her work. When I asked her why she liked our class she replied that there were always so many things to do.

At first she worked at such an unbelievably slow pace that I wondered about the trainable schools. But she speeded up and smiled and giggled at the amount of work that she could do.

At the end of the year her mother called me. Karen had always gone to a summer program for retarded children and her mother wondered if it was right to send her there this summer since she had made so much progress. She thought maybe she would go back again if she spent the summer with all the retarded kids. I said that I thought it was fine to send Karen if she enjoyed the program. Her mother was pleased.

It's strange that Shelley was the most responsible child in the group and yet I never really understood her. I knew from the first day that I had to get to Shelley if I wanted to get the group. She could help put the brakes on. She was over twelve and starting to mature physically and she had two sisters in a special junior high class. It was kind of sad at the end. All year the only real trouble I had with Shelley was mixing it up with James. The last few weeks got real bad. One morning Shelley came up to my desk.

"My mother ain't been home," she said.

"Oh," I said.

"She's been down South a while and she's coming home soon," she added.

"I'm sure you're happy about that," I replied.

"Yeah, I sure do miss her. She's gonna bring me a present. My sister is down there too."

I remembered that she had told me several weeks earlier that her sister had left school. I had never asked why.

"She went down there to get married. She got married last night. She's gonna have a baby."

Her sister was fourteen or fifteen years old. It depressed me. I thought how I was teaching all the wrong things and who needed most of that garbage anyway. I had at least been pretty honest with the girls about the sex education bit. It had been passed from person to person and finally I had done it myself. We started with monthly periods and the girls took it from there. We talked when the boys were in gym and Mary and Karen sat in the back of the room and did their work. But the rest of us had some good talks. When the art teacher started to talk about babies one day Julia said, "Oh, Mrs. Covino told us all about that."

But I hadn't told enough or listened enough or done enough. Maybe next time.

Shelley was the all around best worker that I had. She had a long attention span and usually did her work clean and good. I gave her more respect than any other child. If she said that she didn't feel like finishing her work I quietly let it go. When she and James had a real go at it and I could see that she was so tight that her hands were shaking I would let her go to the library to do her work. I could trust her. I could trust her with anything but James. I never could exactly figure it out. James brought out a bad interplay between himself and the black girls. He lived in a bad house on a bad place and had no father and he had learned to make it on his own. He was an operator and he was something the black girls hated. With Shelley it was way out of bounds. And it was beyond anything that I could control.

At the start of the term I had once said, "Sit down and do your work, Shelley."

"What's the difference," she replied, "don't you see I'm black and retarded and can't do nothing." She didn't say it as though it made a difference to her but as if it was supposed to get a rise out of me. I tried to keep it cool and funny and honest about labels.

"You know," I'd say, "I'm real retarded in rope jumping. I can't jump at all." They liked that and it was true. "Black, white—I'm tired of all that color talk. Look at our arms. We're really just all shades of brown. I wish we were all purple." We all looked and compared and agreed.

When we were painting Halloween pictures and were all covered with orange paint Julia said, "See, Mrs. Covino now we're all the same color like you wanted." I hugged her. I liked that.

Linda was the only child that I ever physically hurt and it made me hate her and me and the whole rotten system. We all played the game of going to the brink and then pulling back. And it made for the give and take, the delicate balance between self-expression and group needs, exploration and control, self-control and external control. Most of the children in a strange, wonderful, and natural way knew how to play the game. But not Linda. I played it with Linda as hard as I could. I gave her more play than any other child because she was the most unhappy and the most lost and needed it. But she was too sick to play. She was in trouble with everyone. The bus driver, the playground aides, the other teachers all had plenty of complaints. Not a constructive suggestion in the lot. I finally spoke to the principal a few weeks before the end of the term. There were only five weeks left but she was getting bad. He said that the system would suspend her for the rest of the school year. When it was put on the line I couldn't do it. I said that I would bear with it. I figured I might just make it. She was going to leave school a week early to go to camp. To show how bad it was, that week meant a lot to me. After that, I kept her near my desk and I hurt her by twisting her arm maybe twice or three times. I twisted just long enough and just hard enough to get her hysteria stopped and back to her seat. If I want to be real honest, a sadistic little bit extra for the pain she caused me. And the worst thing about it is that it worked. For the moment she and I and the group could survive and start fresh the next day.

Linda was ten and very pretty and she needed help. A psychological report written back when she was seven said that she seemed to be reaching out for help. It had that mixed in with a lot of other stuff. Well, by the time I got her she had pretty much stopped reaching. Everyone has a crazy mixed-up family but this one was really it. An older sister in an institution, two brothers in special classes, and a bright struggling mother who was fighting a losing battle and didn't know why. When I called to tell her that Linda had almost been suspended for locking the playground aide in the bathroom she was one up on me.

"What can I tell you," she said. "She is just real bad. I just got home from work and the lady upstairs been telling me she stole candy and hit her three-year-old kid. I'll punish her again."

But after Linda had her tonsils out in the middle of the year, the punishing never really worked. She believed that God would punish her for being so bad and kill her when they took her tonsils out. But when the tonsils were out and she found that she was still here she lost her faith in punishment and that was about all that was holding her back. I remember the first week of school she was always peering out the window.

"What are you looking for Linda?" I asked.

"My mommie say she gonna be out there watching me and I ain't gonna know when she is coming. And if she catch me being bad I sure gonna get it."

Linda's mother never came to school and Linda gave up watching for her.

Until almost the end I really tried. I tried so hard because I knew what she needed. I didn't really like her but I knew what she needed. For a while I even thought that I might be able to swing it.

"My daddy got a cold. He gonna die, Mrs. Covino?" she would ask. The telling and talking wouldn't help. I gave her huge sheets of paper and bottles of finger paint. And she messed a long time and the paper was all dripping and oozing and wet. She cleaned up the mess and herself and she was pleased. But it wasn't enough. She put on puppet shows and invited other classes and did a good job. But it wasn't enough. I brought her food to eat because she was always complaining that she was hungry. But it wasn't enough. She would come and sit on my lap and suck her finger but eventually another child needed me and it wasn't enough. I took her home with me and stuffed her with hamburgers and ice cream and pizza. But nothing was enough. So in the end I twisted her arm because it was better than having her expelled and I knew that her mother didn't want her at home either.

The powers that decide these decisions decided to put her in junior high next year. A sick ten-year-old in junior high because she would be easier to handle there. I called her mother the week after she had left for camp.

"How are things with Linda?" I asked.

"Not so good," her mother replied.

"What happened?" I asked.

"They sent her home from camp after three days," she said. "What will I do with her all summer? I told them at the camp that they got no right to do that but they said they were sorry but they couldn't keep her."

I gave her a talk I had been saving for the right moment. About a clinic that could help Linda. I made it clear. I made it simple. I made it easy to get help.

"Well," she said, "it weren't really Linda's fault being sent home. It was this other girl got sent with her. The junior high teacher will know how to take care of her."

Good-by Linda, little girl reaching out for help. I don't think you'll make it and the fault is mine as much as anyone else's.

IX
RELATIONS WITH RELATIONS

What the Hell Are You Talking About?
And Parents Are Reassured
They Used to Hinder, Now They Help
Help Them Help You
Zeus Says . . .

What the Hell Are You Talking About?

Parents can make or break school innovations. They can undermine your work with their children or support it.

Obviously, good communication is necessary. The best teachers I know call home occasionally to let parents know that their child has done something wonderful that day. It can be a two-minute call, but no parent is immune to the thrill of being told how smart, sensitive, or witty their child is. And, of course, it makes it easier to marshall the parent's support the next week when the child is in trouble.

To make the most of conversations or conferences you should begin with what the parent *wants* to hear. You won't stop at that, but you must *start* where the parent is, just as you do with the child.

A helpful study by doctoral student Ellen Marbach found that, in general, the lower the social-economic class of the parent, the more he or she was likely to value conformity to authority and external standards and a curriculum that was structured and knowledge based.

On the other hand, the higher the social-economic class, the more likely it was that the parent valued self-directedness, peer conformity, and a curriculum that was exploratory and child centered.

Although these generalizations may not hold true for each of your parents, it helps in planning what to share and what to stifle in your initial parent meetings.

You might open by mentioning to one parent what an obedient child she has (this is reassuring) and only *then* emphasize how thoughtful his presentations are, and how wonderfully persistent the child is in seeking answers to questions which puzzle him. To program the mother, you might ask her to note the times he asks her good questions and so stimulate a more open mother-child relationship. Your suggestions will be heard because you reassured this parent first and foremost that you know a "good" child when you see one.

On the other hand, with another parent you might find it's more politic to begin with a compliment about the child's popularity and move on to times the child shows an unusual ability to selectively withstand group pressure and state an unpopular opinion.

Of course, the more relaxed you are, the more relaxed the

parent is. If you don't want to set up a barrier don't sit behind the desk. If you admit some small defeat the parent might feel free to ask questions. If you are anecdotal you can be more secure knowing the parent understands what you said.

So much of the language we education professionals use with one another is made up of jargon. It's often hard for us to recall what's gobbledegook and what's real talk.

The following letter, which appeared in the Ann Landers column, is a great example of what not to do. It's hard to believe someone really strung all these phrases together in one letter home, but I suspect that I might have used them, albeit one at a time, in conversation, and thought I was being understood. Now however, I realize I couldn't hope to further the parent's conceptualization of my goals or enhance and relax our ongoing relationship... Oops!

Ann Landers

DEAR ANN: You are supposed to be a smart cookie. Can you figure this out? I bet my wife $10 you'd flunk just as we did.

The parent of a Houston high school pupil received a message from the school principal concerning a special meeting on a proposed new educational program.

The message read: "Our school's cross-graded, multiethnic, individualized learning program is designed to enhance the concept of an open-ended learning program with emphasis on a continuum of multiethnic, academically enriched learning, using the identified intellectually gifted child as the agent or director of his own learning. Major emphasis is on cross-graded, multiethnic learning with the main objective being to learn respect for the uniqueness of a person."

The parent responded: "Dear Principal: I have a college degree, speak two foreign languages and know four Indian dialects. I've attended a number of county fairs and three goat ropings, but I haven't the faintest idea as to what the hell you are talking about."

Okay, Ann, do *you* know what the principal was trying to say?
—Two Dummies in Fort Worth

DEAR FRIENDS: I don't think you are dummies. That principal needs to learn how to express himself in simple terms.

What he means is: "We are planning a program for students of all races which we hope will encourage the brighter ones to move ahead at their own speed. Grading will be geared to the learning level of the student. In this way we hope to teach and grade each student according to his ability to learn."

This column appeared in *The Chicago Tribune* July 26, 1977. Reprinted by permission of Field Newspaper Syndicate.

P.S. Pay your wife the $10. Or better yet, send it to your local Heart Association.

And Parents Are Reassured. . .

Is it necessary to ignore intellectual precision and logical thinking to be a "humanist"? Bob Gillette, the $100,000 teacher of high school English (so called because of his grant from the New England Program of Teacher Education), thinks not.

Working with potential high school dropouts in their junior year, Gillette, who is concerned that children improve their bad self-image as well as their academic skills, has a record of sending 70 percent of his group on to college.

It's an experimental program that has kids traveling and camping out—the kind of program that might be in trouble now that *basics* is the catchword of the day, but as Bob reports, "The project is still growing and is strong. The new conservatism hasn't affected us because we always stressed basic skill development all through the nine years of the program."

NEA Journal

It was a hot day and everyone in the group was exhausted. They had biked and hiked nearly 50 miles through the foothills of the Berkshires in western Connecticut. Now, as they approached the last lap of the journey, the boys and their teacher saw a steep cliff of a hill ahead. Everyone looked up to survey the new effort required of them.

Suddenly, Joe let out a monstrous groan and roundly cursed the hill, his tired legs, his teacher, and the whole trip. He announced that he couldn't go any farther—that, in fact, he was going to die right there.

The boy's teacher suggested that he die on the side of the road—"out of courtesy to the Department of Public Works." Joe responded by threatening to throw his bike into a nearby stream. The group ignored this threat and pressed wearily on, leaving him behind.

This story has a happy ending, Robert Gillette, the hiking-biking teacher, reports. "As I struggled up the hill," Mr. Gillette recalls, "I thought about my student and friend who had given up. My heart pounded, not only from the exertion of the climb, but also from the risk I'd taken in pushing on without him.

"Then, about half an hour later, I heard a shrill whistle—the kind that only a teenage boy can muster. I turned to see Joe pushing up the hill and slowly gaining on us." The conversation, Bob Gillette remembers, went like this:

This article was originally published as **"Operation Turn-On,"** in the *NEA Journal* (December 1972). Copyright 1972, The National Education Association. Reprinted by permission.

"Hey! Wait up!" Joe panted, his face all smiles.

"What happened?" the teacher asked. "I thought you died back there. Did a truck pick you up?" Joe's response, Mr. Gillette insists, will always remain clear in his mind.

"I looked up that hill," the boy said, "and I saw a big weeping willow tree about a quarter of the way up. I told myself I'd go that far and then decide if I could go on. When I made it to the tree, I saw a big red barn further up and decided to make it that far. Well, now I'm almost to the top!"

Joe paused and then added, "You know, when you look at a long hill or something like that you want to give up. But if you break it up into small goals, you can make it!"

Mr. Gillette comments: "I doubt that any experience within the walls of the traditional classroom could have led Joe to this new perception of himself and of reality. Only the real world of real experience can teach such important lessons about growing up." He adds, "And just think—it was through a school experience that Joe was able to encounter himself."

A school experience? Yes, the bicycle trip through the Berkshires is one of many outdoor experiences Bob Gillette has initiated over the past four years. An English teacher at the Andrew Warde High School in Fairfield, Connecticut, Bob Gillette calls his program Operation Turn On. Warmth and genuine concern for the growth and welfare of his students comes through when he recounts the genesis of this program.

Four years ago, Gillette was asked to work with a group of eleventh grade boys who were turned off on school. They lacked self-esteem and were frequently in trouble; some were about ready to drop out. Given freedom to experiment, the teacher decided to do just that. He began by asking himself some important questions—and answering them.

How do kids learn best? Obviously, they learn best when they are involved in reality.

How can a teacher help kids grow up? He can help by giving them responsibility and the chance to make mistakes.

What do kids like to do? They like to engage in physical activity and to test their capabilities.

When Gillette asked these eleventh graders what they would *like* to do, they indicated that they would "like to get out of here"—the "here" being school. It was then that he decided to go "tripping" with his class, Huck Finn style—to undertake a series of adventures which would combine the curriculum with challenging real-life experiences.

After having all the boys take a physical exam, his first move was to set up a fitness program to get the group in shape for the trips "out there." Among other things, he had the boys run around the track field each day—in full sight of the other students at work in their classrooms. This strenuous workout developed a feeling of group identity, attracted considerable attention, and began the process of building up the boys' self-esteem as well as their physical fitness. In addition, a basis was laid for the feeling of camaraderie that developed on the hiking and biking trips which followed.

In preparing for the trips, the boys began to take pride in their studies as they researched various aspects of diet to help them plan food for an expedition or looked up historical, literary, and geological information about the area they planned to visit. "Putting it all together this way gave them a good idea of the interrelatedness of knowledge," Bob Gillette says.

In time, members of this class became virtual celebrities at school, and when they returned from their expedition, they began to produce in all their classes. Potential dropouts did not drop out; truancy all but disappeared. Obviously, the students saw themselves—and the world—in a new light.

Bob Gillette and his OTO program attracted a good deal of attention in Fairfield. Today, however, he is known internationally. Letters from teachers, students, and administrators have poured into the Gillette home from all over the world.

Last May, Bob received a $100,000 grant from the New England Program of Teacher Education (NEPTE), centered in Durham, New Hampshire. He will receive an additional $200,000 over the next two years if Operation Turn On retains support. The money is practically a no-strings-attached grant. Gillette is quite free to use the funds as he sees fit to implement a variety of educational programs for students, although he works closely and effectively with Lewis Knight, the NEPTE project officer. He cites NEPTE as an agency with courage and a flair for futuristic thinking in education. (There are two stipulations—that the program funds not be used to buy major physical equipment for the school and that his salary be $1,000 more than that of his superintendent!)

The idea of the grant was the brainchild of Dwight Allen, dean of the University of Massachusetts School of Education and a member of the NEPTE board, who proposed it by saying: "Let's see if this experiment captures the imagination." (Captures the imagination? "You can blow your mind just thinking about it!" one of Gillette's students commented. And a stunned administrator remarked, "One hundred thousand dollars—to a *teacher?*")

Robert Gillette believes the award has reinforced the importance of the classroom teacher. "The teacher is the most important member of the learning situation—next to the student," he notes. "If the teacher is so close to the learning happening, it seems only reasonable that he should assume a decision-making role in the expenditure of monies which are translated into programs and experiences for kids."

In his original proposal to NEPTE of what he would do if he had the money and freedom to teach as he wished, Gillette asked two questions: How can we develop an educational program which shakes the student loose from his "zombie" state and which sensitizes him to himself and the society around him? How can we integrate a program of studies so that the student can experience himself and the group in real ways, thereby encountering the real world, which is largely viewed by students as existing outside the classroom?

Operation Turn On is an answer to these questions. It is not a utopian dream or a possibility for the future. It is a real program now in its fourth year of existence. It operates every day, and it succeeds in measurable and sometimes astounding ways.

The present OTO program includes girls as well as boys and both low and high achievers. The girls carry 35-pound packs and sometimes outdo the boys in mastering skills. This heterogeneous group shows great diversity in attitudes, family backgrounds, and plans for the future. Bob Gillette believes that everyone can benefit from the OTO experience, and it is his dream that his approach to learning can be instituted throughout the educational system—from kindergarten through high school.

He is ably assisted by Patricia Clark, who deals with the science aspects of the program, and by Charles Hussey, who deals with the social studies aspects.

Operation Turn On places students in situations and environments which allow them to mature—to grow in a natural way and in a way highly charged with the idea that no individual lives alone in this cosmos; rather, he functions and is fulfilled by the fact that he is a social animal, growing within the human community.

Bob Gillette points out that the program is not an alternative school or a "nonschool school." He feels that the students' activity is "much like a spiral which circles and threads the world of 'out there' into the world of in here.'"

"Students shouldn't have to cut class to get where the action is," Mr. Gillette comments. "Schools ought to help students experience real life with the tools of examination and perspective."

The underlying concepts of OTO are simple: First the teacher finds out what the students want to do most. Then he shows them that what they want to do is actually learning about reality.

"Students want to travel. They want to experience the world on their own terms. They want to get away from the routine of home and school; they want to learn what they think is really important," Gillette believes. "They want responsibility and they are usually willing to live with their own mistakes on the road to maturity. Students can discover that learning and real understanding are exhilarating—though frequently difficult and demanding."

Bob Gillette has a story to illustrate this point. On one hiking trip, the group was late in getting back to the base camp and everyone was famished.

The cooks were doing their job—but not fast enough to suit everyone. Suddenly, some of the hikers couldn't wait any longer; they grabbed the food and began to gobble.

The teacher watched the scene without making a move. "It reminded me of men gone mad," he says. "The boys were turned into animals by their inability to control themselves. The food was quickly devoured—but some of the hikers, including the teacher, didn't get a bite." As the students stood there, looking at each other, one boy began to swear and to accuse the others of selfishness. Suddenly, a teenage voice seemed to cut through all the biting and snapping.

"This is a bad scene," the boy said. "We guys aren't going to survive unless we all stick together."

"I didn't have to say anything," Gillette notes. "No comment on how people survive together was necessary. From that point on, the trip went smoothly. The boys settled on a division of labor that was both strict and effective. They had learned the lesson of community responsibility. I don't think anyone will ever erase that lesson from their minds—and they learned it through school."

Obviously in a program like Operation Turn On, the teacher must assume a low profile. He can raise questions, but he must allow the students to make their own mistakes. He must be able to sit quietly and let the students grapple with the real problems of organizing the adventures they want.

"Decisions made by a group come with difficulty and sometimes with disagreement and heartache. The teacher must be supportive, helping students develop a positive self-image. At the same time, he must remember that no teacher turns on any student; the student turns himself on. All the teacher can do is to provide an environment for real experience and growth," Gillette explains.

Bob Gillette admits that the academic aspects of his expanding classroom are at times very rigorous and demanding. He says: "In this sense, I would term myself a traditionalist, for I do not feel that in order to humanize a classroom one must sacrifice or ignore intellectual preciseness and logical reasoning." Evaluative devices serve to check the students' progress toward specific goals. Traditional testing, numerous papers and research exercises, plus more informal presentations, such as a dance interpretation and multimedia art creations, chart the students' way.

Whether it's a backpacking trip in October, a winter camping and cross-country skiing trip in February, or a white-water canoe or cycling trip, each adventure brings together various aspects of the curriculum into an integrated, total understanding of the region and its people. Economic, political, ecological concerns, historical research, and literature on survival fuse into an overview through the students' research, both on an individual and group basis.

Parents were cautious and skeptical at first about the OTO program. Can this be real education? Should my child really like to go to school? Can I believe my son when he says he can't wait for vacation to end so he can get back to the program? These were frequent questions.

The answer seems to be "Yes" in every case. Parents have responded with vast enthusiasm, Gillette says. They support the program verbally and by their attendance at OTO parent meetings, which are usually briefings about upcoming trips or discussions about past activities.

Parents, in fact, are the outspoken supporters of the program, for they see positive results in terms of their children's growing sense of responsibility and new interest in learning and setting goals for themselves.

One parent, a mother, made a statement which doesn't seem particularly surprising. However, to this family, the change in their boy was momentous. "My son smiles now!" the mother happily explained. "He never used to smile, but now he does."

In his talk with parents each year, Bob always stresses the point that the students must earn their own way. He is sure that part of the experience of growing up is to set goals and then work for their attainment.

"This means that the program is self-supporting. The kids earn money to cover most of the costs of our adventures. Car washes, cookie sales, raking leaves, and washing windows—we do anything to raise money," Gillette reports. "Parents do not have to spend money for our OTO activities."

The hardest lesson for parents to accept is that students are allowed to make mistakes. The only time the teacher steps into the picture is in the event that physical harm or impending financial disaster are foreseen.

'We've gone hungry because the students didn't plan correctly," Bob says with a smile. "But nobody can be injured because of an occasional empty stomach. I continually stress that the goal of the teacher is to teach that the teacher is not needed anymore. The same thing goes for the parent. It's a difficult concept for parents to understand—the fact that they gain lasting fulfillment by programming themselves right out of the picture."

What about the future? First, the OTO program will expand—now that funds are available for new experiences. Gillette stresses, however, that the earn-your-own-way philosophy will be retained with regard to student expenses and that almost any other high school could afford to set up a similar program because the costs have been so low thus far.

Next summer Gillette hopes to take a group of students on an exploration of Long Island Sound. Plans call for the students to travel in boats they will refurbish themselves. A recreational and educational summer program for students who live in the inner city of neighboring Bridgeport has proven most successful. Already Gillette is expanding his involvement in a community organization representing low-income, mainly Spanish-speaking students in cooperation with the Recreation Department of Bridgeport.

All told, twenty-five Gillette-sponsored projects are now under way, including:

Communication skill programs for teachers, parents, and students

Whole-person effectiveness training programs for the football team

A creative music program that will draw together students from the two high schools in Fairfield and place them in a composing environment with professional composers

A program that will adapt OTO principles to the study of German

A new municipal government internship program for high school students in both Fairfield and Bridgeport

Summer learning experiences for students who will then assist teachers and lead younger students in nature studies

Bilingual program in Spanish for practical use.

Kenneth Petersen, the headmaster at Andrew Warde High School, and Vincent Strout, the assistant headmaster, are enthusiastic about the program. (Both men were Bob Gillette's teachers during his own high school days in Fairfield.) They have confidence in their staff and want their teachers to be fulfilled in their teaching duties. An atmosphere of experimentation with a rationale or purpose is evident in this 2,000-pupil school.

Mr. Gillette says it's great to work with teachers who are excited about the grant and its implications for their own teaching over the next three years. Ideas for programming stream forth constantly from fellow staff members. As Bob notes, "Our high school will never be the same."

They Used to Hinder, Now They Help

Preparing the child to succeed in school was one of the objectives of Head Start. But there was always a critical factor not squarely faced—the problem that the home environment might wipe out gains made in the centers. When progress made by the children in Head Start programs eroded, the initial enthusiasm for Head Start crashed.

Several fresh attempts are being made now to develop workable preschool programs. These projects offer fresh hope, because they are being carefully documented and even replicated in cities across the nation. We may have found new techniques for aiding mothers to teach and support their children in ways that will continue to enhance their learning ability.

Beatrice Gross and Ronald Gross

A bold experiment is going on in six major cities, to give low-income mothers the strength and skills to cope with their own problems and to become better parents. "Parent-Child Development Centers" (PCDCs), funded by a combination of federal and foundation funds, are operating in New Orleans, Birmingham, Alabama, and Houston, with their work being "replicated" by mirror-centers in Detroit, Indianapolis, and San Antonio, Texas.

This article was originally published as "Learning the Art of Mothering," in The Christian Science Monitor, Oct. 31, 1977. Reprinted by permission from The Christian Science Monitor. © 1977 The Christian Science Publishing Society. All rights reserved.

Each center serves some sixty to eighty mothers and their young children, starting when the children are two to twelve months old. Trained psychologists, social workers, health professionals, and early childhood specialists—as well as "para-professionals" from the community—comprise the staff. The centers are supported by some $2 million a year from the U.S. Office of Child Development and the Lilly Endowment.

"I'M DIFFERENT TOO"

"I didn't think they learned at such an early age and so fast," says Carol Marion, a young New Orleans mother of three. "I raised my first two kids by myself—but the PCDCs been like an advisory council for my third. She's more assertive and faster than the others because of what I learned to do with her. And I'm different too: I never used to voice my opinion at PTA meetings. I would just sit back and listen, but not now. The people here showed me how to be myself, 'cause mothers have to talk up for a lot of things in the child's life, and you can't just sit back and let it pass you by."

The centers test, teach, and demonstrate the most potent techniques of child rearing derived from the research of the past fifteen years. They stress the importance of talking, playing, stroking, and fondling infants in their first three years, plus better nutrition and a stimulating environment.

Half the client's time at the centers is spent in discussion and laboratory session where parents learn about research findings, test hypotheses about children's development, and refine their parenting skills. The mothers are trained to play simple games with their children that sharpen perceptions and thinking, see themselves at "play" with their children on videotape, and critique one another's behavior.

The other half is spent in acquiring the tools to enable the mothers to seize control over their own lives. By taking high school equivalency courses, studying consumerism, cooking, toymaking, sewing, driving, group dynamics, and counseling, they learn to cope better themselves, to help neighbors, and to take advantage of the underutilized social services in their community.

INCREASING RESPONSIBILITY

In Birmingham, where mothers begin at the center when their children are three to six months old, each participant receives an increasing stipend as she takes on increased responsibility. At the start, mothers attend the center 12 hours a week, but after two and a half years they may be spending as much as 40 hours a week there, managing small nursery groups and teaching newer mothers, at a stipend of $300 a month.

In Houston, the center is geared to a bilingual Chicano population with a strong family orientation. In Houston and in San Antonio, its replication site, the whole family is involved in regularly scheduled weekend workshops from the time their baby is one year old. They are visited at home that first year, then attend the center four mornings a week when the child is two, receiving a stipend of $3 a morning until they leave the program when the child is three.

"Although methods differ, certain results have been demonstrated in all three centers," reported staff research consultant Janet Blumenthal recently at a meeting held at the Bank Street College of Education, the replication management organization chosen to oversee the experiment. "You can see it when you walk into the waiting room. Mothers are explaining more to their children, using more logic, and are more encouraging. You see them stroking and touching their children more. I rarely visit a program mother at home who just sets her child in front of the TV when we talk. They always take the time to set up the pots or silverware for the child to play with."

TEST SCORES HIGHER

Four-year-old children were tested in New Orleans one full year after leaving the program. While a control group's standard-Binet IQ scores had dipped from 98 to 95 (3 points in the year since they were last tested), the program children's scores had stabilized at 108, leaving a significant 13-point difference between the two groups. Apparently continued stimulation at home kept the children's thinking active 12 months after the mothers were no longer actively involved in the centers' programming.

A typical center child talks more and uses more complex sentences than his age-mate who has not been exposed to the program. When he enters school, he'll ask more questions and answer questions more clearly, make better use of materials in his classroom, and be friendlier to other children and adults he meets.

LONG-TERM RESULTS

Most often the first wave of an experimental program is the most successful—"everything works once," as professionals in the field say. But in the case of the PCDCs, five years of evaluation records demonstrate that the successive waves of mothers have learned faster. They have grown increasingly confident in their own judgments; they question more, and even challenge the authority of "experts"; they speak with more confidence about the needs of their particular child; and they feel that the rest of their lives have been enriched.

"Our goal isn't just to create another mother-infant training program that works," says Mary Robinson, the federal coordinator of the program in Washington. "What we're after is proof that the methods will work in any community that adopts the program. Our country just can't afford the money or the time to continually support programs on a hit or miss basis."

Help Them Help You

Dorothy Rich tells us that over 80 percent of the parents polled in 1971 said they wanted the school to tell them what they could do at home to help their children. Ms. Rich, founder and director of the Home and School Institute, shows what we can do to help parents help us. It is a fine list of projects you can start tomorrow to set the foundation of a real partnership between home and school.

Dorothy Rich

. . . The Home and School Institute has developed a number of specific strategies, which have recently been published under the title *101 Activities for Building More Effective School-Community Involvement.** The sampling of activities and ideas that follows highlights educational outreach programs that involve no cost, little time, and a small staff:

From awareness to action. Start with ways to make it possible for parents—even working parents who have little free time during or after school hours—to use the resources of the school. When scheduling volunteers for some of the events below, think of before-work hours, early evening, or even Saturday mornings. Try to avoid the usual kind of evening meetings, and don't assume that the principal and the full staff need to attend all of the events set for parents. Of course, if your school has a full-time home-school coordinator, so much the better. But the activities described here can be managed without additional federal or other funds; what they take is planning and ingenuity.

Family room in the school. Convert an underused or unused classroom into a family room. Ask for furniture donations from parents and businesses—they're tax deductible. Try for easy chairs, lamps, and a rug; then, if you can, add a typewriter for parents who don't have one at home, a sewing area, and, if possible, a washer and dryer that parents can use while they observe their children in the classrooms, take part in workshops, or do volunteer work. Child care can also be provided in the family room. Set up a system using older elementary school children or teenagers from a nearby high school to provide babysitting. Linking up with the local high school's home economics program in child development will provide practice for the high schoolers, as well as an educational program for the preschoolers who are brought to the family room.

*For information on this publication and other HSI materials and courses, write to the Home and School Institute, Trinity College, Washington, D.C. 20017.

This article was originally published as **"The Family as Educator: A Letter to Principals,"** in *The National Elementary Principal* 55:5 (May–June 1976). Copyright 1976, National Association of Elementary School Principals. All rights reserved. Reprinted by permission.

Book and toy lending library. This service can be run in conjunction with the family room. Arrange for donations of books and toys from homes and businesses; what isn't donated can be made by parents and teachers. Parents can check out card games, books, homemade reinforcement activities in the basic skills, and so on, for use at home. A lending library is particularly appreciated by working parents whose hours do not permit them to attend workshops at school to make such materials themselves. Schedule the library hours to include at least one after-work period weekly. Set a time limit on the use of the materials and stick to it. Assess a fine for each day the toy or game is kept longer than the limit, and make it a rule that materials returned damaged must be replaced.

Make-it-and-take-it workshops. Here's a way to involve parents in making inexpensive learning materials to use at home with their children—especially those in kindergarten or the primary grades. Select items that all parents can make easily from low-cost art materials, such as days-of-the-week wheels, bingo games, alphabet trays, or number wheels. If possible, ask the parents and teachers to make some extra materials for use in the lending library.

Las Vegas night. Hold an evening session to acquaint parents with the many ways that games can be used for teaching. Set up tables, Las Vegas fashion, around the auditorium, and ask teachers to be the "croupiers." Have a different game going at each table—such as Black Jack Math and Phonics Roulette. Parents can spend a few minutes at each table and then talk to the teacher about how to use such games at home.

At-home meetings with neighborhood parents. Ask a "host" parent to invite neighbors in to meet the school principal. An informal, at-home meeting can help build administrator-parent rapport. For more structure, ask one member of the group to present ideas for home learning activities or tips on solving behavior problems in the home.

Principal's open house. Announce an open-door time when you'll be available to listen to parents on school related matters. Provide coffee and shut off the phone. Encourage parents to drop in and out freely and to bring new residents and friends with them. Ask teachers who are free to join you. If specialists are needed to follow up on concerns parents raise, they can be called in for future meetings.

Constructing learning centers. While some parents like to talk, others would rather build. They can help teachers construct needed school equipment and, at the same time, find out what learning centers are all about. A teacher who wants more learning centers provides a model, plus a list of suggested topics. Parents can either duplicate the model or come up with ideas of their own—which might range from the steps in writing a friendly letter to the care and feeding of goldfish. All that's needed are tagboard, magazine pictures, magic markers, and enthusiasm.

Tutors teach, parents learn. Parents can be invited to observe the school's tutoring program in action and to exchange with the tutors ideas and experiences in teaching children reading or other skills. These open house tutoring sessions needn't be run with "problem" children, who might be embarrassed at such identification. The sessions are designed to help parents learn how to tutor by observing the process and discussing it afterwards.

Book swap. This activity saves money for everybody and encourages parents and children to read more. The school community is asked to donate old or new books for the swap. Each parent and child is entitled to a new batch of books equal to the number of books he or she has contributed to the swap. During the last half-hour of the event, all unclaimed books are up for grabs. It's astonishing how popular reading can be when it's a bargain!

Parents and teachers share expectations. Just as books can be traded, so can expectations. What do parents hope children will learn? What, in fact, will the school curriculum include in the coming year? These questions can be dealt with in a discussion forum *before* they become issues. Send out a questionnaire to both parents and teachers, to be answered anonymously. Use the results as the basis for opening the forum. Parents who know what their children will be studying during the year can integrate home learning activities, including trips, with the school curriculum. Through a discussion forum, teachers can come to better understand the children's home backgrounds and the hopes and expectations of their parents.

Feature family of the week. Here's a way to "bring" a family into school without actually bringing them in. Set up a family bulletin board. Each week, each class selects one family to feature. Information about family members is compiled by the student and accompanied on a poster with Polaroid snapshots of the family. Information for the bulletin board can come from a family file assembled at the beginning of the school year, with each family jotting down only as much information as they want to share—such as the parents' jobs, how many children in the family, family pets and hobbies, and so forth. The Polaroid pictures can be taken at PTA meetings and kept on file.

Parent-community resource file. To make sure that the school uses the talents of its community fully, keep a file on parents and others indicating their readiness to share their special talents, skills, or experiences with the children. This file, open to all teachers and revised often, will identify adults who can demonstrate crafts, give travel slide shows, or lead tours through their work places. A teacher should feel free to contact any person listed in the file, whether or not that adult has a child in the teacher's class.

Mystery storyteller. Even someone with no special talent has a lot to contribute to the school—perhaps as a mystery storyteller for children in the primary grades. Once a week, a new mystery storyteller comes to class. It might be the school custodian, the barber in the shopping center, or the college-age sister of one of the students. The storyteller signs up for a fifteen-minute reading. The story to be read can be old or new, and the teacher can check to see if the teller needs help in selecting a tale. The excitement over this small, ongoing project runs high among both the children and the adults involved. Take pictures of the guests (always keep a school camera handy and working) as a special souvenir of the day.

Family evening. Have a family field trip for the whole school family. See a play or movie together, for example, to open channels for meaningful discussions among children, parents, and teachers. An effort should be made to correlate the event with in- and out-of-school discussion activities, including "assignments" for the family dinner table. (A pool of parent and teacher "buddies" can accompany children whose own parents are not able to join the event.)

Family information center. The information center doesn't need to be a room; it can be a shelf of books for loan or pamphlets to share, or even a newsletter sent out regularly, compiling sources of information on family life. Assembling an up-to-date list of resources in the community, along with news of books and materials on parenthood, is a needed service for busy families and can be an excellent project for a volunteer or PTA committee. Of course, the information center can be located in the family room, if there's space; otherwise, use a corner of the school library. Use the regular school newsletter to announce what's available in the center.

Summer learning and activity package. Notes about summer reading recommendations and a list of interesting places to visit in the area make a nice summer present for youngsters to take home when school lets out. Add some references to low-cost games for long summer days and some tips on home learning activities and staple everything together in book or calendar form. Children will enjoy decorating the covers of their own summer learning packages. This low-cost item is good education for the child and parent and good public relations for the school.

Strategies such as the ones outlined here emphasize the roles of the parent and the home as critical educational change agents for the child. When parents are in the school, they're learning the how-to's of teaching and making or learning about materials they can use for more effective home teaching. The school becomes a center for helping parents implement out-of-school learning for their children. The use of school facilities, personnel, and volunteers are all directed toward that goal; after all, home learning will ease the burden on the school, not make it harder.

The observant reader will have noticed a number of references to "home learning activities" throughout this article. These activities, developed by the Home and School Institute, appear to have significant impact in raising children's achievement in basic skills.

In a study of four randomly selected first-grade classes in the Washington area, conducted in 1974–75, eight home learning activities were sent home, one every other week. The study was designed to find out whether the use of teacher designed home learning activities alone (there were no meetings, no home visits, no workshops for parents) would raise student achievement. And, in fact, it was found that the youngsters who worked with their families in these "kitchen-style" reinforcements of reading and math, as a group, achieved significantly higher scores in reading than did the four classes in the control group, who were doing otherwise similar first-grade work.

This study, based on the research cited at the beginning of this article, was designed to be completely replicable by any teacher or school system: it involved no extra monies, no extra personnel, and very little time. It has pointed to the possibility—and the practicality—of helping teachers to help parents in their role as teachers at home and in using the home and community to supplement—not duplicate—the school.

The home learning activities used in this study were each written recipe-style on a single sheet of paper. They were short, easy activities involving, for example, grocery lists for math and newspapers for reading—ordinary items found in any home. Anyone over the age of ten could work with the first graders in doing these activities.

Basically, the home learning program provided a way in which families could become directly involved in the education of their children. While research has not yet pinpointed a specific relationship between this kind of activity and increased school achievement, it may well be that what happens in school outreach programs is an enhancement of the family process itself. It may not matter what the specific activity is or in what order it is presented. What may ultimately matter is that children come to realize that the school really cares about the child's educational achievement and about the family itself.

HOME LEARNING ACTIVITIES

Teachers can use the following model and examples to develop home learning activities:

Name of activity. Be imaginative here to capture the child's interest.

Why do it? The objective or purpose of the activity—what it teaches—can be anything from hand-eye coordination to reinforcement in math or other basic skills. Avoid such general objectives as "to have fun with your child."

Materials needed. Keep the materials simple, inexpensive, and readily available. Try to use materials that are found in most homes but not necessarily in the school.

How to do it. Give a step-by-step, recipe-style approach to the activity. Be as brief as possible and as clear as you can. Have a friend or colleague read the directions over to be sure they are easy to follow.

How much time the activity takes. Keep beginning activities short—about five to ten minutes—and time your activity to be sure you have estimated correctly.

What age child the activity is for. Try the activity out with your students to be sure.

Evaluation. How will the parents know that this activity works? What are the signs, the yardstick, by which parents can judge its effectiveness?

Adaptations. How can the activity be varied with only a few minor changes? Adaptations get more mileage out of an activity and inspire children's and parents' creativity.

Here are two examples of home learning activities that were developed by teachers in the Washington, D.C., area.

Word Detectives

Why do it? To build observation and reading skills.

Materials needed. Magazines, newspapers, scissors, cardboard, and paste

How to do it. Ask the child to look for different kinds of words—for example, words beginning with *b* or ending in *g*. For older children who are more aware of grammar, ask them to look for "action words," and so on. Ask the child to cut out the words and paste them onto cardboard, which can be displayed at home or in the classroom.

Time. About fifteen minutes

Age. Early primary for simple phonics; later school years for more difficult words

Evaluation. Set varying numbers of words to find and then check the words the "detectives" have found for correctness.

Break Down

Why do it? To teach the child the names of simple machines; to acquaint the child with taking things apart and putting them back together; to develop fine motor coordination

Materials needed. Simple machines that are no longer being used, such as a coffee grinder, ice crusher, clock, or pencil sharpener, and a screwdriver

How to do it. Discuss with the child what needs to be removed first. Allow the child to take the object apart, naming the parts in the process, and then put it back together.

Time. About ten minutes

Age. Six to eight

Evaluation. Does the child want to do more? Does the child recall the names of machines and parts? Can the child locate other machines in the environment?

Adaptation. Ask the child to take apart two or more objects at the same time and to compare the parts.

Zeus Says . . .

Beatrice Gross

In ancient Greece when a soldier or politician wanted to take action and found opposition, he would cite Athena's advice. The opposition would counter, "Ah, but Zeus says. . . ."

Since teachers are frequently assaulted with dictums derived from authoritative studies, they also frequently need some equally strong counterargument. You could cite Zeus, but you might find that "Benjamin Bloom says . . ." carries more weight nowadays.

Much of the research now available can be of help to parents and teachers alike. While teachers get the journals that report research, parents often don't. It would be a service to your parents to share what you learn with them. This can be done at meetings, or through a class newspaper column, and it will be appreciated.

Sometimes though, parents, anxious to do well by their children, will pick up the latest pop psychology fad and lose all perspective in their attempt to follow the new recipe for raising good, competent children. They'll worry because the third child is likely to be less self-sufficient than the only child or panic because they do (or don't) pay their child for service to the home.

To put parents at ease about some of their concerns you might mention some of the studies that I've come across which puts research into perspective.

Did you know that fifty years ago it was thought that too much education for females reduced the size and function of their wombs? A researcher "proved it" by showing how college-educated women had fewer babies and many had none.

More recently a well-respected researcher found that fluorescent lights adversely affected children's learning capacity and increased the incidence of out-of-control behavior. About four months later the study was refuted.

According to Professor Adon Gordus of the University of Michigan, students at the low end of the academic scale have a "higher-than-normal iodine content in their hair," while those at the highest grade-point level have a "higher-than-normal zinc and copper content in their hair."

On the Berkeley campus of the University of California about 50 percent of the incoming freshmen fail the famous Subject A examination. What was it like in the good old days? Back in 1950 about 50 percent of incoming students failed the test as well. (So much for declining capacity.)

Research on the value of laughter might be considered more seriously. Avener Ziv of Tel Aviv University says that laughter enhances creative ability and liberates the flow of creative ideas.

One of the most positive studies done of late is that by Benjamin Bloom, the notable educational psychologist, who questioned the need for any failure in the schools. In his book *Human Characteristics and School Learning*, he claims that all normal children could be "A" students if they got the time and attention they needed. He explains that the student must be well grounded in early concepts and techniques; trouble develops when students miss (due to absence, inattention, or requiring more time) a part of the necessary basic information. They fail to fully understand and keep failing more and more since they are missing an essential part of the structure.

If a child is having difficulties, the best thing to do is go back over the basics. How can we motivate a nine-year-old to review his blends or a thirteen-year-old to practice addition, without bruising their delicate egos?

One way is to capitalize on another serious study showing that when children teach children, the *tutor* gains far more than the *tutee*, better than twice as much in fact. So for children who are having difficulty, suggest to the parents they find a younger child who needs help and hook them up. Both kids will benefit.

X
EPILOGUE

Epilogue in Xanadu

You, the teacher, are under pressure. You must satisfy the majority of children in your class, your supervisor, your class parents, your mandates from the Board of Education, your critics in the media and, to remain sane, your current perceptions of what's most needed.

What if those pressures disappeared and all that worried you was how to turn Karen on to math or teach John to clean up after he painted?

Imagine, if you will, a place where each teacher teaches the children he or she can best reach, using techniques that feel most comfortable. A place in which each child is able to get the quality and amount of attention, movement, experience, and control that he or she needs.

I would not have thought of checking out Minneapolis, Minnesota, to seek Xanadu, but that's the place where alternative schools are so accepted there is no longer any "regular" program.

I'm told that because there is no regular program, there is no battleground, no need to fight for or against testing, basics, or humanistic education. No need to tear down *their* position to affirm *yours.*

As educational currents change in Minneapolis, one school expands to serve more, another contracts to accommodate fewer, allowing children and teachers to choose a method that best suits them.

The Southeast Alternatives Program, once federally funded, is now supported both financially and philosophically by the community, a typical city community with the usual urban mix, but different in that its members have been educated to make choices for children by having been given choices to make.

It could, with hard work, be replicated in your community.

Here is the program in brief as it is introduced to "new parents."

CHOOSING A SCHOOL IN SOUTHEAST ALTERNATIVES

Choice making has become a way of life in Southeast Minneapolis. For those new to the Southeast Alternatives project there are often questions on

This excerpt was originally titled "**Questions Parents Ask** . . ." and reprinted with permission from *Southeast Alternatives 1974,* Copyright 1974 Southeast Alternatives and Sally French, Minneapolis Public Schools.

how that choice making operates. The brochure is an effort at describing what the SEA project offers. Here are some frequently asked questions which may help as parents consider enrolling their children in the Southeast Alternatives program:

What are the choices of alternative schools? Parents and students may select the SEA school they wish to attend. Five choices are available, four on the elementary level (Contemporary, Continuous Progress, Open and Free), and two on the secondary level (Free School and Marshall-University High School). Three choices are available for Marshall-University junior high students (grades 6-8) through the transitional program, which provides options that are extensions of the Continuous Progress, Contemporary and Open programs.

Who can enroll? Children in Southeast Minneapolis and the Cedar-Riverside area may have their choice of schools. Through Open Enrollment and Urban Transfers and Principals Agreement students may transfer from the city to Southeast if there is room in the school and if the racial balance of the sending and receiving school is enhanced. Students from outside the Minneapolis Public Schools area may enroll but must pay tuition.

How do students enroll? Students may enroll by contacting the counselor in the school of choice, or, if transferring in from outside Southeast and Cedar-Riverside, by securing an application from the Student Support Office—telephone 376-4573 or by calling SEA office at 331-6252.

How can we receive more information about choices of schools? Call the Southeast Alternatives office and ask for public information. The office staff will be happy to answer questions. One of the best ways to determine what choice should be made is to visit the school you are interested in to gain first-hand knowledge about the school. Counselors, administrators and community resource coordinators are always happy to talk with parents about the alternative that will best answer the needs of the individual child.

Can my child receive transportation? Elementary children who travel outside their neighborhood may receive transportation within Southeast as well as children who come from the rest of the city into Southeast. Currently we are transporting over 800 elementary children to the elementary programs. Secondary students must provide their own transportation. Open Enrollment and Urban Transfer students may receive assistance from the Board of Education in individual cases where there is financial need.

How do I know my child will receive a good basic skill education? There is a commitment on the part of all schools to provide an excellent basic skill training no matter what the philosophy. Testing and reporting on a regular basis make it possible to determine how a child is progressing.

How is discipline handled? Each school handles discipline on an individual basis. However, the opportunity to match learning styles, philosophies and attend to the needs of the individual child have made "discipline" in the old sense of the word less of a concern than helping a child to achieve his/her full potential through personal satisfaction and self-discipline.

As a parent, if I am dissatisfied with my choice can my child transfer? Yes. Transfers from one program to another are accommodated through the year as parents, teachers, counselors and students work together to find the best learning environment for each child.

How do parents become involved in the schools? Parents are invited and welcomed in all programs as participants in the various governance models (described in the brochure) as well as in the classroom so that the teaching/learning process becomes one in which families and schools work as co-partners. Through newsletters, personal invitations and making one's availability known, parents and community members are sought as valuable partners in school life.

and most important of all. . .

How do I know which program would be best for my child? Parents must assess the personality, attitudes and needs of the individual child. Often children in the same families work well in different environments because they have different needs. Counselors and the public information person will be happy to discuss which of the SEA schools would best suit the individual child's needs.

AUTHOR INDEX

SUBJECT INDEX